RACE, NATION, AND
WEST INDIAN IMMIGRATION
TO HONDURAS, 1890–1940

RACE, NATION, AND WEST INDIAN IMMIGRATION TO HONDURAS, 1890–1940

★ GLENN A. CHAMBERS ★

LOUISIANA STATE UNIVERSITY PRESS
BATON ROUGE

Published by Louisiana State University Press
Copyright © 2010 by Louisiana State University Press
All rights reserved
Manufactured in the United States of America
First printing

DESIGNER: Michelle A. Neustrom
TYPEFACES: Minion Pro, text; Cg Futura Maxi, display
PRINTER AND BINDER: Thomson-Shore, Inc.

Chapter 6 first appeared, in somewhat different form, as "The Deportation of West Indian Workers from Trujillo, Honduras, and the Construction of Race and Nation in a Banana Republic,
1934–1939," *Wadabagei: A Journal of the Caribbean and Its Diasporas* 10 (Spring/Summer 2007):
56–81, and is reprinted by permission of Lexington Books, a division of Rowman & Littlefield
Publishing Group.

LIBRARY OF CONGRESS CATALOGING-IN-PUBLICATION DATA

Chambers, Glenn Anthony.
   Race, nation, and West Indian immigration to Honduras, 1890–1940 / Glenn A. Chambers.
      p. cm.
   Includes bibliographical references and index.
   ISBN 978-0-8071-3557-0 (cloth : alk. paper) 1. Blacks—Honduras—History—19th century. 2.
Blacks—Honduras—History—20th century. 3. West Indians—Honduras—History. 4. West In-
dians—Ethnic identity—Honduras—History. 5. Immigrants—Honduras—History. 6. National-
ism—Honduras—History 7. Honduras—Race relations—History—19th century. 8. Honduras—
Race relations—History—20th century. 9. Honduras—Emigration and immigration—History.
10. West Indies—Emigration and immigration—History. I. Title.

   F1517.B55C48 2010
   304.8'7283072908996—dc22

                                                                                    2009022092

CONTENTS

Map of fruit companies on the North Coast
of Honduras appears on page 28.

TABLES

ACKNOWLEDGMENTS

It is impossible to conduct a project of this magnitude without incurring numerous debts along the way. This book represents both the culmination of many years of study and the fulfillment of a lifelong goal to contribute in my own way to the history of the African diaspora and the role migration continues to play in redefining its parameters. I first became interested in history as a profession at the University of St. Thomas in Houston, Texas, where under the guidance of the many professors in the history department my interests in colonialism, migration, nationalism, Latin America, and the Caribbean were given the intellectual space to develop.

This project was first conceived in graduate seminars at Howard University in Washington, D.C. Selwyn H. H. Carrington and Vincent Peloso alerted me to the dearth of scholarship on the Caribbean and Latin America. Through their distinct approaches to the region, each encouraged me to see the historical and cultural interconnectedness of the two regions and the ways in which immigration and migration influenced social, political, economic, and cultural developments. Alan McPherson challenged me to broaden my trajectory and to view Honduras within the context of U.S. foreign policy debates by looking at the role U.S. corporations and their political influence played in the movement of peoples in the region. While working as his graduate assistant, I was introduced to various research methodologies that proved essential in facilitating a project on which there was so little written. The skills acquired while working as his assistant have served me well not only with this project, but also in the historical profession. Special thanks are in order as well to

Emory Tolbert, Edna Medford, Elizabeth Clark-Lewis, Daryl Scott, Ibrahim Sundiata, Orlando Taylor, Barbara Griffin, David DeLeon, Franklin Knight, and all who assisted me through the various stages of this project.

I would also like to extend my gratitude to the countless librarians, archivists, and staff at the numerous research libraries and facilities in the Washington, D.C., metro area. I am indebted to Georgette Dorn at the Library of Congress and her staff for awarding me a research fellowship in the Hispanic Division in 2004. The fellowship afforded me the opportunity to survey the holdings of the library related to this topic as well as provided a forum to engage prominent international scholars in the field, most notably those from Honduras. Some of my first contacts in Honduras were forged during this period. While working in the Library of Congress, I had the pleasure of making the acquaintance of Mario Argueta, Olga Joya, and Darío Euraque, all of whom provided insight into Honduran history and the location of pertinent archival materials in Tegucigalpa and on the North Coast. Prior to my arrival in Honduras to conduct the bulk of the research for the book, Darío Euraque of Trinity College assisted me with vital introductions to Honduran scholars. I am most indebted to him for granting me access to his personal archival materials that were no longer available in Honduras and were instrumental to understanding the economic and cultural dynamics on the North Coast.

The archivists and staff at the National Archives and Records Administration in College Park, Maryland, as well as librarians at Howard University, Moorland-Spingarn Research Center, Georgetown University, the University of Maryland, College Park, and George Washington University assisted with locating numerous microfilmed government records as well as pertinent books and newspapers. I am grateful for their unyielding patience and expertise.

This project necessitated extensive archival research in the United Kingdom and Honduras. No project of this scale could be conducted without considerable external financial support. The history department at Howard University generously provided me with graduate assistantships throughout my M.A. and Ph.D. programs. Field research in Honduras was financed through a Fulbright fellowship during the 2004–2005 academic year. The Fulbright provided the opportunity to devote all of my attention to the project without financial distress, a luxury that cannot be taken for granted in the humanities. While in Honduras, Karla Fiallos de Castañeda, Reverend Albert Brooks, Edwardo Hendricks James,

Rand Garo, German Alvarez, Cruz Bermudez, Gilberto Bermudez, Jorge Amaya, Alma Nuñez, Roberto Nuñez, Wendy Griffin, German Chavez, Martin Lambert, and countless others assisted with navigating the logistics of Honduran society on the North Coast and Tegucigalpa and challenged me to be true to the history of Honduras and its diverse people.

Following the year in Honduras, a dissertation fellowship at DePauw University in Greencastle, Indiana, aided in the completion of the project. The research funding from the fellowship afforded the opportunity for me to commit to writing and also to conduct additional research at the British Public Record Office. Special thanks to Neil Abraham and his staff for making financial resources available to continue my research. Several members of the history department at DePauw, Yung-chen Chiang, Glen Kuecker, Mac Dixon-Fyle, and Robert Dewey, as well as Emmanuel Harris and Teresita Hernandez of the modern languages department, were encouraging throughout the writing process and offered sincere advice, friendship, and constructive scholarly criticism.

My colleagues in the history department at Texas A&M University have often been my points of reference for making the transition to the professoriate and navigating the publishing process. I am indebted to the department for extending research funding that allowed me to conduct research at the Howard-Tilton Memorial Library at Tulane University and the Nettie Lee Benson Latin American Collection at the University of Texas at Austin. Conference funding provided the opportunity to develop several ideas for the book while presenting on panels throughout the United States and the Caribbean. Walter Buenger, Albert Broussard, Walter Kamphoefner, Harold Livesay, and numerous others have been excellent mentors. Special thanks to Carlos Blanton and Jason Parker for reading various drafts of chapters, as well as Rebecca Hartkopf Schloss, for her advice on teaching and research.

I am forever grateful to my graduate school colleagues and dearest friends, all of whom have been instrumental in this process: Louis Woods, Nathan Carter, Keith Craig, Walter Hosey, Quito Swan, Michael Firven, Santiago Mauer, Abraham Smith, Sharita Jacobs, LaShawn Harris, Sheila Aird, Christina Jones, Gordon Gil, David Gosse, Abba Baez, Jahi Issa, and Radell Tankard. They understand the level of dedication and sacrifice endured to see this project to completion, and we helped each other through when it seemed like no one else would. I thank Vera Baquet and Victoria Rundberg-Rivera for embracing me as their own and for being that constant positive influence that all of us desire, but most are unwilling or unable to seek out.

My family has offered continuous support at crucial stages along the way. Many thanks to my Washington family: Bernie, Cydne, Amiri, Paulette, John, Cliff, and Joyce. They were my first introduction to the area, and I know that I could not have made it all of those years without them. Because of them, Washington has become as much my home as the Texas of my birth. I wish to thank my mother, Toxi, and my sisters, Caire and Samaria, for their unconditional love and encouragement through the many endeavors I have embarked upon over the years. This book is as much a testament to their hard work and sacrifice as it is to my own. Finally, words cannot express how much the constant love and support of my wife, Terah, have meant to me. Thank you for being my safe place.

RACE, NATION, AND
WEST INDIAN IMMIGRATION
TO HONDURAS, 1890–1940

INTRODUCTION

The Caribbean coast of Central America is home to numerous English-speaking communities of British West Indian descent. From Guatemala to Costa Rica, the enclaves created by West Indians and their descendants represent the failure of nationalist ideologies to fully incorporate this population into the scope of their respective nations. Allegiances to Caribbean language, culture, religious traditions, and broader political and social traditions of the African diaspora serve as both historical and cultural reminders that modern Latin American nationalistic notions of *mestizaje,* or an exclusive mixed race identity, as championed during the early decades of the twentieth century, had limitations. The Republic of Honduras, like many of its Central American neighbors, embraced a concept of *mestizaje* that emphasized the Iberian and indigenous biological and cultural heritage of the nation. With this focus solely on the interaction between the Spanish and the indigenous, all other elements of Honduran culture were ignored or denigrated. As a result, the historiography of Honduras is devoid of many black participants. While some scholars concede that this absence in the literature is the result of Africans and their descendants being selectively ignored in the historical debate, others insist that the African presence in Honduras left little lasting impact on the racial and cultural landscape of the country. However, in recent years significant scholarship has emerged that focuses on the formation of communities of African descent in Honduras. Primarily ethnographic in nature, these studies emphasize the Garífuna (Black Carib) community and its indelible contribution to the cultural fabric of Honduras, particularly along the Caribbean littoral of the nation.[1] Absent from this discourse is mention of the sizable population of Hondurans of West Indian descent who often settled in the same coastal cities as the Garífuna. It is the Garífuna who maintain the monopoly on black identity in Honduran cultural discourse, due largely to the fact that they represent the majority of the population of Afro descent in the country and have resided in Honduras continuously for over two hundred years. However, the West Indian experience, which dates from the late nineteenth and early twentieth centuries, also contributed to the racial discourse in Honduras by challenging Honduran responses to immigration, labor, and foreign influence, as well as preexisting discourses on race and identity.

The process of identity transformation among people of African descent in Honduras is best examined through the assessment of the liberal reform period. Traditional Honduran historiography dates the beginning of this multifaceted modernization process from 1876 with the inauguration of the liberal regime of President Marco Aurelio Soto (1876–1883). This is seen by many as a watershed in Honduran economic and political development due to innovative legislation such as the suppression of the tithe, the introduction of public education, and the codification of legal commercial mining and administrative laws.[2] This is also the period that saw the development of the multinational banana industry and the subsequent importation of West Indian workers into the country. Mario Argueta suggests that the internationalization of the Honduran North Coast began with the liberal reforms, during which the Honduran government offered economic incentives to foreigners to aid in the modernization and industrialization of the country, primarily through agriculture.[3] These reforms served as the catalyst for the mobilization of foreign capital (mainly British and U.S.) into the country and the subsequent introduction of black migrant labor to work on the foreign-owned railroads and fruit plantations. An examination of the reforms also raises questions about how the local population viewed the arrival of a foreign, majority black work force into the region. In the case of the North Coast of Honduras, some workers arrived initially from the United States, but the overwhelming majority came from the numerous British Caribbean islands, most from Jamaica, followed by neighboring British Honduras (Belize).

The status of the immigrant black population in Honduras was often uncertain. The anti-black political and social climate of Honduras, which traditionally targeted the Garífuna and other Afro-mestizo populations, was the initial reason for the tense relations among locals and West Indians. However, this apprehension about West Indians did not begin with the labor policies of the fruit companies. The Anglophone and Protestant blacks of the Bay Islands claimed British citizenship well into the twentieth century despite the incorporation of the islands into the Honduran nation in the 1860s. Ross Graham, among others, asserts that Bay Islanders clung to their "Britishness" in order to exclude themselves from the nationalist politics of the time, to maintain the rights and privileges of British subjects, and to differentiate themselves from the dominant Hispanic population.[4] They were not anxious to become Honduran citizens. Bay Islanders saw no advantages to switching citizenship any more than the Honduran modernizers found it advantageous to include them as citizens. Some forty years later with the arrival of thousands of West Indians seeking employment in the fruit industries, the old British/Honduran citizenship debate or the Anglo-Hispanic conflict as described by geographer William Davidson that was historically relegated to the Bay Islands reemerged on a national scale to accentuate the social, political, and economic realities of the growing foreign presence on the North Coast.[5]

HISTORIOGRAPHICAL CONCERNS

The subject of blackness has received increased attention in recent years in both Honduras and the United States. The historian Marvin Barahona asserts that Honduran identity emerged as a result of miscegenation among Native Americans, Europeans, and Africans.[6] Consequently, by acknowledging the role of African-descent peoples, both enslaved and free, Barahona recognizes that Honduras, like most nations in the Americas, is a heterogeneous, multiracial, and multicultural society. Covering the period from the Spanish conquest through the onset of the banana industry in the late nineteenth and early twentieth centuries, Barahona expands interpretations of blackness in Honduras to demonstrate that black identity did not begin with the arrival of the Garífuna, Bay Islanders, or West Indian banana workers. Following in this tradition, Darío Euraque has opened up the theme of race in Honduran historiography to specifically address concepts of blackness within the Afro-Honduran, particularly Garífuna communities and its relationship to the more predominant discourse on *mestizaje*.[7]

The legacy of the transatlantic slave trade surfaces with any in-depth discussion of communities of African descent in the Americas. Edmund T.

Gordon maintains that slavery serves as the "key generative historical experience in most constructions of African or black diasporic identities."[8] Honduras is no exception. A long history of African slavery existed in Central America dating back to the establishment of the Spanish American empire in the early decades of the sixteenth century, in which gold and silver mining helped provide the capital to spark Spain's growing power on the world stage. Slavery in Honduras dates back to the first sizable cargo of 1,000 to 1,500 enslaved Africans brought to the region of Olancho in the 1540s to mine gold for the Spanish.[9] The institution existed in the mining regions of central Honduras, and in various locales along the North Coast, particularly Trujillo, Puerto Caballos (later Puerto Cortés), and San Pedro, where some gold deposits were found. Slavery was officially abolished in 1824. As in most societies that opted for the enslavement of Africans to satisfy their labor needs, the enslaved population of Honduras was diverse, composed of the African-born, creoles, and those imported from other regions of the Americas. The patterns of enslavement proved similar to those of other areas in Central America where precious metal extraction was the primary focus of Spaniards.[10] Absent from Honduras is the legacy of sugar and slavery, or other labor-intensive, commercial monoculture ventures like many in Latin America, the Caribbean, and the American South.

On the North Coast of the country, where scholars have documented the existence of a minor plantation economy, African slavery was instituted sporadically. The coast was on the periphery of the Spanish empire, and its fortification was a constant struggle. This Atlantic coastal area remained overwhelmingly the territory of indigenous groups, Maroon communities, and European (mostly Dutch and English) pirates. Many scholars such as Linda Newson have maintained that the relative autonomy of the North and Mosquito coasts of Honduras contributed to an anti-authoritarian mentality in the region. Newson's study of the conquest of Honduras further reveals a situation in which *marronage* and miscegenation were rampant along the North and Mosquito coasts as early as the sixteenth century. The creation of the Zambo-Mosquito peoples, an Afro-Indian ethnic group, gives testament to the relatively small, yet enduring presence of people of African descent in Honduras. Combined with the long history of piracy and *marronage,* the region remained an obstacle for the Spanish colonial powers.[11] However, this region would prove instrumental to understanding the complexity of national identity in Honduras as it pertains to people of African descent.

No comprehensive monograph exists dedicated solely to the history of the West Indian community in Honduras that emerged as a result of the multinational banana industry. Darío Euraque and Elizet Payne Iglesias have made considerable advances in integrating the history of West Indian immigration and its effect on broader discussions of race, nation, and identity in Honduras.[12] Euraque's work in particular emphasizes the complexities of black identity in Honduras during the period of study and the often ambiguous designation of the term *black* as it applied to West Indians, Bay Islanders, and the Garífuna. Since West Indians were a relatively small segment of the population in North Coast cities, opting to settle in communities with other West Indians, the majority of the "negros" in Honduras that intellectuals and anti-black immigration proponents emphasized were in fact Garífuna and Bay Islander citizens.[13] This points to the uniqueness of the social and political fallout from West Indian immigration to Honduras, given that the group was such a small segment of the black population in the country.

Most historians of the West Indian diaspora in Central America have chosen to direct their efforts toward communities in Costa Rica, Panama, and to a lesser extent Nicaragua due in part to the dearth of readily accessible archival sources available in these countries in addition to those in the United States, Great Britain, and the various British Caribbean islands. Many of these studies have focused on the political and economic relationship of West Indian labor to U.S. corporate interests. The situation in Honduras displayed some similarities to other Central American republics with sizable minorities of African descent. However, the longstanding complexities of black ethnic identity in Honduras among both the Hispanophone and Anglophone populations, combined with the peculiar intersection of race, language, class, and culture on the North Coast, separate the country from its neighbors. This study centers on the development of a West Indian community and its experiences within the Honduran political and social environment of the late nineteenth and early twentieth centuries. The goal is to bring the history of West Indians in Honduras from the periphery into the growing literature on the multidimensionality of the black experience in the nation.

Despite the unique nature of the Honduran situation, the broader literature on West Indians in Central America is helpful in understanding the complexity of anti–West Indian sentiment prevalent in the region throughout the twentieth century and the attitudes of locals to the foreign labor force. In her assessment of Costa Rica, Aviva Chomsky suggests that "fruit company plantations and migrant West Indian workers challenged national conceptions of small land holding and racial homogeneity that led to the development of Costa Rican nationalism and anti-imperialism."[14] In Honduras, the rise of anti-black, anti-immigrant sentiment did much to rally the nation around *mestizaje* as indicative of Honduran national identity. However, unlike Costa Rica in later decades, West Indians in Honduras never reached a point where they were completely embraced by locals and redefined as nationals. They remained outside the concept of the nation for much of their history in the country.

Michael Conniff's assessment of Panama describes West Indians subjected to the nuances of discrimination at the hands of both their North American employers and Panamanian society. The study of Honduras reveals examples of North Americans exporting their "brand" of discriminatory policies that further divided West Indians and mestizos within the banana enclaves. North Americans preferred West Indian laborers because they spoke English and many had prior experience in the banana industry in the Caribbean. Because of their experience, many West Indians were employed in overseer and more skilled positions initially. Hondurans and other Central Americans often served in a laborer capacity and were relegated to lower-paying positions in the early years of the industry, although salaries on the North Coast were generally higher than in other parts of the country. This remained a point of contention for Honduran labor organizers and their followers in later decades. John Soluri argues that Spanish-speaking migrants to the banana zones "forged collective identities to both the hegemony of the U.S. fruit companies and the presence of their black and foreign laborers."[15] This created a situation in which all labor conflicts and the substandard circumstances under which many Hondurans lived contained elements of racial and class antagonisms directed at West Indians.

Unlike in Panama and Costa Rica, West Indians in Honduras rallied around a collective identity and did not allow interisland jealousy and nationalism to prevent them from building a strong sense of community.[16] This was necessary in order to stave off the barrage of attacks from all facets of Honduran society. The tendency within the community was to unite based on a pan-Caribbean and British identity. West Indians created separate neighborhoods, social networks, cultural organizations, and religious institutions that thrived on racial and ethnic exclusivity. The number of West Indians in Honduras consistently ranged between 5,000 and 10,000 people throughout the period of the study (depending on the sources), thus facilitating the need to coalesce around commonalities.[17]

Studies of West Indians in Central America often discuss this population as an appendage to larger studies on the nature of U.S. corporations in the region. This notion of the black migrant as an accessory to U.S. corporate interests immediately relegates this group to problem status within the scope of the national debate centered on race and nation. West Indians and other nonwhite immigrants were viewed by Central American republics as part of a racial problem within Central America, rather than as allies in a common struggle for cultural and political autonomy.

Studies centered on West Indians in Central America almost always focus on issues of labor organization as a central theme. This is understandable given that the primary reason West Indians left their home islands for Central America was to gain employment. However, the West Indian experience is almost always more than a story of labor. It encompasses families both in Honduras and in the West Indies, communities, governments, cultural interactions, and a host of social and political consequences.

Both Aviva Chomsky and Philippe Bourgois emphasize the importance of West Indians to the labor movement in Central America.[18] In the Honduran case, there was an absence of West Indian involvement in the labor movement. Echeverri-Gent maintains that the United Fruit Company (UFCO) created a policy of oversupply "in which they imported more workers than they needed or could absorb."[19] In addition, the UFCO and Standard Fruit curbed steamship passenger travel between Honduras and the West Indies, ensuring that potential workers remained at their disposal. This kept labor costs low and prevented workers from organizing because there was always a surplus of potential employees waiting to take the place of strikers. Mario Posas hints at the lack of labor organizations in Honduras during the period. He indicates that mutual aid societies that supported members in cases of sickness, unemployment, or death emerged in Honduras around 1899 throughout the country. These societies were antecedents to the labor movement that emerged in the mid-twentieth century. However, the organizations were loosely organized and poorly funded, and at no point did the national membership exceed 1,700 people.[20]

The goal of the UFCO labor management strategy as outlined by Echeverri-Gent was to maintain complete control of their work force. Langley and Schoonover assert that the fruit companies employed a

foreign labor force initially because it was "easier to squeeze extra profits from alien workers who were poor, considered racially inferior, and
lacked the intellectual ability and determination to rely on the family,
community, or the law for legitimate protest."[21] Many of the institutions
that normally encouraged labor organization were challenged by the migration of West Indians to Honduras. Initially, families were fractured
and the law often sided with the fruit companies. Honduran politicians,
most notably President Tiburcio Carías (1932–1948), historically had no
interest in improving the situation for banana workers, whether Honduran or West Indian, and worked with the UFCO and Standard Fruit to put
down strikes and labor organizers for fear that they would challenge the
authority of the regime.[22] Moreover, any disruption in fruit production
by organized labor risked jeopardizing Honduran government proceeds
from an industry that by 1944 accounted for nearly four-fifths of total
exports from Central America to the United States and three-fourths of
all imports from the United States.[23] As a consequence, Carías suppressed
the labor movement in Honduras during his dictatorship and true organized labor did not emerge until after 1948.[24] Evidence suggests that as
late as 1951, there existed no organized labor movement among banana
workers on the North Coast.[25] Most West Indians had since left the country due to the immigration laws of 1929 and 1934, which curtailed and
later prohibited black immigration to the country, thus explaining in part
the lack of West Indian representation in the movement.

Although government-sanctioned labor unions did not emerge until
after the Carías government, Honduran workers on the North Coast repeatedly organized informally to combat the unfair labor practices of the
fruit companies. Mario Posas documents strikes in the banana enclaves of
the North Coast from 1916 through 1932 through which Honduran workers sought increased wages and better working conditions.[26] In these early
strikes, fruit companies often employed West Indians as strike breakers
or scabs, thus facilitating an enduring suspicion of and animosity toward
West Indian labor by Hondurans.[27]

WEST INDIAN IMMIGRATION AND ITS IMPLICATIONS
FOR THE AFRICAN DIASPORA

The experiences of West Indians in the historical narrative of Central
America have been consigned, due largely to phenotype, culture, and

employment, as oppositional to the construction of homogenous Central American national identities. However, as Francisco Scarano suggests, "the historical experiences of people of African descent have often been buried beneath a homogenizing discourse of national unity in a popular undercurrent of anti-black intellectual thought."[28] In the case of Honduras, not only have the experiences of West Indians been submerged beneath an "all-inclusive" nationalizing agenda, but also through the homogenization of blackness in the literature that emphasizes the Garífuna experience above all others. Scholars have adequately demonstrated the pivotal role of the Garífuna in defining the discourse on blackness in Honduras. Since they were in Honduras long before the arrival of West Indians, the Garífuna bore the brunt of anti-black sentiment and continue to experience racism and prejudice that marginalizes them within Honduran society politically, socially, and economically.[29] In some instances, particularly in the banana zones of the North Coast, Garífuna and West Indian experiences overlapped due to an oversimplification of definitions of blackness. The goal of this project is to underscore the West Indian experience within the debate on blackness and its role in challenging Honduran notions of race and nation.

Michael Conniff describes the West Indian community in Central America as a microcosm of the African diaspora in which blacks had been scattered abroad by the forces of slavery, poverty, and white supremacy.[30] Paul Dosal depicts a similar scenario in his assessment of Puerto Barrios, Guatemala, in which he posits that the formation of black culture in the Atlantic coastal city forms part of a "larger socio-historical phenomenon in the second stage of the African Diaspora" involving Jamaicans that spans the entire Caribbean coastal region of Central America.[31] The history of West Indians in Honduras initially followed a similar course. The majority came to escape the lack of opportunity in the Caribbean following the collapse of the sugar industry during the mid-nineteenth century. Most West Indians worked for American-owned fruit companies and their subsidiaries. However, unlike other nations where the divisions within the African-descent communities centered on the adversarial relationship between West Indians and Spanish-speaking blacks, or where interisland rivalries permeated much of the discourse, the communities of Afro descent in Honduras represented a unique situation.

By the time West Indians arrived in Honduras during the late nineteenth and early twentieth centuries, two distinct cultures converged in the cities along the North Coast of Honduras to form a mélange of interpretations of Honduran and African diasporic identities. The aforementioned Garífuna represented the most significant ethnic group because of their unique racial and cultural heritage. Their origins stem from miscegenation between captive Africans shipwrecked on the island of St. Vincent in the seventeenth century and the indigenous Carib Indian population that embraced them. The culture and language of the Garífuna reflect this mixture and represent a distinct New World identity based on African and Amerindian cooperation. This alliance manifested itself in the establishment of Maroon communities in St. Vincent, which disrupted the colonization efforts of the French and later British for almost a century.

Garífuna history in Honduras began when the British, after successfully defeating the Garífuna, deported the population from St. Vincent to Roatan in the year 1797 in order to rid the British settlement of the possibility of future reprisal and disruption to British hegemony on the island. From Roatan, the Garífuna resettled to Trujillo on the Honduran mainland, where the colonial Spanish government employed them to defend the coast against outsiders. Eventually the population spread along the Caribbean coast of Central America, extending as far north as Belize and as far south as Nicaragua.

In addition to the Garífuna, an established Honduran population of West Indian descent which dates to the 1830s resided in the Bay Islands archipelago of Honduras. This group shared much in common with later West Indian arrivals. The Bay Islanders were descendants of earlier Caymanian and Jamaican families who migrated independently to the region in the 1830s following the formal emancipation of slavery in the British Caribbean. Many of the early Caymanian settlers were of either white or mixed African and European ancestry. They maintained Caymanian notions of race that embraced a hierarchy structured along color and class lines. However, despite color differences in the Bay Islands population and later West Indian migrants, the anti-English, anti-Black sociopolitical environment in Honduras during the twentieth century facilitated the aligning of the two groups based on their British Caribbean cultural heritage and notions of citizenship. Although a part of Honduras since 1859, the Bay Islands had been ruled informally as a British possession since the 1840s at the urging of the local population and after 1852, as a crown colony. Crown colony status was shortlived as the islands were handed over to Honduras in 1859 as a result of an agreement among the United States, Honduras, and Great Britain.

The British conceded to American pressure over the British violation of the Monroe Doctrine. With control of the Bay Islands rendered to Honduras, the inhabitants became Honduran citizens. The terms of the treaty guaranteed that the culture of the Bay Islands remained British due to stipulations that the English language and Protestant religion be given preference. Through the first half of the twentieth century, many in the Bay Islands, unwilling to accept Honduran citizenship, continued to identify as British subjects and disavowed any political or cultural association with Honduras. Bay Islanders continued to identify with the British West Indies and maintained strong economic and social ties to British Honduras. Bay Islanders willingly embraced West Indian workers who arrived in Honduras throughout the late nineteenth and early twentieth centuries, often marrying them and thus reaffirming their ties to the Caribbean.

An all-inclusive Afro-Honduran identity never emerged. Culture, language, and history were the primary means by which black identity developed in Honduras. Most divisions on the surface were based on these factors. However, ethnicity proved instrumental in exposing the complexities of identity on the North Coast. On the one hand, the Spanish-speaking Garífuna community comprised the largest and most dominant population of Afro-Hondurans. On the other hand, the English-speaking population of West Indian descent, composed of British West Indian banana workers and Bay Islanders, forged its own distinct community. The Honduran government, with its majority mestizo population of Spanish and Amerindian descent, made little distinction between West Indians, Bay Islanders, and Garífuna.

Studies by Mark Anderson, Nancie Gonzalez, Salvador Suazo, Darío Euraque, and others have traced the effects homogenizing discourses on race have had on the solidification of Garífuna identity. William Davidson's history of the Bay Islands remains a seminal work in understanding the cultural and geographical circumstances that facilitated the formulation of a Bay Island culture and identity. No such monograph exists for the communities of West Indian descent that trace their ancestry to the workers who arrived from the 1890s to the 1930s to work for the Cuyamel Fruit Company, the United Fruit Company, and the Standard Fruit and Steamship Company in various skilled and unskilled labor capacities. This study focuses on the emergence of this community in Honduras and aims to position the history of this population within Honduran historiography. Between 1890 and 1934, West Indians from various British colonial holdings—primarily Jamaica and British Honduras (Belize)—converged in the Caribbean coastal region of Honduras. Though they were never a majority of the workforce in the banana zones, their presence in the country raised questions about Honduran notions of identity centered on the concept of *mestizaje* as definitive of the Honduran "race."

Several interests clashed in this political and racially charged environment. From the beginning of American dominance in the fruit industry, both the Honduran elite in Tegucigalpa and West Indians on the coast forged a web of political and social relationships that challenged Honduran national identity. The West Indian workers in particular brought with them a culture that was oppositional not only to the Spanish-speaking, mestizo culture, but also to the culture of the more dominant Garífuna and Honduran conceptions of blackness. This opposition served as a contributing factor to the inability of people of African descent in Honduras to forge a common identity.

West Indians fought to maintain their identities as fruit company workers, Protestants, and English speakers. The West Indian was clearly an outsider in Honduran society, owing to the many racially motivated notions of the Honduran government that defined acceptable immigration as "white only." An unintended consequence of these political patterns was the emergence of a clearly defined and separate West Indian community that proved to be in many ways antagonistic toward native Hondurans. This ultimately was detrimental to West Indians, who were blamed for many of the labor, economic, and social problems on the North Coast of Honduras. An explanation of how this occurred is the goal of this book.

THE SIGNIFICANCE OF COLOR AND CLASS WITHIN
THE WEST INDIAN DIASPORA

West Indian conceptions of ethnicity and group identity in Honduras were influenced by postemancipation realities in the British Caribbean. Studies on identity within the African diaspora often focus on the transformation of "New World" societies by enslaved Africans through the recreation of their African past in new environments and through the reconceptualization and assimilation of non-African traditions. Moreover, new identities and cultures were formed as a result of new realities. Therefore, debates centered on ethnicity must incorporate postemancipation realities that delve into issues of identity formation in the colonial and postcolonial world. As Stephen Glazer suggests, in areas like the Caribbean following emancipation, ethnicity was a "declaration of political and historical consciousness."[32]

Although the Caribbean world comprised a majority population of either African or mixed African and European ancestry, colonial elites were instrumental in the construction of national identity. In this system, Caribbean societies were constructed along color and class lines with European racial and sociocultural norms accepted and African ancestry relegated to a subordinate position. Within this framework, there was the creation of a middle group of mixed-race individuals known as the "colored" class. This group was regarded by whites and themselves as a completely separate racial category.[33] Members of the colored class in the Caribbean often disassociated themselves from the black masses. As Bonham Richardson maintains in his study of Barbadian society prior to large-scale migration to the Panama Canal Zone, "clothing, mannerisms, religious affiliations, social relationships, reading preferences, and many other variables all combined with skin color separated brown Barbadians from their black cousins."[34] Barbados was not unlike other islands in the Caribbean during this period in which rigid social and cultural barriers inhibited black and colored cooperation. Because many of the West Indians who immigrated to Honduras aspired to colored social norms or reinvented themselves along those lines upon arrival in Honduras, their actions inhibited cooperation based on being black. This is evident in the fact that early twentieth-century, pan-Africanist movements such as the Universal Negro Improvement Association (UNIA), which boasted a sizable membership within the West Indian migrant communities in Panama and Costa Rica, never gained a large following in Honduras. Instead, religious organizations (Methodist and Episcopal), Masonic lodges (male and female), and mutual aid societies, in addition to other cultural organizations and events, had a more sustained impact on the West Indian community in Honduras. Close proximity to British Honduras reinforced many of these Caribbean traditions in addition to the British colonial education system.

West Indians in Honduras struggled to garner support outside of their communities for their distinct cultural identity within the context of a national discourse on immigration and race that viewed them as the other. In many ways, the existence of a West Indian identity and the hostility of Honduran intellectuals to it fell within the binary relationship of power prevalent in the study of structuralism. In an assessment of similar circumstances in late nineteenth and twentieth-century Egypt, Eve Troutt Powell maintains that in an effort to create a language that would unify Egypt, nationalists had to incorporate social and political contradictions to offer a centralizing method of expression.[35] The application of such principles in Honduras can be seen in the homogenizing discourse of national unity in a society that historically had no tangible concept of either race or nation. On the one hand, Honduran intellectuals attempted to soften the effects of a national discourse against immigration through legislation. On the other hand, they sought to maintain a distinct cultural identity for West Indians separate from a Honduran national identity but compatible with it.

While an effort has been made to integrate this study within the growing discourse on identity and nationhood in modern Latin America, unlike previous studies on identity, this one will not be read simply as a variable in an adversarial relationship between the powerful and the powerless. In order to assess adequately their situation in Honduras, West Indians must be seen as agents in a process of cultural construction, a process that involved the historical combination of several different strands of ethnic and social differentiation into a sense of community.

ECONOMIC REALITIES OF IMMIGRATION AND THE CREATION OF TRANSNATIONAL IDENTITIES

In addition to its focus on race and ethnicity within the African diaspora, this study of the West Indian community in Honduras is a migration study encompassing a North American, Caribbean, and Central American analysis of black identity within a postemancipation context. The economic incentives offered to North American entrepreneurs by the Honduran government to aid in the modernization and industrialization of the country led to the creation of the banana industry that served as the primary pull factor to entice West Indian laborers struggling to survive in a depressed Caribbean economy. Many of the West Indians, especially the Jamaicans, had previous experience in the banana industry owing to the early development of that industry on the island by both local growers and later the Boston Fruit Company, the predecessor to United Fruit. The banana plantations of Honduras offered promises of opportunity for these workers and the possibility to better their economic condition.

The economic benefits of the banana industry and the transnational migration that ensued "must be analyzed within the context of global relations between capital and labor."[36] In Honduras, the emergence of the West Indian community was sparked by the labor needs of American businesses and their desire to gain financially from their investment exploits on the Caribbean coast there. In addition to the labor and capital component, Linda Basch and others also assert that transnationalism is a process by which migrants, through their daily life activities and social, economic, and political relations create social fields that cross national boundaries.[37] By maintaining cultural traditions and ties to home countries, the West Indian community in Honduras was able to retain much of its identity. Also, by disassociating themselves from the more dominant Garífuna and mestizo populations, West Indians created a situation in which they were susceptible to being singled out in the anti-immigration political discourse of the period. However, because the community found itself in a Central American environment that was foreign both geographically and culturally, it was changed by the encounters with the local population. The children of the first wave of West Indians born in Honduras represented a dual nationality in more than just the diplomatic sense. Culturally they were West Indian, but politically their interests were becoming Honduran.

West Indian workers were viewed as outsiders by Hondurans. Their status as black (by Honduran definition), English-speaking, and employed by the fruit company pitted them against the majority of society. In many instances, Hondurans defined themselves in opposition to the West Indian and used legislation and violence to eradicate the West Indian presence from the country. However, in their home colonies the West Indian migrant workers were seen as a source of revenue through fees gained by the various colonial treasuries placed on those contracting labor as well as through the remittances sent back by workers themselves to support relatives.

The West Indians who immigrated to Honduras in order to work for the North American–owned banana companies on the Caribbean coast never intended to become Honduran. Their preservation of the English language, Caribbean cultural heritage, modes of religious worship, and social organization, in addition to their own ethnocentrism, are just some examples of how West Indians opted to maintain their distinct identity in a Hispanic-dominated environment. Hondurans clearly saw West Indians as outsiders and agents of a North American economic machine that grew rich at the expense of the Honduran worker. This study is not simply another case study of West Indian workers in a Latin American context. The goal is not only to demonstrate how immigration shaped the way in which the Honduran state saw itself as a result of the influx of West Indians, but also to show how West Indians managed and negotiated their existence in their new environment.

* * *

The bulk of this study centers on the West Indian experience in Honduras between 1890 and 1940. The turn of the twentieth century witnessed the expansion of the banana industry in Honduras and the development of the United Fruit Company and Standard Fruit into multinational corporations with significant political and economic influence in Latin America and the Caribbean. However, in order to understand this phenomenon and how it relates to the West Indian situation, the first part of the book incorporates an analysis of the 1876 legislation of the liberal reform period in Honduran history and its impact on the migration of West Indians to the country. The legislation of the liberal party initiated by then-president Marco Aurelio Soto promoted foreign investment in the country, and the legality of American companies in the region was sanctioned. The last chapter ends in 1934 with the deportation of West Indian workers from the cities of Tela, Trujillo, and Puerto Castilla as fruit companies bowed to local government pressure to transition their labor force to a completely Honduran one. However, the events at Trujillo and Puerto Castilla had implications for the next decade in terms of the eventual decline of the West Indian population in the country. Geographically, this study is centered on the banana enclaves and communities surrounding the coastal towns of Tela, La Ceiba, Trujillo, and the Bay Islands, each of which at some time were major centers for banana production.

Chapter 1 traces the development of Honduran liberal reforms and their connection to the development of the banana industry. Special attention is given to the development of the liberal ideology of race and the role it would play in shaping Honduran views of West Indians. Chapter

2 analyzes Honduran immigration law and the impact it would come to have on the North Coast of Honduras and the West Indian population. This chapter highlights the systematic ways in which blacks were legislated out of the concept of the nation and the role immigration had on the development of the Honduran economy and its fostering of an anti-black political agenda. Chapter 3 is dedicated to the arrival of the West Indian labor force in Honduras and the impact West Indians had on the development of the banana industry. The arrival of the community immediately sparked anti-black and anti-immigrant sentiment in the country. Steps were initiated to eradicate this group from the country and curb the fruit companies' influence over Honduran affairs. Such tactics culminated in the deportation of large numbers of West Indians from Honduras. This theme is also discussed in chapter 6, with special emphasis on the situation in the coastal town of Trujillo.

Chapter 4 is dedicated to an understanding of the cultural and social dynamics of the West Indian workers in Honduras. It provides a window into how a sense of community developed despite obstacles created by outside forces. Of special importance are the institutions that grew there that demonstrate the cultural continuities between the West Indies and the community in Honduras. Central to this chapter is a discussion of the cultural and racial dynamics that played out among Bay Islanders, West Indians, and the Garífuna. Chapter 5 looks at the West Indian experience in Honduras within the larger context of the British Empire and emphasizes West Indian perceptions of Englishness as juxtaposed with the British government's notions of dealing with subject peoples. The epilogue addresses the period between 1934 and 1950 by exposing the realities of West Indian return to the Caribbean region after deportation from Central America and the implications for understanding the modern Caribbean diaspora that later emerged in Britain, Canada, and the United States during the second half of the twentieth century.

1

THE HONDURAN LIBERAL REFORMS
AND THE RISE OF WEST INDIAN MIGRATION

The initial stages of the West Indian migration experience in Honduras are best understood within the context of the liberal reform period in Honduran historiography. Banana companies and economically minded Honduran liberals used the reforms to create an extralegal environment in which fruit corporations benefited economically from the political and social agendas of the nation. Because West Indians were an imported labor force hired specifically by the fruit companies, they remained in a quasilegal position that left them outside the scope of the state. This was clearly a benefit to the corporations that were able to control West Indian labor on the North Coast, but it proved to be a mixed blessing for the West Indians, whose fate in Honduras was often decided by others. Scholars in the United States and Honduras such as Darío Euraque, Héctor Pérez Brignoli, Mario Argueta, and Mario Posas have examined the complexities of the liberal reforms and their impact on the political, economic, social, and labor dimensions of the modern Honduran state.

This chapter focuses on the reforms as they relate to the emergence of the West Indian migrant population in Honduras and their settlement in the banana enclaves of the North Coast. By adhering to established analyses of this period, I do not seek to reinterpret the existing literature on the liberal reforms in Honduran historiography, but rather to provide the context for a better understanding of the political, economic, and social climate West Indians entered on their arrival.

The liberal reforms represent a major shift in the history of migration in Honduras. The fallout from the political and economic legislation during the period constitutes perhaps the most comprehensive example of population shift in the history of the modern state of Honduras. Among those arriving on the North Coast of Honduras were North American businessmen seeking to benefit from liberal economic policies in agriculture, Honduran elites shifting from coffee-producing regions to the easily accessible banana lands and commercial opportunities of the North Coast frontier,[1] European and Middle Eastern immigrants capitalizing on the expanding mercantilist economy as a result of the expansion of agribusiness, West Indians seeking employment as laborers and skilled workers, and Hondurans and other Central Americans fleeing from the interior to the North Coast in search of more viable means of making a living. All of these groups were seeking to share in the liberal vision of a Honduras deeply integrated into the global economy and the modernization and industrial processes.

Honduran historiography dates the beginning of the liberal reform period from 1876 with the inauguration of the Liberal party candidate Marco Aurelio Soto (1876–1883) as president of the republic. Kenneth Finney suggests that 1876 was a watershed year for Honduras owing to such innovative legislation as the suppression of the tithe, the introduction of public education, and the codification of legal commercial mining and the passage of administrative laws aimed at the promotion of economic development within the country.[2] Marvin Barahona maintains that, in order to allow access to agricultural lands, the reforms also called for the separation of church and state and the nationalization of church lands in an effort to curb the *latifundia* systems that monopolized land and inhibited the development of natural resources for the benefit of the nation. Furthermore, the system hindered the development of large-scale agricultural enterprises believed by liberals to be the catalyst for economic growth.[3]

Perhaps the greatest legacy of the reforms as they relate to the emergence of the West Indian community in Honduras is their facilitation of new ties between Honduras and the world economy by offering incentives to both Hondurans and foreigners to develop and expand the export agricultural industry.[4] The reforms served as the catalyst that ignited the banana boom in Honduras by regenerating the Honduran agricultural industry and redirecting the economic orientation of the nation from the interior to the North Coast.[5] Darío Euraque asserts that Honduran efforts to establish banana plantations on the North Coast between 1870 and the first decades of the twentieth century represented an obstacle for the legislature in Tegucigalpa to develop other possibilities for agriculture.[6] The reforms established the North Coast of the country as the economic center of the nation and encouraged an influx of both human and economic capital into the region.

Hondurans from all parts of the country converged on the North Coast to take advantage of the numerous job opportunities and higher wages offered in the region. At the height of banana production, employment on the North Coast was ten to fifteen times higher than in the interior.[7] The prospect of lucrative wages that attracted Hondurans to the North Coast also attracted thousands of West Indians to the region. With its relative economic prosperity and long history of cultural and ethnic pluralism, the North Coast appeared to be an area where West Indians would thrive. Because the export banana industry was in its early stages in the late nineteenth and early twentieth centuries, some scholars have argued that West Indians were in prime position to monopolize the Honduran labor market due to their prior experience with banana production in their home islands and to the racial sensibilities of North American employers who relied on subordinate black labor. Hector Perez Brignoli highlights these sentiments in exposing views shared by many fruit company executives that blacks, particularly West Indians, were the only group predisposed to work in railroad and plantation construction in the extreme heat because of the affinity of African-descended peoples to warm climates.[8] Despite the racist notions of North Americans and some Hondurans, West Indians were never the majority population on the North Coast and constantly found themselves at odds with Hondurans over competition for employment. Table 1.1 lists the number of documented West Indians available through Honduran immigration and census records. However, these numbers may not represent all West Indians because many entered the country as temporary workers for the fruit companies, rather than as immigrants seeking resettlement in Honduras.

Justifiable demand for jobs on the part of Hondurans was often the root cause of anti–West Indian sentiment. While the economic agenda of the liberal reforms accounted for an influx of foreign capital and business ventures into Honduras, the reformers did not realize that their efforts toward modernization would translate into racial and ethnic tension with a foreign labor force. They did not foresee the vast importation of foreign

TABLE 1.1 Estimated Number of Documented West Indians on the North Coast, 1887–1935

YEAR	NO. OF WEST INDIANS
1887	1,033
1910	4,710
1926	3,673
1930	4,215
1935	2,083

Sources: Honduras, Censos de Población (1910–1935), and Mario Argueta, *Los alemanes en Honduras* (Tegucigalpa, Honduras: Centro de Documentación de Honduras, 1992), 11.

labor into the country. West Indians and their descendants were never the intended beneficiaries of liberal policies. There was no reason for reformers to believe that fruit companies would not favor local Honduran labor. Such was the case in most instances. However, West Indians in the early days of the foreign-dominated industry did receive considerable advantages in terms of higher-quality and often higher-paying jobs, and a better overall quality of life that most Hondurans were not afforded. Mario Posas has documented extensively that most Hondurans were not granted such advancements in the banana zones without protest through strikes and other forms of collective resistance, a reality West Indians never experienced.

Many scholars of the West Indian diaspora in Latin America have mistakenly viewed the competition between West Indians and the local citizenry as only an economic or labor issue. Such an analysis does a disservice to the study of the Honduran situation in that labor and economic uncertainty quickly manifested into political pressures. The West Indian presence on the North Coast in many instances challenged the agenda of reformers. Although Marco Aurelio Soto is often credited with establishing the economic agenda of the Honduran liberal reforms, his strategy also had political implications. Soto, along with his cousin Ramón Rosa, instituted a political approach based largely on the latter's efforts to unify the territory of Honduras politically and culturally. Rosa, in an effort to sustain the territorial integrity of Honduras and promote political stability, sought to unify the nation on political and constitutional models from North American and European democracies.[9] The establishment of public education, the debate over the national image of Honduras, and the liberal strategies of social development can all be traced back to the positivist-influenced thinking of Ramón Rosa. The economic approach of Marco Aurelio Soto, while credited for providing the policies that led to the influx of foreign capital into Honduras, surpassed the efforts of Rosa in terms of lasting impact. Some scholars have argued that both approaches did very little to change the fundamental structure of Honduran society. The economic and political visions of the country were changed, but the social and cultural structure based on a hierarchy established by the Creole elite from colonial times remained intact.[10]

Reform did not promote the surge in modernization that reformers hoped. Honduras remained a weak state, and the revenues collected from the developing agricultural industry were rarely enough to strengthen the economic and political structure of the national government.[11] In no place was this more evident than on the North Coast. The enormous profits garnered by the fruit companies most often made their way back to New Orleans, Boston, New York, and other U.S. cities where the fruit companies were headquartered. Elizet Payne suggests that the inability of Liberals to create a strong centralized state in the region inadvertently indebted the nation to North American investors.[12] The government created new departments on the North Coast in an effort to politically consolidate the region under the umbrella of the state, but it did not have the infrastructure in place to enforce the laws. Countless examples throughout this study demonstrate disconnect between Tegucigalpa and the North Coast. Government representatives in the North Coast departments often held short tenures, and most mail and telegraph correspondence was irregular. This would pose serious challenges in immigration issues concerning West Indians, as most department officials were not competent interpreters of laws and procedures and handled issues such as deportation haphazardly. Because of an inadequate state presence in the region, the fruit companies were able to utilize this environment to their benefit and circumvent labor and immigration laws regarding hiring West Indians, a theme that is discussed further in subsequent chapters.

Prior to the institution of the liberal reforms, the Honduran economy was at subsistence level. Forestry and mining aided in sustaining the local economy and by 1855 accounted for two-thirds of the country's exports.[13] However, these industries were mostly unregulated and failed to spark an export-oriented economy that would achieve larger financial gains for the nation.[14] In addition, industries such as forestry and the contraband trade were historically dominated by the British and other Europeans in contested regions such as La Mosquitia and the colony of British Honduras during the colonial period. Taylor Mack has demonstrated the role of Hondurans as smugglers in this enterprise and the far-reaching impact of the trade from Trujillo and La Mosquitia through established networks to Comayagua and Tegucigalpa.[15] The mining industry of Honduras in the regions around the capital city of Tegucigalpa had an enormous foreign presence in terms of investment capital.

The North American—specifically, the United States—presence in Honduras increased tremendously following the Clayton-Bulwer Treaty between Britain and the United States in 1850.[16] Kenneth Bourne maintains that the British entered into the treaty with the United States in the hope of securing free and equal use of a future interoceanic canal in the region. The British also hoped to present a formal barrier to the territorial expansion of the United States.[17] Unfortunately for the British, the treaty did neither. Honduras did not become the site of the canal, and disputes over British expansion in the region, stemming from debates over the Monroe Doctrine, eventually led to the loss of British territories in La Mosquitia and the Bay Islands.

The increased U.S. presence in Honduran political affairs set the stage for future intrusion into the Honduran economy. The political situation in the emerging nation fueled much of this. Honduras was unable to achieve economic success and promote large-scale development in line with the liberal reforms due to continued political instability within the country. In 1897, Albert Morlan, an independent American traveler to Honduras from Indianapolis, Indiana, wrote that many of the local fruit developers, in an effort to monopolize control over the local banana industry and maintain their contracts with New York– and New Orleans–based importers, often employed the local militia in order to intimidate the competition.[18] Such actions promoted a bellicose environment in which local business competition led to wide-scale armed conflict in certain regions. Writing in 1914, Frederick Upham Adams maintained that within a fifteen-year period, there had been six revolutions in Honduras.[19] In such a political climate, with constant in-fighting over control of the resource-rich mining and agricultural areas, unregulated exploitation of wealth by Honduran elites and their U.S. cohorts was common. Ironically, during the same period, Euraque notes that some thirty-seven land and railroad concessions were granted to North American, primarily U.S., capitalists.[20] Some dependency theorists contend that this factor contributed to the underdevelopment of Honduras and the subsequent dominance of foreigners in the economy.[21]

Despite the political uncertainty and the inability to develop an industry that would produce viable returns on the international market, many Liberals felt that agriculture still offered the best conduit for economic development and coffee was the chosen product. For Liberals, the emerging coffee industry presented an opportunity for Honduras to enter the world economy.[22] However, a Honduran coffee boom was over before it began because, in addition to being in competition with Puerto Rico, Brazil, Colombia, and various other countries for a share in the market, Honduras also lacked the infrastructure necessary to transport the coffee bean crop from the mountainous regions to the coast for export.[23] In addition, the emergence of the banana industry on the North Coast of the country and its enormous success relegated coffee to second place.[24] Although the efforts of Marco Aurelio Soto, Ramon Rosa, and other notable Liberals were laudable, their initial reform measures were the least successful in Central America at achieving basic institutional and economic transformation.[25] Some scholars maintain that this was because the Honduran elite lacked the investment capital and entrepreneurship of the North American and European societies they sought to emulate.[26] While foreign investment had been detrimental to many aspects of Honduran political and economic vitality, it was still necessary to build a modern, industrial nation. Therefore, to promote development, the Liberal government of Marco Aurelio Soto began to offer incentives to North Americans and Europeans to immigrate and invest in Honduras.

Liberals saw immigration as the solution to Honduras's economic misfortunes. In the Honduran constitution of 1880, as Alison Acker describes, the Liberal government maintained that the state would do everything possible to increase the welfare and development of the country by stimulating progress in agriculture, industry, and trade, by attracting immigration, colonizing arid land, building railroads and highways, helping new industries, establishing leading institutions, and bringing in foreign capital.[27] What emerged from these efforts was the integration of Honduras into the world economy, although not always on equal terms with other nations.

TABLE 1.2 Direct Investment of the United States in Honduran Agriculture and Mining Industries, 1897–1950

YEAR	AMOUNT (U.S. DOLLARS)
1897	$2,000,000
1908	2,000,000
1914	9,500,000
1919	19,400,000
1924	40,200,000
1929	72,000,000
1936	36,000,000
1940	38,000,000
1943	37,000,000
1950	62,000,000
Total	$318,100,000

Source: Juan Aranciba C., *Honduras: ¿Un estado nacional?* (Tegucigalpa: Editorial Guaymu-ras, 2001), 40.

To promote the new immigration policy, the Honduran government offered various incentives to both Hondurans and foreigners to develop Honduran agriculture, such as free land to any foreigner who would de-velop it for agricultural or industrial purposes, and a property tax exemp-tion for farmers as well as a tax exemption on the import of machinery and tools, along with numerous other exemptions.[28] Although the laws stated that both Hondurans and foreigners were entitled to the conces-sions, most Hondurans did not benefit from this policy because they lacked capital.[29] Between 1882 and 1915, 276 concessions were granted to businessmen to develop industries in the country.[30] These concessions were accorded primarily to promote the development of the mining in-dustry. The Honduras and Rosario Mining Company offers one of the few noteworthy examples of Honduran interest in an industrial enter-prise that benefited from the liberal reforms. However, the Hondurans involved in the enterprise were members of the elite and detached from the interests of most Hondurans.[31] Some have argued that the small Hon-duran elite lacked the level of national consciousness that was necessary in order to promote the interests of the entire nation. Instead, this group utilized the mechanisms of the state to advance their personal agendas of acquiring individual wealth.[32]

THE DEVELOPMENT OF THE HONDURAN BANANA INDUSTRY

Foreign-owned businesses profited enormously from these new policies and incentives. In no case was this more pronounced than on the North Coast of Honduras with the development of the banana industry. According to the historian James Mahoney, during the first two decades of the twentieth century, bananas accounted for one-half of all exports from Honduras. The other half was shared by the mining industry. By 1930, the banana industry represented 90 percent of all of the country's exports, with the United Fruit Company accounting for nearly 70 percent of the banana exports.[33] As table 1. 2 demonstrates, this rise in fruit production also led to an increase in the amount of U.S. capital investment in Honduras.

The substantial increase in U.S. investment in Honduras from 1897 through 1929 as denoted in table 1.2 stemmed largely from investment in the mining and agricultural sectors of the Honduran economy. Investment decreased after 1929 primarily as a result of the global economic depression of that year. However, investments eventually rose after the global economy recovered. The figures do not indicate that most of the investment in the country during this period was centered on the banana industry.

In the twentieth century, a banana industry that once was dominated by small and independent local producers soon became the domain of a handful of North American entrepreneurs.[34] Mario Posas among others maintains that the control of banana production prior to the twentieth century was in the hands of local Honduran producers who challenged foreigners by offering competitive prices for bananas that were in turn shipped to the port of New Orleans.[35] The fact that private citizens, primarily through their business dealings, became the most important vehicle in shaping the role of the United States in Latin America has been the focal point of numerous works by U.S. foreign relations historians. Emily Rosenberg articulates this trend most thoroughly in her theory of liberal developmentalism, in which she maintains that traders eroded cultural and political barriers that enabled investors, missionaries, philanthropists, international societies, and purveyors of mass communications to galvanize U.S. expansion abroad.[36] In addition, an industry that was once dependent on local labor soon became the domain of immigrant workers imported from throughout Central America and the Caribbean.

Steve Striffler argues that six factors gave rise to the growth of multinational corporations in Latin America in the twentieth century: opening up of new lands by Latin American governments, scientific research demanded by newly developing tropical agriculture, the development of extensive canal networks, the construction of railroads, the purchase of modern machinery, and the global transportation of a perishable commodity.[37] While focusing specifically on the United Fruit Company in Ecuador, Striffler's model holds true for Honduras because it was there that the United Fruit Company and several other North American–owned fruit companies developed the business strategies that were implemented throughout Latin America.

The cultivation of bananas in Honduras, specifically the Gros Michel variety, was initiated on the Bay Islands and on the North Coast of Honduras in the later decades of the nineteenth century. From roughly 1860 to 1900, the industry remained almost completely in the hands of local growers. In coastal cities such as La Ceiba, these local growers were mainly independent farmers descended from migrants from the department of Olancho who settled the coast in search of better economic opportunities. The farmers cultivated the banana and sold the fruit to North American merchants who had access to seafaring vessels. Some estimates indicate that roughly 320,000 bunches of bananas were shipped to the United States per year between 1891 and 1899.[38] According to U.S. diplomatic correspondence from the 1890s, La Ceiba emerged as the center of a large district devoted to the production of tropical fruits for export to the United States. It was estimated that some ten to twelve American steamships called at the port every month from New Orleans and New York.[39] These North American merchants had access to an untapped market for "exotic" tropical fruits. In addition, the large ports of the northeastern and southern United States, combined with a transcontinental railroad system that linked the entire United States, set in place the necessary infrastructure to market the fruit throughout the country.

While the number and size of North American–owned fruit companies in Honduras varied throughout the late nineteenth and early twentieth centuries, ranging from small independent companies to large multinational corporations, three companies proved essential to defining the dynamics of the North Coast of Honduras: the Vaccaro Brothers (later Standard Fruit and Steamship Company), the United Fruit Company, and the Cuyamel Fruit Company. Most West Indians on the North Coast worked for one of these three companies. The Standard Fruit and Steamship Company eventually controlled the fruit industry in the region in and around La Ceiba, while the United Fruit Company, after merging with the Cuyamel Fruit Company in 1929, and through its subsidiaries in Tela and Trujillo, controlled the fruit industry from west of San Pedro Sula to La Lima and Tela and from Trujillo to Puerto Castilla.[40]

The three major fruit companies on the North Coast all shared an ability to obtain and manipulate government concessions. The Honduran government awarded the Vaccaro Brothers and Company a concession in 1905 to export fruit from La Ceiba in exchange for a promise to build canals in the region served by the Salado and Porvenir rivers. In addition, the company was to build jetties, docks, and structures necessary for the development of the region. Smaller local companies acquired access to the canals and the ports and were exempt from customs duties on imports and exports.[41]

The Cuyamel and United Fruit Companies gained access to the North Coast through similar dealings with the government. The history of the Cuyamel Fruit Company often focuses on its controversial founder, Samuel Zemurray. A Mobile, Alabama, banana merchant of Russian Jew-

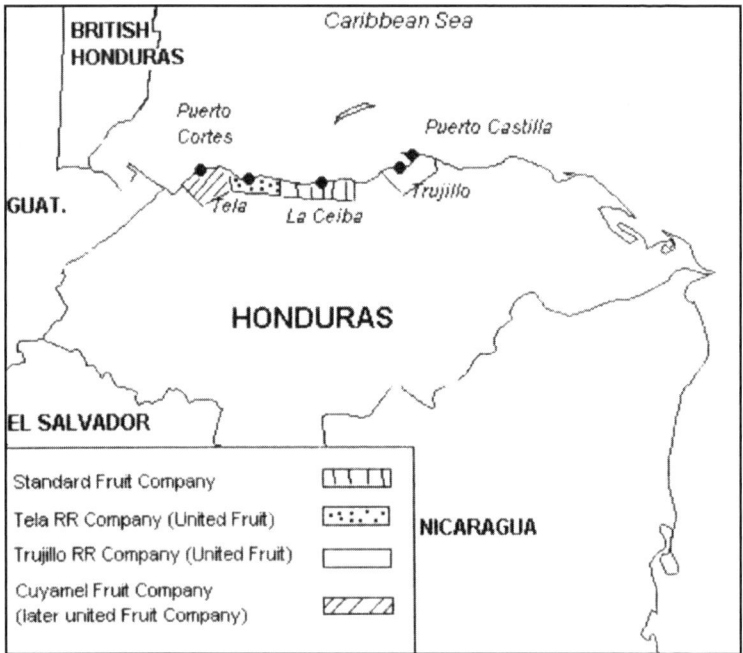

Fruit Companies on the North Coast of Honduras, 1905–1954

ish immigrant origins, Zemurray began his career by buying bananas in railroad cart loads and selling them to local dealers. Later he moved to New Orleans and contracted himself out to the United Fruit Company to sell bananas that had ripened aboard ship and needed to be disposed of quickly in order to avoid a total loss. Eventually in 1910, Zemurray and his partner, Ashbell Hubbard, raised enough money to purchase 5,000 acres of plantation land in Honduras near the Cuyamel River, marking the beginning of the Cuyamel Fruit Company. The firm owned land in the region around the port city of Omoa and built railroads to transport its product to seafaring vessels. The company also built shops and developed a town in the area. The Cuyamel Fruit Company owed its expansion in large part to its construction of canals to enhance agricultural development. Samuel Zemurray also obtained land concessions by allying himself with future Honduran president Manuel Bonilla and financing his revolutionary efforts. As a result of Bonilla's success, Zemurray received large tracts of additional lands and the Honduran government waived his tax obligations.[42]

Cuyamel acquired more land through private business transactions. In 1904, the company bought five thousand hectares of land near Omoa from William Streich, an independent American entrepreneur who had previously been involved in Honduran government ventures to attract white American and European immigrants to the country. Streich had acquired the land only two years prior through a concession granted by the Honduran National Congress for the establishment of an agricultural and industrial enterprise.[43] The Cuyamel Fruit Company was able initially to benefit from the many concessions granted by the Honduran government. And since the company was the largest in the region at the time, it was able to force smaller enterprises, both local and foreign-owned, to sell out or face financial ruin.

Cuyamel came under strong criticism in the Honduran press for what was seen as its strain on the local economy. It was compared to a "boa constrictor breaking the vertebrae of the local economy," and many Hondurans viewed the presence of Cuyamel with anger.[44]

The Cuyamel Fruit Company acquired the right to use a government port to conduct private business. Unlike the United Fruit Company subsidiaries in Tela and Trujillo and the Standard Fruit Company in La Ceiba, Cuyamel used the national port at Puerto Cortés instead of building its own. Criticism arose when the company began to commandeer national resources for private use. The company owned and operated a port at Omoa; however, Puerto Cortés allowed the possibility of more revenue owing to its larger size and additional shipping destinations. While Omoa continued to be important to Cuyamel, the expansion into Puerto Cortés was a cause of concern to many Hondurans because local exporters were unable to export their products without Cuyamel approval. Many called for Hondurans to reclaim the port or else lose it to foreigners. It was suggested that if Hondurans did not fight to retain control of the port, they risked being denied access to it by a dark-skinned Jamaican employee of Cuyamel.[45] Blacks were often hired by Cuyamel as regular employees, but more importantly as strike breakers to maintain production when there was labor unrest with Honduran employees.[46] Clearly, the reference to the dark-skinned Jamaican played to the racist inclinations of Honduran society at the time. Rather than focus on the real issue of why Cuyamel was able to expand into Honduran territory, it was easier to reduce the issue to race, a recurring theme throughout this study. West Indians were a convenient scapegoat.

In addition to the concessions made to Cuyamel, the government of Honduras granted United Fruit exclusive rights to the lands on the west side of the Tela River in exchange for the company's construction of railroads, shops, office structures, hospitals, and other buildings.[47] The company also tested soils and the water and applied scientific remedies in order to increase agricultural production. More important, the eradication of the mosquito aided in the transformation of the swamps and jungles of the North Coast into food-producing areas.[48]

The manipulation of the original railroad concessions into agricultural developments was done in several ways and represented the beginning of the banana industry's dominance over the Honduran national state. From the beginning, there was no resistance to the ingressions of the fruit companies into Honduran territory on the part of a strong Honduran national government because one did not exist. In addition, the heads of the banana companies were able to acquire and maintain power by forming systems of alliances with local and national economic and business leaders. They also made local governments financially indebted to the companies by extending loans to government officials in the name of the state and in actively financing revolutions.[49] More important, since the home offices of the fruit companies were located in the United States, the companies were subject to the protection of the U.S. government. In many instances, these companies served as "representatives" of the U.S. government in Honduras.[50]

The dominance of the banana companies in the local economies of the North Coast and subsequently, in all of Honduras was not limited to banana production. From 1876 to 1954, the interests of the companies expanded into banking, business, new agricultural production, shipping, and communications.[51] For instance, the Standard Fruit Company founded Banco Atlántida, monopolized sugar production with its Honduras Sugar and Distilling Company, made beer and other refreshments through the Compañía Industrial Ceibeña, produced soap and vegetable oil under the Fábrica y La Blanquita and shoes under the Sole Leather and Shoe Company, and engaged in cigarette and tobacco production, just to name some of the industries the company controlled.[52] In addition to the Tela and Trujillo Railroad Companies, the interests of United Fruit included many of the same industries as did Standard Fruit, and United Fruit also maintained control of many of the most important rail and shipping lines in Central America. The company also ventured into communications and established radio and telegraph lines as well as newspapers such as the *Diario Comercial*.[53]

Immigration was another area in which the fruit companies were able to circumvent the law. At no point in Honduran history were immigration policies liberal toward people of African descent. West Indians entered Honduras as employees of the banana companies and were thrust into an environment in which issues of race and immigration were at the forefront of political debate. The experiences of the West Indian workers were directly tied to the dominance of the banana industry in the political and economic affairs of the country.

LIBERALISM AND THE IDEOLOGY OF RACE

Honduran perceptions of race during the liberal reform period and the subsequent expansion of the banana industry, particularly as they relate to the Afro-descended populations, share many similarities to larger political and intellectual movements in Latin America centered on the implementation of a "modern, scientific" approach to nation building. Steeped in the liberal traditions of Europe and the United States, Honduran reformers sought to recreate the industrial successes of northern Europe and the United States through the adoption of northern European and North American cultural norms and ideas based on notions of European racial superiority. Payne suggests that the United States was seen as the model of development for Honduras, particularly the North Coast.[54] According to Richard Graham, Latin Americans during the liberal period generally aspired to an even closer connection to Europe and the United States and sought to follow their leadership in every realm.[55] Unfortunately, a major aspect of U.S. society during this period was the exclusion of "undesirable" elements of the population through the promotion of racist policies. In the United States, this was most visible in the discriminatory policies aimed at African Americans.

The Honduran concept of nation building along racial terms was not new in Latin America. In many instances, the policies enacted by Liberal governments in Honduras paralleled the strategies employed by other nations in the region to address its racial composition. Nancy Appelbaum maintains that liberalism as a philosophy generally presumed an unmarked, raceless, even genderless citizenry, yet nineteenth-century liberals on both sides of the Atlantic described the ideal qualities of citizens and nations in implicitly racial and gendered terms.[56] Literacy, property ownership, and individual autonomy were associated with whiteness and masculinity by the Creole elite.[57] In addition to blaming the ills of Latin American societies on politics, dictators, conservative plots, the Church, and various other institutions, liberals adopted the views of conservative social Darwinists who maintained that the high level of poverty and lack of industrial growth in Latin America was due to the inherently inferior racial and genetic makeup of its multiracial populations.

Historically, regions designated as black or Indian in Latin America were labeled backward in comparison to whiter areas.[58] Regions such as the Caribbean coast of Central America or the Indian lands of Guatemala or Mexico remained on the political and cultural periphery. While *mestizaje* was promoted by many nations, as a way of dealing with a multiracial, multiethnic society to varying degrees since the Spanish colonial era, the existence of this multiracial or nonwhite population was problematic for liberals after independence. Some liberals attempted to develop ways of dealing with the dilemma of promoting development and progress within a society viewed by many as lacking the core racial elements necessary for success. In this regard, the criticism that the liberal perspective disparaged the social importance of nonwhites and Indians in postindependence societies holds some validity.[59]

Much of the debate surrounding race and the degeneration of Latin American society can be tied to the eugenics movement that began in mid-nineteenth-century Europe and North America. Eugenicists adopted a Lamarckian view of genetics and believed that it was possible to obtain "racial improvement" scientifically. Focusing primarily on the family and reproduction, eugenics in Latin America linked health, sanity, alcoholism, diseases, and various social ills to the presence of inferior racial groups and their behavior within society. Efforts were made to attract white immigrants from Europe to counterbalance the African and Indian populations in the region that were the perceived causes of the social ills. David Bushnell describes this period as one in which racist attitudes were briefly made respectable by "science."[60] However, very little of the eugenics debate was grounded in scientific investigation.

In part as an attempt to quell feelings of inadequacy on the international scene, many Latin American intellectuals began to adopt notions of a homogenous culture in which a true nation was defined by a common language, culture, and national identity.[61] The ills of society were blamed on the degeneration of the masses caused by the inferiority of nonwhite populations. Some leaders accepted European racial theory at face value, while others chose to arbitrarily define themselves according to what seemed to fit the particular situations within their country. In countries with a large indigenous and mestizo (mixture of Spanish and Indian) population such as Mexico, liberal thinkers like Jose Vasconcelos claimed the mestizo identity as the apotheosis of human development and created the concept of the "Cosmic Race" in which racial mixture was championed as the ideal.[62] In Brazil, intellectuals such as Gilberto Freyre held race mixture as a national achievement for which Brazil should be proud.[63] In this instance, the mulatto and *mestiço* became the representation of Brazilian identity.

In this perspective, education was seen as a way to combat racial inferiority and ultimately led to notions of a racial democracy in which one could move beyond the stigma of race through education and economic prosperity.[64] If nations could not conform to the national image genetically, then they could do so culturally by cleansing themselves of the "degenerate" traditions and cultures of Africans and Indians. In the case of West Indians in Honduras, this meant the deportation of undesirable elements from the country.

In Central America, liberals were initially concerned with establishing a link to the North Atlantic economy rather than developing notions of national identity. Achieving this goal was seen as the key to the region's success.[65] While liberal governments in the region sanctioned the policies of whitening the population through immigration and the promotion of a Hispanic identity and culture, the development of strong economic and industrial ties to the United States and Europe superseded the national identity debate. The concept of embracing the multiracial character of the population and the efforts to eradicate many of the social and economic ills of society through education came much later. In Honduras, the eugenics argument did not fully manifest itself until the increase in nonwhite immigration during the banana period.

Liberalism proved unsuccessful in Central American countries such as Honduras. This was due in part to the fact that Honduran liberals failed to debate the political and social aspects of society. According to Lowell Gudmundson and Héctor Lindo-Fuentes, liberalism was unable to articulate a credible program for nationhood and national identity despite the identification with an independence movement justified by a cosmopolitan mixture of ideas favoring freedom of thought and action in a reformed society.[66]

The Honduran plan for liberal reform was overwhelmingly an economic plan that benefited those directly tied to the market, foreign companies, or policymakers.[67] The masses of Hondurans remained on the economic periphery. The Honduran liberal elite did attempt to develop a national identity that promoted multiracialism. However, as in the cases of Mexico and Brazil, the promotion of a mixed race identity automatically excluded those whose racial identities were more African or Indian.

The promotion of a mestizo identity in Honduras gained some government recognition in 1916 when the national census replaced the seven racial categories used in previous census reports to identify the population with only two. Hence, white, black, yellow, mulatto, Indian, ladino, and mestizo were replaced with Indian and ladino. In Honduras, the term *ladino* became synonymous with mestizo in that it meant a person of mixed Indian and Spanish ancestry. In addition, the term was also applied to a hispanicized Indian. While such a broad definition of ladino recognized the validity of a large segment of the Honduran population, the term excluded most people of African descent. Those of undeniable and discomforting African ancestry were excluded outright in Honduran census records. The African ancestry of many ladinos, the result of many centuries of miscegenation among Africans, Spaniards, and Indians, was ignored. According to a census taken in 1910, 61.1 percent of the population was ladino, 9.6 percent was mestizo, and 3.3 percent was mulatto. The census of 1926 did not use racial categories and in subsequent years, the population of Honduras, according to census records, was almost 99 percent mestizo.[68] Whereas in countries like Argentina where the large black and mulatto populations were systematically eroded primarily through war and intermarriage, the mulatto population of Honduras was redefined by the government and placed within a broader mestizo category. In Honduras, the pen accomplished the same goal as the battlefield in Argentina.[69] Most blacks, however, remained outside the concept of the nation.

The absence of the black population from the debate over national identity is no more evident than in the establishment of the Indian cacique Lempira as the symbol of Honduran identity in the 1920s. Famous for fighting against Spanish conquerors in the sixteenth century, and regarded as the first martyr in the fight for the sovereignty of Honduras, Lempira was elevated to the status of national hero and used as a vehicle to promote the myth of Honduras as a mestizo nation. The fusion of Spanish and indigenous heritage, a result of the miscegenation that took place between the two groups during the Spanish colonial era, was praised.[70] The image of Lempira was placed side by side with the image of notable Honduran Creole statesmen such as Francisco Morazán and Marco Aurelio Soto. This elevation of both the oppressed and the oppressor to national hero status in Honduran mythology is a testament to the ambiguity of identity politics in the nation.

Though Honduran notions of *mestizaje* recognized Africans and Indians as instrumental to the historical and cultural traditions of the nation on an intellectual or mythological level, their actual role in Honduran society never achieved the same heights as the Spanish or mestizo elements of society. The nineteenth and twentieth centuries witnessed the further development of political and cultural ideologies of *mestizaje* in which integration and assimilation of Indians and Blacks was the goal. However, biology was not the only means by which this transition was to occur. Though the government adopted policies of European immigration to "improve the race" (*mejorar la raza*) of its citizens by infusing European blood into the population, the Hispanicization strategy of the government through the introduction of schools and missions, particularly among the indigenous population, achieved varying degrees of success. The government promoted the mestizo ideal throughout the first half of the twentieth century. Marvin Barahona argues that the Honduran state used its influence to bestow upon or deny rights to its citizens based on its interpretation of *mestizaje*. This ultimately affected women, Blacks, Indians, and anyone not a part of the dominant population.[71] In other nations in Latin America and the Caribbean during this period, nonmestizo populations were deemed invisible, but this did not occur in Honduras to the same degree. Though the civil rights of Afro and Indian descent populations and their fundamental contributions to the national identity and ethnic constitution of Honduras were negated, these populations persisted and continued to challenge the homogenizing discourse aimed at their exclusion.[72]

In Latin American societies where mixed-race identities were glorified, whiteness never ceased to be held in high regard. In fact, people of European descent were viewed as a necessity in the miscegenation process and white immigration was encouraged. Consequently, African and Indian identities continued to be shunned. Peter Wade maintains that the ideology of *mestizaje* can be used to exclude those considered unmixed. People of African and Indian descent, depending on the national project, run the risk of being defined as outside the bounds of the nation.[73] In the case of the North Coast of Honduras, the debate over national identity took on a decidedly racist and xenophobic tone. Many intellectuals and government officials conceptualized blackness as something both foreign and threatening to the social and cultural integrity of the nation.

This book, by focusing on the black West Indian immigrant population recruited to work in the North American–dominated banana industry, attempts to discern how a community that was foreign, English-speaking, and black was able to maintain itself in a nation that had no plan for its integration into society. Because West Indians remained foreigners and arrived with conceptions of race and nation that differed from Hondurans', to some extent, their history in Honduras is removed from the *mestizaje* debate centered on integration and assimilation. However, the presence of this population on the North Coast raised serious questions on the nature of immigration to Honduras and its effects on the social, political, economic, and cultural aspects of society.

2

HONDURAN IMMIGRATION LEGISLATION AND THE RISE OF ANTI–WEST INDIAN SENTIMENT

For much of the modern history of Honduras, the government viewed immigration as a means by which Honduras would obtain the human and economic capital essential for modern development and entrance into the world economy. Many Honduran intellectuals shared the racial determinism of the era—the belief that the historical realities of individuals, nations, and peoples were determined by their racial ancestry.[1] Although U.S. corporations encouraged West Indian immigration to Honduras, Honduran liberals did not. At no particular point in the debate on immigration did intellectuals and politicians ever envision that the majority of immigrants to Honduras would come from non-European origins. The assumption was that, like its neighbors in North America and South America, Honduras would attract primarily European immigrants. However, such conjectures were not borne out by reality. This chapter assesses Honduran efforts to entice European immigration into the country and demonstrates how immigration policies were designed to exclude certain sectors of the world population, specifically West Indians of African descent. The analysis emphasizes the anti-black component of Honduran immigration policies in order to highlight how Hondurans were unprepared for and unwilling to accept the growing West Indian presence on the North Coast.

For a brief period in the 1880s, white North Americans, as well as English, German, French, Italian, and Spanish immigrants, moved to Honduras. However, their numbers remained insignificant compared to other groups. According to Jorge Amaya, other Central Americans, primarily Guatemalans and Salvadorans, represented the largest percentage of immigrants to Honduras prior to 1910.[2] For instance, in the year 1887 only 390 North American and European immigrants were registered as opposed to 4,060 Guatemalans and Salvadorans. The number of English immigrants was listed as 1,033; but it is impossible to determine the number of those from the British Isles within this group because this figure also included those persons with British passports from the British West Indies and other colonial possessions of the British within their massive global empire.[3] In subsequent decades, Arabs, Palestinians, Chinese, and black West Indians contributed to the growing numbers of non-European immigrants to Honduras. Their numbers increased to the level that, at varying times throughout Honduran history, laws were passed that excluded all of these groups from entering the country. The increased presence of these nonwhite populations was thought by many to be a threat to the racial composition and moral fabric of the nation.

The oldest law of immigration in Honduras dates back to 1866 and was promulgated in the time of President José M. Medina.[4] The consensus of scholars is that it did very little to promote immigration, and the government revamped it in later decades. The constitution of 1865 specified that foreigners were not obligated to accept Honduran citizenship. Also, there were no government mechanisms in place to support massive immigration.[5] According to Marvin Barahona, in the years following passage of the immigration law of 1866, immigration sparked recurring legislative debates during four different periods: the liberal reform period of Marco Aurelio Soto and Ramón Rosa (1876–1883), the constitution of 1894, the legislative reforms of 1906, and the new immigration laws initiated from 1926 to 1934.[6]

The liberal reform period is the first in which the government systematically created an agenda to attract European immigrants. Leaders and intellectuals such as Ramón Rosa articulated the desire for European immigration by maintaining that Honduras needed large currents of immigration to bring the spirit of business and liberty like that sustained in the United States of America.[7] In fact, the Honduran constitution of 1873 was one of the most liberal in terms of allowing immigrants to acquire Honduran citizenship. In order to be naturalized, immigrants needed only to do one of five things: Obtain from the legislative body of the country a letter of naturalization, acquire real estate in the country valued at 1,000 pesos and reside on it for one year, contract marriage with a Honduran or someone who had resided in the country for one year, open a commercial establishment in the country and reside there for one year, or simply reside in the country for two years.[8] With such an open naturalization policy, the government believed that white immigrants would be attracted to Honduras and enter the country at a rapid rate. In fact, many Europeans and North Americans did make the journey to Honduras and settled in the newly modernizing nation.

Despite the unabashed liberalism of the constitution of 1873 toward immigration, mechanisms remained in place to deter certain groups from entering the country. One such vehicle was the religion clause of the constitution. Chapter 3, article 7 of the constitution stated that the religion of the Republic of Honduras was the Christian, Apostolic, and Roman Catholic Church and forbade the public exercise of any other faith. While the government maintained that it would not interfere with private worship as long as it did not disrupt the public order of society, there was little room for outward religious expression for non-Catholics. Only the National Congress possessed the authority to allow the public worship of other Christian denominations or religions, and this was only in cases where the social demand required it.[9] Reasonably speaking, non-Catholics possessed few rights regarding religious freedom. Such policies had the effect of curtailing the immigration of less desirable groups such as the Chinese, Jews, and primarily Orthodox Christian Arabs, who would later immigrate to the country in large numbers after the immigration reforms of 1894 and 1895. However, the policies proved to be attractive to those immigrants from Catholic areas of Europe looking to escape the stranglehold that poverty and class placed on them in their respective countries.

At varying stages between 1876 and 1910, the Honduran government made efforts to attract Irish and German immigrants to the country in order to promote the ethnic and economic mobilization of a fledgling Honduran nation. The liberal policies associated with legislative reforms and the language of the constitution had some success in stimulating immigration. Though several citizens from European nations arrived in Honduras as permanent settlers, their numbers remained relatively small in comparison to other nations in Latin America. Nations within the Caribbean and the Southern Cone offered more viable economic opportunities for immigrants. Honduras's stage of development was rudimentary compared to these areas and it could not compete with the industrialization agendas of its Latin American neighbors. George Reid Andrews, in his study of Afro-Latin America, affirms this by maintaining that most

Europeans favored the United States and Canada or Australia and New Zealand over poorer, less developed countries of Latin America. If Europeans did immigrate to Latin America, they usually went to Argentina, Brazil, Cuba, and Uruguay.[10] In Honduras, many European immigrants perished from tropical diseases, relocated to more developed countries in Latin America, or simply assimilated into the general population. They left only small relics of their existence in the country. This is most evident in the case of 250 Irish immigrants who arrived in the Caribbean port of Trujillo in 1879, only to disappear mysteriously from the public record a few years later.[11]

The constitution of 1894 differed considerably from that of 1873 in that the government no longer took an official position concerning religion. More important, the new legislation established the position that Honduras would be an ideal nation for all persons who sought refuge in the country from the harsh economic conditions of Europe and extended the same civil rights to Honduran citizens and foreigners alike.[12] This liberal immigration policy promoted by President Policarpo Bonilla (1895–1899), combined with the liberal naturalization policies maintained from the 1873 constitution, sparked the subtle increase in European immigration. It also initiated the arrival of the first major group of Arab immigrants. The naturalization procedures of 1894 were more liberal than they had been in 1873. Title II, article 9, of the 1894 constitution listed only three criteria for obtaining Honduran citizenship: Hispanic Americans who had one year of residency in the country and wished to become naturalized needed only to acknowledge this before the proper authorities, other foreigners needed only to have two years of residency in the country and present their desire to become naturalized before the proper authorities, and other prospective residents needed a letter of naturalization according to the designated laws.[13]

Though the constitution of 1894 did much to change the nature of the immigration debate in Honduras, it was the Immigration Law of 1906 that served as the catalyst for what would unfold on the North Coast for the next three decades. The law created the Honduran Board of Immigration and Agriculture responsible for proposing new immigration and colonization projects in the country.[14] Consisting of the Ministries of Development and Government, an expert in livestock, an agronomist, and a businessman, the main function of the board was to facilitate the introduction of both European and U.S. investment and immigration into Honduras.

Despite the preferences for Europeans and North Americans, the law did not impede the presence of foreigners from all over the world.[15] An unintended consequence of the 1906 legislation was the increase in nonwhite immigration to Honduras. Many foreigners came to Honduras to acquire free land and establish agricultural enterprises built on cheap skilled labor. Such labor demands were easily filled by not only local Hondurans, but foreign labor from other Central American countries and the Caribbean as well. A concession issued to one James Adam Muerch on September 21, 1906, shortly after the passing of the Immigration Law of 1906, indicates the ease with which lands were acquired by some.

The Honduran government conceded to Muerch 500 hectares (1,235 acres) of national land in an area around San Pedro Sula in order to cultivate bananas. The only stipulation was that Muerch would not cut down the mahogany, cedar, rubber, and pine trees that he found on the land. Such trees remained viable commodities in the logging industry that in previous decades had sustained sectors of the Honduran economy. If it was necessary for Muerch to cut any of the trees in order to develop the land, he would be required to pay a fine of five pesos in American gold to the Honduran government for each mahogany, cedar, or rubber tree that he felled. In terms of the productivity of the land, the concession called for the payment of twenty-five cents per year to the national government for each hectare of land not cultivated and ten cents for each hectare cultivated.[16] In no part of the concession was the issue of labor ever mentioned. The government concentrated only on the development of the land and the receipt of revenue. Whether James Muerch used local or foreign labor was of no consequence. Foreigners like Muerch, particularly North Americans, were able to acquire such enormous concessions because they were considered desirable immigrants. According to the 1906 law, immigrants were divided into three classes.

First-class immigrants, those without a contract and seeking to invest in the country, were given preference in many of the individual concessions, such as Muerch and other North American businessmen. Moreover, first-class immigrants were entitled to a minimum of three hectares of national land (about 7.5 acres) as long as they agreed to cultivate one-third of that land for use in some type of industrial project. For their efforts, these immigrants were given access to water, wood, and whatever other construction materials they needed to develop their holdings.[17] Second-class immigrants, comprising those contracted by the government, were

given most of the same legal rights as their first-class counterparts. However, national land entitlements and other intricacies of immigration law,
such as an exemption from taxation, were left solely to the discretion of
the government.[18]

The most important group to the subject of this book, the third-class
immigrants, consisted of those contracted by private citizens, societies,
or companies for colonization or the performance of jobs. These immigrants had very little access to the privileges extended to both first- and
second-class immigrants.[19] Most were contracted by various companies
to perform certain occupational tasks and return home when finished.
Initially, there was no inclination on the part of the Honduran government, the employers, or the third-class immigrants themselves to establish permanent residency in the nation. Third-class immigrants were a
temporary solution to the labor problems within the country. The law
maintained that businessmen who were engaged specifically in agriculture, or any other industry, could contract foreigners to fill positions
within their companies. The government agreed not to intervene in their
contracts, or in the organization of the areas established by the companies
for their foreign workers.[20] The Honduran government gave the companies complete autonomy over their foreign labor force. This fact is critical
to understanding the political and social dynamic within the fruit companies for much of the period. Foreign workers, specifically West Indians,
were more beholden to the fruit company officials than they were to the
local Honduran government because, according to the 1906 law, the fate
of foreigner workers in Honduras was very much predicated on the actions and interests of their employers.

The legislative reforms of 1906 were not limited to immigration. Efforts were also made on the part of the government to clarify many of
the ambiguities in previous legislation. There was an effort to consolidate
laws governing the police and foreign consuls, two potential impediments
to settlement and sources of assistance to the burgeoning West Indian
population on the North Coast.

The 1906 Police Law, while not specifically aimed at the West Indian
population, was often used as justification for castigating this particular
group. Crimes attributed to West Indians in the Honduran press, such
as public scandal, inebriation, and conduct leading to the decline of the
moral fabric of Honduran society, were often cited as reasons why West
Indian immigration to Honduras should be suspended. Instances of West

Indians being deported for minor offenses permeate police records from the North Coast during this period.

Chapter 3, article 43, of the law forbade the playing of dice, roulette, and all games associated with luck or chance. Offenders of such crimes could be either fined or jailed.[21] In one particular instance, four West Indians in the coastal city of Puerto Castilla, Walter Lowell, Israel Smith, Segismond [Sigmond] Lindo, and Allan Gayle were deported to British Honduras for the crime of playing dice.[22] Revealingly, the lone Honduran in the group, Lázaro Dolano, was not reported to have received any punishment for his crime. By committing the crime of playing dice, the West Indian men were in violation of the Police Law and should have been subject to a mere fine. However, local authorities labeled their crime pernicious, thereby making it a violation of the laws pertaining to foreigners. Violation of such laws was grounds for immediate deportation.

Though the West Indians in the previous examples were guilty of gambling, the question remains as to whether there was equal treatment for West Indians and Hondurans under the law. This issue surfaced in most deportations of West Indians. In the few instances where West Indians were incarcerated instead of deported, many found themselves in precarious circumstances. The case of Henry McLaren of La Ceiba is a testament to this. In a letter appealing for a commuted sentence of a fine rather than deportation for her brother, Rachel McLaren maintained that she was forbidden by authorities to provide her brother with food and basic treatment while he was incarcerated. She insisted that his crime, which was never fully disclosed, did not warrant the penalty of deportation.[23] Another example of deportation employed as a punishment for petty crime is the case of Carlos Anderson of Trujillo, who was detained on charges of pick-pocketing. For his crime, the authorities recommended that Mr. Anderson and his cohorts either remain in jail indefinitely or be expelled from the country. However, according to the records, the reason for the expulsion was not due to the fact merely that the subjects were criminals, but that they were "criminals who happened to be Jamaican blacks."[24] Given the highly racial climate of Trujillo in the period leading up to the mass deportations of West Indians from the territory in 1934, the accused were quickly deported to Jamaica.

Deportations of West Indian workers were numerous during this period because most West Indians found themselves on the wrong side of the justice system. Many were law-abiding citizens who became victims of police harassment. As evidenced from one instance in La Ceiba, dark skin often warranted suspicion from local authorities. In a report from police in 1927, two blacks were arrested for attempting to sell three pairs of shoes on the street. While street vending was not a crime, the arresting officer maintained that he would investigate "from where the two blacks had stolen the shoes."[25] It was assumed that black men surely had stolen the merchandise.

The practice of associating blackness with criminality is not uncommon in former slave societies with sizable populations of African descent. Blacks were often believed to possess genetic and cultural deficiencies that predisposed them to a life of crime. Rather than assess the relationship between crime and economic deprivation, it was easier for society to associate the problem with racial inferiority. Honduran society was no exception in this regard. In the areas of the North Coast with large West Indian populations, workers in the camps were often blamed for the increase in criminal activity in the country.[26] However, the available police records from the period that specifically list the nationality of offenders demonstrate that most of the crimes on the North Coast of Honduras were committed by Hondurans rather than West Indians.

From the available statistics, the number of crimes committed by West Indians was relatively low. Of the fifty crimes committed in Trujillo during 1934, a period in which accusations of heightened West Indian criminal activity persisted, only five were attributed to West Indians. The breakdown of the offenders reveals much about the nature of criminal activity among West Indians on the North Coast. Within this group, only

TABLE 2.1   Crimes Committed by West Indians in Trujillo, Department of Colón, 1934

NAME	NATIONALITY	AGE	CHARGE	SENTENCE
Rafaela Gram	British Honduran	30	contraband	6 days in jail
Eduardo Desus	Jamaican	25	robbery	8 days in jail
Edward Mickey	Jamaican	26	robbery	8 days in jail
A. Smily	Jamaican	28	robbery	8 days in jail
Carlos Anderson	British Honduran	17	vagrancy	1 day in jail
Reginal McNeil	British Honduran	58	drunkenness	2 days in jail

Source: Legajo: Correspondencia Recibida de la Policía Nacional, June–December, 1934. Archivo Nacional de Honduras.

TABLE 2.2 Crimes Committed by West Indians in Puerto Cortés, Department of Cortés, 1934

NAME	NATIONALITY	AGE	CHARGE	SENTENCE
Horacio Grindley	Jamaican	37	drunkenness	fined 2 lempiras
Carolina Strat	British Honduran	25	public scandal	fined 10 lps.
Archibal Lotano	British Honduran	26	drunken scandal	fined 2 lps.
Hector Desck	Jamaican	31	fighting	fined 5 lps.
Juan Mony	Jamaican	31	fighting	fined 5 lps.
Lamberto Fraser	Jamaican	40	immoral acts	fined 10 lps.
Andrés Anderson	Jamaican	60	undetermined	deported

Source: Legajo: Correspondencia Recibida de la Policía Nacional, June–December, 1934. Archivo Nacional de Honduras.

one of the offenders, Rafaela Gram, was female and only one, Reginald McNeil, a mechanic, was married. Crime in these cases appears to have been the realm of younger, single men. The crimes most frequently committed were petty theft such as pick-pocketing, drunkenness, or those that fell under the term *immoral acts* and were most likely sexual in nature. Table 2.1 lists the crimes committed by individuals reported to be West Indian in the department of Trujillo for the year 1934.

The trends witnessed in the case of Trujillo prove to be almost identical to those in Puerto Cortés during the same period. As seen in table 2.2, of the 129 crimes listed for the port city, only 7 were committed by West Indians. In this case, only one of the offenders was a woman, charged with "public scandal," while the other crimes were committed by single men and involved drunkenness, fighting, or "immoral acts." Such crimes as "immoral acts" and "public scandal" were probably sexually related, but authorities did not elaborate on the nature of these offenses. There was only one instance in all the North Coast departments registered during the period in which the punishment of deportation was rendered. Ironically, the department of Atlántida, which boasted the largest West Indian population in the country, reported the smallest number of violent occurrences of all North Coast departments. The city of La Ceiba boasted the arrest of one West Indian for drunkenness during the period.[27]

The types of crimes committed by West Indian offenders represented the nature of criminal activity on the North Coast during this period. With the exception of the three murders committed by Hondurans over a four-month period in La Ceiba in 1933, the criminal activity in the region was limited primarily to petty theft and alcohol-related offenses.[28] Table 2.3 breaks down the nature of criminal activity for the years 1933 and 1934. When we compare the data in these tables with the data above from tables 2.1 and 2.2, it is clear that West Indians were not a major criminal element within North Coast society.

The only instance in which Honduran leaders may have gained some credence for their allegations of higher criminal activity among West Indians was in the case of the island of Roatan in the Bay Islands dating back to 1916. Roughly 213 crimes were committed in the islands during the period.[29] However, determining whether the Bay Islanders of this period were in fact West Indians or Honduran citizens of West Indian descent is difficult because of the ambiguity of the citizenship claims of the island inhabitants throughout history. Also, with the exception of the island of Guanaja, the police statistics on the islands did not emphasize nationality to the same extent as they did on the mainland, due largely to the fact that the Anglo/Hispanic debate had not yet permeated the discourse on the island to the same degree.

All of the crimes committed on Roatan were assessed with fines paid to the treasury instead of deportation or incarceration, indicating that the severity of the offenses was relatively minor. The only exception was in the propensity for murders within the islands. While the number of assassinations reported was "relatively high for a department with such a small population," only two offenses were linked to West Indians.[30] One incident involved the killing of a pastor, his wife, and baby daughter by a man identified as a Jamaican in the Flowers Bay district of Roatán. The other involved the killing of a woman by a Jamaican man in Guanaja.[31] There were several isolated incidents of criminal activity on the part of West Indians during the period. These cases were in no way representative of the majority of the West Indians in Honduras. By and large, criminal activity on the North Coast and the Bay Islands was a local affair and did not reflect any inherent cultural affinity for criminal behavior by a particular immigrant population, as was often suggested by local authorities. Specifically on the islands of Utila and Guanaja, most of the crimes were committed by either sailors or day workers whose residence on the islands was temporary.

In the case of Roatán, the occupational breakdown of the offenders revealed that most of the crimes were committed by day workers and la-

TABLE 2.3   Number of People Found Guilty of Crimes by the Police, 1933–1934

	ATLÁNTIDA	CORTÉS	COLÓN
Drunkenness	80	121	9
Scandal	10	31	15
Fighting	10	4	1
Animal Vagrancy	52	11	64
Discharging of Firearm	3	19	0
Vagrancy	0	0	0
Failure to Comply	10	14	36
Security Issues	0	7	3
Disobedience	3	16	12
Disrespect	4	3	8
Lack of Normalcy	4	8	1
Prohibited Games	0	7	0
Prohibited Weapons	5	37	2
Totals	181	278	151

Source: Legajo: Informe de Estadísticas de Policía. Número de personas juzgadas por falta de policía en los departamentos de Honduras en el año 1933 a 1934. Archivo Nacional de Honduras.

borers. However, a sizable number of crimes were committed by middle-class workers such as businessmen, writers, musicians, teachers, tailors, and other "respectable" professionals.[32]

The rate of criminal activity was not high among the West Indian population. However, if members of the group found themselves in a legal predicament with local Honduran authorities, there was often insufficient diplomatic assistance available to them because the Honduran government sought to limit the influence of foreign governments (except the United States) within its borders. This is most evident in the Law of Foreign Consulate Missions of 1906. The legislation acknowledged the right of foreign consulate offices in Honduras to represent the rights, interests, and property of its citizens inside the limits of Honduras. These consulates were not recognized as representatives of their respective governments nor were they considered diplomatic agents. Their function was solely to represent the interests of private citizens.[33]

Unfortunately for the majority of West Indians residing on the North Coast, there was no consistent diplomatic representation of the British government to attend to their needs in the event that they became involved in disputes with authorities. The diplomatic representation for the British was headquartered at the legation offices in Guatemala City, Guatemala. There were satellite consular offices available at various intervals throughout the period of this study at the ports of Trujillo and La Ceiba, but the representatives assigned to these locales were for the most part situated on the periphery with limited resources at their disposal. With the exception of the British consulate at Trujillo, the only viable option for West Indians was to seek assistance from either the governor of British Honduras if they were citizens of that colony or the British *chargé d'affaires ad interior* in Tegucigalpa. Many sought assistance from the United States consular agent in La Ceiba, but the U.S. diplomat had no jurisdiction over British subjects. One U.S. consul reported that he often received requests from West Indians to assist them in resolving their grievances with the Honduran people. It was his observation that "the West Indians and local Honduran population hated each other and that the former were partly to blame based on their insistence that they were entitled to certain privileges because of their British citizenship." The consul maintained that he gave what advice he could but ultimately referred the West Indians to the nearest British Consulate.[34] Any perceived allegiance between the representatives of the United States government and West Indians based solely on a shared language was quickly shattered. West Indians were left to defend themselves in many instances.

It was not until 1928 that a consul general of Great Britain was established in the department of Atlántida, the area with the highest concentration of West Indians claiming British citizenship in the country.[35] Prior to this development, the concerns of the British government were primarily centered on protecting British economic interests in the Honduran mining industry, and not on the fate of its colonial subjects.[36]

This lack of concern is most evident in the case of the attack and murder of Jamaicans by private citizens and government authorities in 1924. Whites were occasional victims of abuse from the Honduran authorities. However, local retaliation against whites, specifically white Americans, was almost always limited to mere threats. There were a few noted exceptions, the most famous of which was in 1924 when twelve Englishmen and Americans were kept prisoners in their own company towns while Honduran troops paraded the streets after successfully suppressing an attempted coup d'état. Because the whites and their United Fruit Company employers were suspected of supporting the opposition, many Honduran officials felt that the treatment of the employees was justified. However, the United States government felt that the local government had over-stretched its authority and quickly sent in marines to protect American life and property.[37]

The situation of West Indians in the same position proved distinctly different, as foreign governments, mainly the British, were much more insensitive when the lives threatened were simply those of black labor-ers. The same article detailing the incidents involving the government troops and the white company workers noted that Jamaicans were killed "for no apparent reason" by local militias according to witnesses. More important, the article reported that the British government failed to see the gravity of the situation and risked having its prestige in the region destroyed if there was no government retaliation for the mistreatment of its citizens.[38] British concern was focused more on the reputation of its government than on the lives of its Jamaican subjects in Honduras.

In 1924, a strike directed against West Indian labor was initiated in Trujillo by local Honduran laborers. In correspondence between the U.S. State Department and the British Embassy in Washington, it is clear that the two governments believed that the situation had the potential to get out of control. The State Department advised the British ambassador that it would be in the best interest of the British government to prepare a warship to be sent to the area to protect the lives of the black population.[39] Nevertheless, only two days later, the Foreign Office sent correspondence to the British ambassador in Washington that the government should take no action to protect the lives of its black subjects in Honduras. A later report by the consul at Trujillo informed that another British subject was seriously wounded by strikers and that alone he was powerless to protect British subjects from future attacks.[40] From the correspondence between the Foreign Office and the British ambassador, at first it appears that the events surrounding the strike and the targeting of black West Indians caught the British government off guard. However, a week earlier the British consul at Trujillo informed the Foreign Office of the com-mencement of the strike and its implications. This illustrates the lack of concern on the part of the British government for its subjects abroad.[41]

The increased attacks on Jamaican residents were not a surprise con-sidering that anti–West Indian sentiment was most prevalent in Honduras during periods of economic depression. More staggering is the lack of con-cern about West Indian life by those in positions of power designated to protect it. This nonchalant attitude on the part of the British government did change somewhat in 1932 when it presented claims for substantial compensation to the Honduran government on behalf of the dependents of one Percy Tucker and C. F. J. Everard, two of six British subjects killed by Hondurans. However, the racial identity of the two men and their country or colony of origin was not listed. Tucker died under circumstances very similar to many black victims of Honduran violence; he was returning home from a dance in La Ceiba and was shot by Honduran police.[42]

From a legislative standpoint, the period between 1906 and 1928 was uneventful in terms of rulings on immigration. It was not until the passage of the 1929 immigration law that a drastic shift in the racial dynamics of the North Coast occurred. The law stated that blacks could enter the country if they possessed 5,000 Honduran pesos ($2,500 U.S.) upon entry and deposited 500 pesos ($250 U.S.) with the Honduran government. Because West Indians were leaving a depressed economic situation on their home islands to seek employment in the banana enclaves, the likelihood that they possessed enough capital to fulfill the new immigration requirement was doubtful. Through this excessive financial burden imposed on potential immigrants, West Indians and other undesirable groups were excluded from admission into the country. The 1929 immigration law demonstrated extreme xenophobia and racism and effectively impeded the entrance of foreigners of certain ethnicities and nationalities into Honduran territory.[43] The shift in immigration policy resulted in a heightened awareness of racial issues on the North Coast.

Building on the precedents of the 1929 immigration law, chapter 3, article 14 of the 1934 immigration law strictly forbade the entrance of blacks, East Indians, gypsies, and Chinese into Honduran territory.[44] Article 4 of the law extended the ban to prohibit issuing tourist visas to excluded groups. The government also began to crack down on the registration of immigrants with the proper authorities. Visa information in Honduras listed foreigners by place of birth, date of birth, residence, profession, marital status, hair, eye, and skin color, as well as height and stature and identifying marks. In records issued after the 1934 immigration law, West Indians, specifically Jamaicans and British Hondurans, were represented within the group of immigrants screened by Honduran authorities. Most entered the country either through the ports of Puerto Castilla or La Ceiba and arrived in the year 1928, just prior to immigration reform. Surprisingly, those West Indians who bothered to register with the proper authorities were men with trades as opposed to fruit company employees or laborers.[45]

On further examination of the records, the references made to the physical features of the West Indians went beyond mere descriptive observations. References to "big mouths," "strong black skin," and "frizzy" hair suggest a preoccupation with race and phenotype by immigration workers. Many within the government maintained that the new Honduran immigration policy was the result of a need to defend the social integrity of Honduras and was not based on attitudes of racial and ethnic discrimination.[46] However, the fact that only certain groups were targeted in the legislation suggests racist overtones.

In the few years following the 1934 immigration law, the number of West Indians declined significantly. Many returned to their former countries. However, a greater number resettled in the United States, Canada, and Great Britain during the Second World War. The wartime defense and agricultural industries in these countries sparked the need for additional sources of labor. According to oral accounts of West Indian descendants in Honduras, those who did not leave Honduras in the period following the immigration restrictions of 1934 ultimately left the country following the labor strike of 1954, which forced companies to reconsider their policies in Honduras for the benefit of local labor.

The strike began on May 3, 1954, when the workers of the Tela Railroad Company, a subsidiary of the transnational United Fruit Company, declared a cessation of work until better working conditions and benefits were extended to them and their families. The strike lasted for some sixty days and spread to include workers in Puerto Cortés, La Lima, La Ceiba, and Batán, ultimately encompassing almost every sector of society associated with the banana industry on the North Coast.[47] It sparked reform not only within the fruit industry, but in Honduran labor organizations and politics as well.

The newfound spirit of Honduran nationalism and worker solidarity the movement ignited placed most West Indians at odds with the local population because the former had sided overwhelmingly with the companies not only during the strike, but throughout their entire history on the North Coast.[48] North American workers preferred West Indian workers because of their ability to speak English and their perceived submissive nature. As a result, West Indians often held positions within the fruit companies that were higher in pay and status than those of the local Honduran population, such as loaders, shopkeepers, gardeners, and in a few instances as suppliers and supervisors. Most local Hondurans worked as laborers in the banana fields ten to twelve hours a day for little pay.[49]

The companies also protected the West Indians from extreme cases of discrimination at the hands of local authorities and businesses in the banana zones and contributed in many ways to the feelings of superiority exhibited by West Indians over the local or "indio" population (as Hondurans were often called by foreigners). According to one account, West Indians were even protected by the fruit companies in instances of civil war within the country. The workers simply retreated to the confines of the banana zone until local conflicts subsided.[50] The banana zone offered a safety net to West Indians that was not available to the local population. Clear distinctions such as these led many strikers to demand that there be more of a Honduran presence within the hierarchy of fruit company management and skilled positions. They wanted bosses that were either Honduran or at least Central American. They did not want to work directly for foreigners who could not relate to the situation of the masses of workers.[51] Moreover, the idea of preferential treatment for Hondurans in hiring practices and business-related endeavors was debated from the inception of the first concessions given to foreigners during the liberal reform period and continued to resurface at various periods during the first half of the twentieth century. In fact, just a few years prior to the 1954 strike, small business owners suggested that all businesses and commercial concerns, including the banana industry in Honduras, should be in the hands of native-born Hondurans of Indo-Spanish origins.[52] However justified such demands of local ownership might have been, this concept excluded from ownership those Hondurans of other ethnicities, most notably the indigenous populations, the Garífuna, and the Bay Islanders. Not only were these groups eliminated from the debate, but they were not even regarded as an integral part of the nation.

Because the fruit companies could not afford to lose their entire labor force, they ultimately complied with many of the demands of the workers. Most of the thirty demands centered on improving the conditions of workers regarding better pay, housing, medical care for families, the restructuring of the work day, labor conditions, and other issues pertinent to creating a positive work environment.[53] One issue that stands out in the discourse regarding the need for better working conditions was the demand on the part of workers to integrate more Hondurans into positions formerly held by West Indians. Some West Indians remained in Honduras and continued to work for the fruit companies alongside Hondurans. Those who remained were forced under the circumstances to assimilate into the local population and embrace Honduras fully. However, rather than give up their status and identity, many chose to flee. There were instances in the oral record of West Indians, forever defiant, opting to leave the country and return to the Caribbean rather than train local Hondurans to perform their jobs.[54] Tensions among the West Indian population and Hondurans were responsible in many instances for the ill will between the two groups in the first place. The strike simply exacerbated poor relations.

Beginning with the immigration laws of 1866 and extending through the strike of the banana workers in 1954, the legislative policies of the Honduran government defined the West Indian presence in the country. Throughout the legislative history of immigration, varying degrees of acceptance were given to nonwhite immigrants. When the fruit companies exerted influence, the status of the West Indian in Honduras was favorable. However, when foreign businesses and investment were threatened, the West Indian community became the target of intellectual and political attack. While simply disallowing their entrance into the country was feasible to authorities and aided in the reduction of West Indians on the North Coast, such governmental policies alone did not halt the immigration process. It was not until the masses of Honduran workers challenged the hegemony of the fruit companies in the country that the West Indian presence in Honduras was diminished.

3

COUNTERING THE "BLACK INVASION"
The Intellectual Response to West Indian Immigration

The arrival of West Indians on the North Coast of Honduras sparked more than immigration reform. The presence of this mostly black, English-speaking, and skilled labor force gave rise to a social and economic debate about race, identity, and the competition for much-needed employment. The Honduran press provided the platform for much of the intellectual discourse centered on nationalist rhetoric and the protection of Honduran workers' rights from undesirable immigrants. Labor leaders and thinkers of the day often viewed the presence of West Indians on the North Coast as an attack on Honduran sovereignty, portraying West Indians as invaders intent on destroying every aspect of Honduran life.

As early as 1913, reports of the importation of black laborers to Tela to work for the Tela Railroad Company sparked criticism from the press on the basis that hiring West Indians to fill company positions displaced local Honduran workers.[1] The Honduran intellectual Froylán Turcios declared that not only was the presence of these workers in the country unnecessary in order to fill positions in the burgeoning fruit industry, but that "black labor, particularly from the Anglo-Saxon countries such as the West Indies, constituted a source of unease and neighboring danger."[2] "Black workers," according to Turcios, were "less intelligent, less apt for agricultural work, and due to their physiological makeup were much more prone to violence and crime."[3] In addition, blacks and other immigrant groups were often scapegoated as the reason why Honduras could not maintain a hygienic society. Blacks, Chinese, and other foreigners, due to their "displeasing" customs, were said to represent disagreeable sectors of society and pose a general health risk.[4] According to José Antonio Funes, Turcios's criticisms tended to exacerbate nationalist sentiments in Honduras.[5] A key literary figure in Honduras, Turcios questioned not only the presence of undesirable immigrants in the country, but the effect the North American capitalist system was having on the politics and culture of Honduras. For Turcios, West Indians and their allegiance to both Britain and the U.S. fruit companies were a threat to Honduran sovereignty.

The North Coast, where most of these arrivals settled, possessed a reputation for lawlessness due to the long history of clandestine activity in the isolated area. Disease posed a constant threat because of the enormous amount of pestilence in the region caused by mosquitoes. Racial and ethnic stereotyping of African and Indian descent peoples in the region hinted at the growing role of identity politics in the political and cultural discourse. A Honduran Justice Department report suggested, "as a result of the primitive indigenous influence on Honduran culture and the deviant behaviors associated with poverty, that it would be difficult to improve the life of the Honduran people."[6] Undesirable immigrant groups such as West Indians added to the difficulty of nation building and therefore were discouraged. Many even began to question their ability to perform the duties associated with being fruit company employees by suggesting that black workers were incapable of agricultural labor.

The claim that black workers were ill-equipped for agricultural work is astounding considering the fact that historically, the experience of peoples of African descent in the Americas has been one of plantation labor centered on agricultural production. Turcios's comments were an attempt to justify notions of black inferiority, a doctrine that many within the Honduran intellectual elite espoused. His remark was one of the few instances in which English-speaking black labor was referred to specifically within the national immigration debate.

Despite the racial overtones of Turcios's position regarding black operatives, he was right in discerning that there was a growing West Indian presence on the North Coast of Honduras attributed largely to the hiring practices of the American-owned fruit companies. Even when other Latin Americans were hired, they were in many instances descendants of West Indians. In company towns such as Tela, many black operatives arrived from Colombia and Panama to work for the United Fruit Company.[7] These workers were in most instances descendants of black West Indians arriving from Colombia's Caribbean possessions of Providencia and San

Andrés or from the Canal Zone. Mario Posas maintains that black opera-tives were imported both legally and illegally from Jamaica, Colombia, Panama, Cuba, and Belize because of their prior banana plantation expe-riences.[8] With the exception of Jamaica and Belize, those black workers being sent to Honduras from other Latin American countries were most likely products of earlier Caribbean migrations to the Panama Canal Zone and from American-owned fruit and sugar plantations in Cuba. Workers from Jamaica and Belize were also imported to work for the Tru-jillo Railroad Company, a subsidiary of the United Fruit Company.

As evidenced by the opinion of one newspaper reporter, the arrival of the Jamaican workers would be the source of disputes originating from international claims that the West Indians believed they were immune to Honduran laws and customs.[9] The implication was that West Indians would demand certain privileges and concessions based on their political status as subjects of the British crown and would infringe on the sover-eignty of Honduras and its laws. In another article, the writer maintained that "the presence of Jamaican workers in Trujillo would raise the prices on goods and would also be the source of many disputes between the local population and the West Indians because the latter believed they were immune to the laws of the land because of their status as subjects of a powerful nation."[10]

The concerns of the local Honduran population and the intellectual elite regarding black immigration fell on the fruit companies' deaf ears. By October 1914, the fruit companies were introducing large numbers of West Indians into the region. In one account, the United Fruit Company had been given a concession to import as many as four hundred workers to the North Coast per month. Though initially such concessions were to be allowed for only a three-month period in order to construct a rail-road from Trujillo to Juticalpa, the Honduran government had no means of enforcing such regulations and the workers continued to be imported clandestinely by the fruit companies on a permanent basis.[11]

The ineffectiveness of Honduran law is evidenced by a case in which the United Fruit Company brought in eight hundred West Indians to work on plantations in Trujillo, Tela, and Puerto Castilla. The company's representatives secured approval of then Honduran president Rafael Ló-pez to bring the workers in without the deposit of $100 U.S. in gold per person as prescribed by law.[12] Because of their ever-growing power and influence, the companies acted with impunity and displayed little regard for Honduran law. Their reliance on corrupt politicians on their payroll allowed them to circumvent local legislation. The fact that the concession was for railroads can be misleading considering that railroad concessions were the means by which many of the fruit companies first gained inroads into Honduran territory. The workers brought into Honduras during this period were almost exclusively involved in the fruit industry.

In addition to bypassing laws, the United Fruit Company made life extremely difficult for Honduran laborers. The company was reported to have expelled Honduran workers who failed to sign contracts that restricted their pay period to every forty days as opposed to weekly.[13] The company replaced these workers with noncontract labor, which was overwhelmingly West Indian. One scholar maintains that the importation of noncontract West Indian workers was no accident; they remained at the mercy of their employers and therefore were less likely to organize collectively against the fruit companies.[14] This helped quell the growth of organized labor in Honduras. The strategy employed by the fruit companies ensured that daily operations would not be threatened as they had been in Costa Rica and Panama by a surge in trade unionism among West Indian and mestizo workers organizing collectively to advocate for better conditions.

The writings of Honduran intellectuals and the general press claimed that West Indians were descending on the Caribbean coast at an alarming rate. However, census records reveal that the West Indian presence in Honduras was relatively small compared to other immigrant groups. The earliest record of a sizable British West Indian presence in Honduras dates back to 1887, when it was reported that 1,017 Englishmen resided in the country.[15] These Englishmen were most likely West Indian workers imported to work on the proposed Inter-oceanic Railroad stretching from Puerto Cortés on the Caribbean coast to the Bay of Fonseca on the Pacific coast in the 1870s.[16] Ironically, imported labor for railroad construction was almost exclusively black. No Asians or Europeans were recruited for Honduran railroad projects, as was common in other countries.[17]

The term *Englishmen* was a common moniker for West Indians during this period. The group was often identified based on their language and status as British subjects, rather than by their specific place of origin within the British Empire. Marvin Barahona maintains that the term *ingleses* almost exclusively referred to blacks originating from the British colonies of the West Indies.[18] The major centers of white British settle-

ment in Central America were confined to the colonies of British Honduras (Belize) and the region in and around La Mosquitia. Even in these two
locations, white settlement still remained relatively low in comparison to
West Indians.

In 1910, the number of West Indians residing in Honduras was listed as
4,710.[19] In 1887 and 1910, West Indians represented 70.4 percent and 75.8
percent, respectively, of all immigrants to Honduras. Initially these per-
centages seem rather large. However, considering the fact that the average total population of the North Coast of Honduras was around 40,000
people, the West Indian presence in the region was relatively small in
numbers. Available census data for the years 1926 and 1930 reveal a much
more accurate analysis of the size of the West Indian community in Honduras. Though many immigrants from all over the world elected to settle
throughout Honduras, the North Coast proved to be the domain of the
West Indian. The fruit industry was situated primarily in the coastal departments of Cortés, Atlántida, and Colón. Therefore, it was no surprise
that these regions represented the largest areas of West Indian settlement.

The department of Islas de la Bahía (Bay Islands) also boasted a sizable West Indian population. However, the Bay Island community proved
exceptional because of the ambiguity over whether those West Indians
residing in the department were in fact recent immigrant British subjects tied to the banana industry or Bay Islanders still clinging to a British identity stemming from the mid-nineteenth century when the islands
were a formal British crown colony. In several instances throughout the
period the citizenship of Bay Islanders was in question. United States
consular reports reveal that this misunderstanding regarding the nationality of Bay Islanders was so widespread that a British gunboat arrived
in the islands in 1902 to inform its inhabitants that all persons (and their
descendants) residing in the territory at the time of the 1859 treaty ceding
the islands to Honduras were in fact Hondurans. If the inhabitants arrived after 1859, they were allowed to retain their British nationality. Also,
the British officials made it clear that British passports issued to Bay Islanders in British Honduras (Belize) and the British consulate at Trujillo
were null and void.[20] The British believed that most Bay Islanders would
in fact leave the islands because some four-fifths of all inhabitants had,
until the arrival of the gunboat, considered themselves British subjects
and subsequently entitled to the protection of the British government.[21]
While most Bay Islanders did not abandon the islands, many in fact con-

tinued to cling to their Anglo-Caribbean cultural heritage, despite their legal status as Hondurans.

Bay Islanders clung to their status as British subjects not always in an attempt to deny their connection to Honduras. However, there were numerous instances of Bay Islanders invoking British citizenship when it suited them. As late as 1911, some fifty-two years after the ceding of the Bay Islands to Honduras by the British, one British vice consul in La Ceiba often registered Bay Islanders as British subjects in his offices, issuing certificates authenticating their British nationality. In most cases, those individuals registered had no legal rights to claim such status. The British government voiced concern over such practices and instructed the vice consul at La Ceiba, as well as all other vice consuls in the region, to refrain from granting certificates of British nationality without proper verification.[22] These actions by the British quelled some of the issues regarding the status of the Bay Islanders. However, isolated cases of individuals continuing to claim British nationality surfaced until the 1930s.

While many West Indians continued to arrive in the Bay Islands from Grand Cayman, Jamaica, and other British Caribbean colonies, their numbers were relatively small. One government report from 1917 maintained that their numbers declined considerably after the prohibition of people of color to the region in 1916, the first instance of a formal policy restricting black immigration.[23] Also, by this period most people living in the islands were not involved in the fruit industry to the same magnitude as they had been prior to 1912, when the focus of the companies shifted exclusively to the mainland. Many Bay Islanders migrated to work in the fruit industry, but many others gained employment in the shipping industry.

Despite inconsistencies with ethnic, racial, and national identifications, Honduran census data for the period remain the most reliable source as to the number of West Indians in Honduras at the height of their immigration. In table 3.1, statistics from the 1926 official Honduran census reveal that West Indians represented 3,673 individuals out of a total North Coast population of 99,616. Of the 3,673 West Indians, 173 were transients and the majority resided in the department of Atlántida. The data reveal that by 1926, the majority of West Indians in Honduras resided in the department of Atlántida, home to the Standard Fruit and Steamship Company's Honduran operations situated at the port city of La Ceiba.

The demographic information provides the first glimpse into the settlement patterns of West Indians. The ratio of West Indian men to women was relatively balanced in all of the North Coast departments with the exception of Atlántida, in which there existed a disproportionate number of men to women. Such discrepancies are best explained by the fact that La Ceiba represented the largest city on the North Coast and contained a wide range of businesses and industries associated with the fruit companies. This made it highly plausible for single men to arrive initially in La Ceiba to perform unskilled labor. Also, because La Ceiba was a major port, there was a propensity to have merchant sailors and fisherman in the area as opposed to just fruit company employees. This was markedly different from smaller company towns such as Trujillo and Tela where West Indians were recruited to perform more specialized tasks for the railroad companies. Therefore, they were in a better position financially to settle with their families. The fact that most of the workers in Tela and Trujillo were probably married in the Caribbean prior to their departure for Honduras explains the higher frequency of marriage within this group.

The 1930 Honduran census reveals many of the same trends as the 1926 census. However, the number of West Indians in many of the departments of the North Coast declined due in part to increased anti-immigration legislation targeting blacks. Such legislation had its origins in many of the racist notions prevalent during the period. Honduras's acceptance of this consensus would at first appear questionable considering the fact that the nation was overwhelmingly composed of people of non-European racial heritage. Yet the fact remains that Honduran intellectuals were actively engaged in the growing international debate. Honduras was invited to send a delegation to the Second Annual International Congress of Eugenics in New York City to be held September 22–28, 1920.[24] Although Honduras was unable to send representation due to the short notice of the invitation, the secretary of state did note the importance of such a conference and was "grateful for the honor of Honduras being invited to participate."[25] The interest generated by this conference was just one indication of the views of Honduran political elites regarding race. Much more telling is the debate centering on the creation of more strict immigration laws.

In 1920, Robert Purdy, the American consular agent stationed at Tela, Honduras, wrote a letter to one Frederick Job in response to his inquiry about importing Chinese laborers to work for a Chicago-based company looking to expand in Honduras. Purdy informed Mr. Job that "Honduras, as well as other countries of Central America, did not care for the impor-

TABLE 3.1 Population on the North Coast of Honduras, 1926

| DEPARTMENT | NATIONALITY | RESIDENT | | TRANSIENT | | TOTAL | PERCENTAGE OF WEST INDIANS |
		Male	Female	Male	Female		
Cortés	English	383	264	7	3	657	18
Colón	English	220	173	81	72	546	15
Islas de la Bahía	English	355	347	—	—	702	19
Atlántida	English	1,035	723	6	4	1,768	48
Totals		1,993	1,507	94	79	3,673	100

Source: General Census of the Population of Honduras, 1926. Records of the Department of State Relating to the Internal Affairs of Honduras, 1928, Record Group 59. U.S. National Archives and Records Administration II, College Park, MD.

tation of Chinese, or Negro laborers and did everything to discourage and stop such immigration."[26] Four years later, a proposed law of immigration surfaced that prohibited all individuals or corporations from importing "Negroes or coolies" for labor or any other purpose.[27] Fruit companies received certain concessions to import black workers with specialized skills, a designation under which many of the West Indians fell. However, after the completion of their duties these workers had to return to their countries of origin.

Though this law was not passed in its complete form until 1929, the sentiments it sparked carried strong racial undertones. West Indians were accused of being involved in frequent incidents with the law and, because of their protection under the British government, were allowed to act with impunity. In order to curb this tendency, the government moved to implement immigration restrictions based on race and color. West Indians were undoubtedly the target group. However, the restrictions would extend to Syrians, Palestinians, and other groups under the protection of foreign governments whose agents, so it was perceived, did not respect the laws of Honduras.[28] Such legal actions held some merit, as foreign government officials were more inclined to protect the interests of their countrymen abroad than adhere to local law and custom. However, the fact that the debate over immigration targeted specific groups of nonwhite immigrants is a testament to the true nature of the anti-immigration agenda.

The attacks on West Indian immigration continued to portray them as complicit in the demise of Honduran society. Such claims were continuously employed in order to stave off competition in the labor market. Echeverri-Gent posits that the lure of higher wages offered by the banana companies increasingly encouraged Hispanics from the highlands to seek employment on the coast. She maintains that this created intense competition between Hispanic and West Indian workers for jobs.[29] While competition may have existed on the part of the local Honduran population, black workers were secure in their positions because they had specifically been imported by the fruit companies and were the preferred source of labor in technical positions. The local Honduran worker was without such economic and financial security.

Apart from a few isolated incidents such as the one in La Ceiba in 1905 when disgruntled local residents passed out flyers on the streets in large numbers calling for the burning of the fruit offices of the Vaccaro Brothers (later Standard Fruit) because they offered work "only for blacks and not Hondurans," the concern over West Indian immigration had been reduced to the opinions of a few government officials and intellectuals in Tegucigalpa.[30] However, toward the end of the 1920s, popular support for anti-immigration legislation grew considerably. The government desired a healthy and select group of immigrants that would stimulate Honduran industry and impart the values of a superior, European culture. With West Indians constituting a highly visible percentage of non-European, non–Central American immigration to Honduras along with a growing Arab and Chinese presence, they represented a growing threat to the Honduran vision of modernity.

This nonwhite immigration was considered dangerous and threatened to bring about the expedient degeneration of Honduran society. The government deemed people of color as an unfit immigrant group.[31] Arabs, or *turcos,* as they were called in Honduras due to the fact that most came from the Arabic-speaking countries of the Levant that had previously been a part of the Ottoman Turkish Empire, were regarded dubiously. Chinese suffered from designation as carriers of syphilis and other sexually transmitted diseases, while blacks were stigmatized as having a natural degenerative quality that went against the very social standing of the Honduran race.[32]

After years of debate and discourse, the Honduran National Congress passed a Decree of Immigration on February 28, 1929, that practically excluded blacks as immigrants inasmuch as article 11 of chapter 4 of the law stated that they were required to have 5,000 silver pesos in their possession and to deposit 500 pesos with the Honduran government.[33] However, the U.S. diplomat who reported the news of the law to the U.S. Department of State maintained that "the law did not affect the fruit companies because the blacks employed by them were primarily British subjects and were exempted by Article 3 of the Treaty of Commerce and Navigation signed by Great Britain and Honduras on June 21, 1915."[34] In reality, the treaty was a part of wartime legislation signed during World War I aimed at protecting British seafaring and commercial vessels that were subject to German submarine attacks. Ships from British colonies were allowed to board in Honduran ports during daylight hours in order to avoid the possibility of being attacked by submarine prowlers making use of light signals.[35] In no instance was the treaty interpreted to extend privileges to British subjects working for fruit companies on Honduran soil. However, according to U.S. consular records, the fruit companies were able to take advantage of the loopholes within the treaty and continued to import West Indian workers. The number of West Indians in Honduras remained about the same in 1930 as it had been in 1926. However, the distribution of the workers shifted from being heavily concentrated in the department of Atlántida to a more even dispersal throughout the entire North Coast.

Atlántida continued to boast the largest numbers of West Indians of any department, mainly because it included the cities of La Ceiba and Tela within its limits. The Tela Railroad Company, founded in 1918 as a subsidiary of the United Fruit Company, had begun to embark on large-scale fruit production in the region. More important, the West Indian population of the department of Colón, the base of operations for the Trujillo Railroad Company, doubled in the same time frame. Ironically, it was in Trujillo where the resistance to West Indian immigration would have its greatest impact on the deportation of large numbers of Jamaican and Belizean workers from the area in 1934. This incident is discussed further in chapter 6.

Like the 1926 census, the 1930 census disclosed that West Indian men continued to outnumber West Indian women. The only semblance of a balance between the sexes was within the Belizean community in Atlántida and Cortés. Only ninety kilometers from the Honduran coast, it was

TABLE 3.2 Population on the North Coast of Honduras, 1930

| DEPARTMENT | NATIONALITY | RESIDENT | | TOTAL | PERCENTAGE OF WEST INDIANS |
		Male	Female		
Atlántida	Belizean	251	200	451	11
	English	559	410	969	23
	Jamaican	257	152	409	10
Colón	Belizean	123	110	233	5
	English	230	114	344	8
	Jamaican	358	162	520	12
Islas de la Bahía	English	182	109	291	7
Cortés	English	593	405	998	24
Totals		2,553	1,662	4,215	100

Source: República de Honduras, *Resumen del censo general de población levantado el 29 de junio de 1930* (Tegucigalpa: Tipografía Nacional, 1932).

TABLE 3.3 West Indian versus Total Black Population on the North Coast, 1930

DEPARTMENT	WEST INDIANS	TOTAL BLACK POPULATION	PERCENTAGE OF TOTAL BLACKS
Atlántida	1,829	5,042	36.3
Colón	1,097	8,733	12.6
Cortés	998	2,619	38
Islas de la Bahía	291	3,631	8
Totals	4,215	20,025	100

Source: República de Honduras, *Resumen del censo general de población levantado el 29 de junio de 1930* (Tegucigalpa: Tipografía Nacional, 1932).

both economically and physically easier to transport entire families from Belize than from other British possessions.

The category of transients does not exist in the 1930 census, indicating that there was no longer a significant amount of mobility within the population to warrant tabulation. Perhaps due to concerns over the number of nonwhites in the country, the 1930 census reinstituted the racial categories of *indio, mestizo, blanco, amarillo,* and *negro,* all of which had been absent from the 1926 census. Based on that data, table 3.3 lists the number of West Indians as compared with the total population of blacks in the country. In most cases, when persons of African descent on the North Coast were not West Indian, they were Garífuna.

In no particular department of the North Coast of Honduras does the population of West Indians number half of the total black population. However, this community received the brunt of the anti-immigrant sentiment. The attacks on West Indian labor were often couched in rhetoric centered on the protection of the Honduran worker claiming that much-needed jobs should not fall into the hands of less deserving foreigners. What this argument fails to address is that the majority of the competition for jobs came not from West Indians but from other Central Americans.

The data show that "other" Central Americans in the major departments of the North Coast outnumbered West Indians by a ratio of 2:1. In the department of Islas de la Bahía, Central Americans numbered only 5, but the territory was no longer a factor in the immigration debate. In the department of Atlántida, the total number of Central Americans was recorded at 2,367 as compared to 1,768 West Indians. In the department of Colón, West Indians numbered 546 as compared to 370 Central Americans. However, in Cortés, there were only 657 West Indians as compared to 4,308 other Central Americans. From the census data, it is clear that in two of the three major departments of the North Coast, other Central Americans and not West Indians posed the greatest threat to the job security of the local Honduran worker.[36] However, this group never experienced the same level of attack in the discussions on immigration. Part of the explanation for the lack of concern regarding Central Americans working in Honduras stems from the fact that the five traditional republics of the area, Guatemala, Nicaragua, Honduras, Costa Rica, and El Salvador, were once ruled as a single entity both during the colonial period and after independence as the United Provinces of Central America. As a result, a strong sense of Central American nationalism permeated the region, despite the fact that the countries had been separate republics since the disintegration of the union in 1838. The groups remained linguistically, culturally, and racially similar.

In a survey of newspapers and reports of government agencies from the period, there were no direct references to the large numbers of Central American workers in Honduras, nor were they a target of political or anti-immigrant legislation. In fact, Salvadorans, the most represented of Central American workers in Honduras, distributed pamphlets in Tela maintaining that they were representative of good labor practices in Honduras. Salvadoran aims, they argued, "were to put their valiant contingency in a position to maintain the peace in Honduras just as they had done in their own country."[37] Salvadorans, unlike the West Indians in this instance, lobbied their case to the local population and used Central American nationalism as a vehicle to do so. This ensured that the anti-immigrant sentiment experienced by West Indians did not trickle down to Salvadorans. Political relations between El Salvador and Honduras were faltering during this period as an upsurge in the migratory flow of Salvadoran peasants into largely uninhabited areas of Honduras, combined with an increase in Salvadoran workers in the banana industry, created stiffer competition for economic resources. In an effort to solidify their position in Honduras by appealing to the xenophobic intellectual and political climate, Salvadorans exploited racial, cultural, and linguistic differences between themselves and West Indians for their own economic benefit.

By 1930, the number of Central Americans increased considerably, totaling roughly 10,000 in Honduras.[38] In the manufacturing and industrial center of San Pedro Sula, the number of Salvadorans increased by more than one-third. However, the most noticeable shift in the Salvadoran population occurred in the department of Colón. In 1926, the number of Salvadorans in the region was 199. However, by 1930 that number increased to 1,053. In comparison, the total number of West Indians on the North Coast according to Honduran records amounted to 4,215 as opposed to 9,964 of other Central Americans. Echeverri-Gent maintains that there were actually over 10,000 West Indians on the North Coast during this period based on British documentation.[39] However, because the fruit companies were not required to file records for noncontract workers, it is impossible to be precise. Moreover, most foreigners, particularly West Indians, did not register with the local government upon entry into the country. In fact, between 1898 and 1926, only 189 British subjects registered with the Honduran government as foreigners out of a total of 993 foreigners, representing 19 percent of all foreigners on record.[40] In 1930, the department of Atlántida, which boasted a West Indian population of 1,829 according to Honduran census records, listed only 250 British subjects in the foreign registry, of which approximately 238 were West Indian.[41] Therefore, Honduran census data remain the most reliable source for determining the number of West Indians present in the country for any given period.

From the census data, it is apparent that the West Indian workers imported to work for the American-owned fruit companies were not a sizable threat to the local Honduran population. If there was ever any challenge to the Hondurans for agricultural jobs, this came from other Central Americans. Therefore, the reason for the animosity toward West Indian labor stemmed from another source. The element of racism always loomed in the background. However, the larger issue of job competition between Hondurans and West Indians for the technical positions within the fruit companies always resurfaced. Contrary to the claims of Froylán Turcios, there were not enough Hondurans within the country to supply all of the labor demands of the fruit companies.[42] This insufficient Honduran labor supply persisted because Honduras lacked the infrastructure to educate its citizens properly to perform anything other than agricultural labor.

In a 1926 article, the Mexican intellectual José Vasconcelos maintained that the problems in Latin America did not stem from land, immigration, or laws. According to Vasconcelos, the problem in Latin America was one of "improving the level of education for the masses. With a better education, the secrets of work, industry, and production would be evident to the struggling nations of Latin America."[43] In the case of Honduras, foreign workers would continue to supply the labor for the American-owned companies until the local population could produce workers with the skills necessary to fill the void.

The West Indians who immigrated to Honduras to work for the fruit companies came with skills. Most possessed a primary level of education necessary to obtain gainful employment abroad. More important, they spoke English and came from an Anglo-Caribbean colonial culture that catered to the racial sensibilities of their white, North American managers. West Indians were often viewed by fruit company employees as docile and well-behaved. In many cases, Jamaicans in particular were viewed as the "most respectful of all West Indian workers."[44] Despite racial stereotypes on the part of company executives, West Indians did possess a level of education that gave them a marked advantage over most Hondurans.

In the various islands throughout the British Caribbean, blacks had improved their level of education since the abolition of slavery. When the British colonial government instituted the system of competition for Civil Service positions in 1885, blacks were able to garner many of the highly sought positions.[45] Though the improvement of educational opportunity was commendable, these opportunities did not extend to all within society and remained heavily class based, with the small middle and upper classes obtaining the best education. Immigration abroad was an option most available to those individuals with skills. This is especially the case for West Indians who migrated to Honduras between 1900 and 1934.

From the available Honduran immigration records, it is evident that the majority of West Indians that converged on the North Coast of Honduras did so as engineers, electricians, mechanics, carpenters, train operators, contractors, and in other technical positions.[46] In the period prior to the 1929 immigration law, reports from the various fruit companies reveal this trend.

Table 3.4 reveals that West Indians represented only 4.5 percent of all Tela Railroad Company employees prior to the passage of the immigration law. This demonstrates an inconsistency with intellectual claims of foreign blacks taking jobs away from Hondurans. However, what the numbers indicate is that these workers were part of a small minority of foreigners within the company. In most instances, white Americans held the managerial positions, while West Indians held the technical positions.

TABLE 3.4 Tela Railroad Company Employees by Nationality, 1928

NATIONALITY	NO. OF EMPLOYEES	PERCENTAGE OF TOTAL EMPLOYEES
Hondurans and Other Central Americans	4,526	90.5
Europeans	46	1.0
North Americans	198	4.0
West Indians	229	4.5
Totals	4,999	100

Source: Tela Railroad Company, "Informe de la Tela Railroad Company," in *Memoria de Fomento, Obras Públicas, Agricultura y Trabajo, 1927–28* (Tegucigalpa: Tipografía Nacional, 1928), 116.

Hondurans and other Central Americans performed all other types of manual and agricultural labor. The situation for the Trujillo Railroad Company reveals many of the same trends as their sister company in Tela. West Indians numbered 450 of a total workforce of 5,232 and represented only 8.6 percent of all company workers, still a relatively small minority of the total workforce.[47] Despite the relatively small number of West Indians working for the fruit companies, their presence continued to spark widespread animosity in Hondurans. Since the immigration decree of 1929 had done little to curb the perceived influx of West Indians on the North Coast, the intellectual debate that was initiated in the press prior to the passing of the 1929 immigration law continued until the passing of the 1934 law that was more defined and clearly aimed at ridding Honduras of West Indians.

After it became clear that the 1929 immigration law was ineffective in reducing the number of West Indians entering the country, many anti-immigration proponents adopted a new strategy disguised in the rhetoric of patriotism. Patriotism was the banner under which many racist notions entered into Honduran intellectual thought. In fact, Froylán Turcios employed this practice in most of his early writings.[48] However, following the passage of anti-immigrant legislation, patriotism was used as a vehicle to promote the interests of the Honduran worker. If the lawmakers in Tegucigalpa had no interest in protecting Honduran workers for economic or social reasons, they were obligated politically to address their concerns as citizens. One newspaper article from the period defined patriotism as a "holy virtue" as long as it was not contrary to basic human rights and ideals.[49] In this instance, fighting for the cause of the Honduran masses to ensure that they did not form a "country of slaves" justified the actions of the government against immigrant groups.[50] Modeling it on the national-istic agendas of China, Spain, and Germany, Antonio Zozaya, the author of the piece, believed that Honduras could become a successful nation. Such a strategy created problems in a Central American context because it became necessary to construct a definition of what constituted the na-tion within a multiracial context.

West Indians belonged to a privileged immigrant group in Honduran society and for the most part never desired to be a part of the nation. However, by reducing their complex situation in Honduras to an exclu-sive focus on race, the press, the government, and even local Hondurans vying for their jobs emphasized the history of West Indians on the North Coast within the larger debate centering on race in Latin America.

One way to challenge the presence of West Indians in Honduras was to argue that the community violated immigration policies. This was most easily accomplished by questioning the validity of West Indian passports and visas issued at Honduran consulates in other countries. In 1932, the government questioned the immigration status of two men, D. Smith and John Weberts, both English-speaking blacks of uncertain origin, on the grounds that the only identification these men had in their possession were documents from the western consul of Honduras and a statement from witnesses testifying that the two men were Honduran citizens.[51] Un-der normal circumstances, an official document from a consular agent would have been sufficient to prove Honduran citizenship. However, in the climate of anti-black immigration, these two men were deported to Belize because they did not have a document that stated specifically their place of birth. A group of twenty West Indians suffered the same fate. Honduran authorities deported them to Belize on the grounds that they were in the country without the proper legal documentation. After the discovery of these twenty men, the Honduran authorities sent commis-sions to the various camps in the Tela area to arrest those thought to be evading Honduran immigration laws.[52]

While the place of origin of these workers could not be authenticated by Honduran authorities, the local immigration authorities saw fit to send all of these men to Belize. In the case of Smith and Weberts, it was quite possible that the two men were Bay Islanders or children of West Indians born in Honduras. However, the authorities did not bother to fully investigate the matter. Blackness and the English language, in addition to being associated with British origins, automatically excluded these men and countless others from due process. Within hours, they were shipped out to the nearest British territory, whether they belonged there or not.

English-speaking West Indians were the largest group affected by the question of the validity of passports issued by Honduran consulates overseas, but the problem was not limited solely to this group. Honduran authorities also accused Czechs, Hungarians, Romanians, and other "undesirable" immigrant groups of entering the country with questionable documentation.[53] The major concern with this Eastern European group of immigrants was that they were Jewish and were, therefore, considered inassimilable.

The situation for West Indians legally residing in Honduras remained as unstable as it was for those deported on the suspicion of carrying false documentation. In 1933, a government decree forbade the re-entry into the country of those individuals of the black race who had recently left.[54] In other words, West Indians who lived and worked in Honduras legally could remain. However, if they chose to leave for any reason, they would not be allowed to return. Such restrictions created many problems for the West Indian community on the North Coast because most maintained some connection with their home countries. In fact, the day following the news of the decree, the governing officer in the town of Puerto Castilla raised the question to the Gobernación Política in Tegucigalpa regarding what would happen to those West Indians who often went to visit their families outside of the country. The response was that as long as these individuals were either citizens or had settled in Honduras, and had accidentally left the country for Belize while acting as guides to travelers, they could in fact return to Honduras.[55] This represented a small fragment of the West Indian population, as most traveled back and forth to visit family or to study rather than to accompany travelers as guides.

The case concerning the children of West Indians studying abroad was not so clear. In 1933, Matilde Reid, a West Indian of Jamaican descent residing in Puerto Castilla, solicited permission from the Honduran immigration authorities for her daughters to return to Honduras after completing their studies in Jamaica. Reid maintained that her two daughters, Edna Mary and Lucila, had lived in Puerto Castilla for eight years prior to being sent to Jamaica for their education.[56] The response to this request, like so many others during this period, was lost in the historical record and there is no way to determine whether or not the daughters were ever allowed to return to Honduras. However, Reid's situation reveals that there was no guarantee that once West Indians left Honduras, their re-entry into the country would be permitted. The government regarded re-entry as an entirely new immigration case. Issues concerning the validation of passports, authenticity of immigration documents, re-entry, and all other concerns relative to immigration illustrate the fact that many Honduran officials felt that a more precise immigration law was needed to control the presence of blacks in the country. They believed that a new immigration law should favor the Honduran worker above all else and guarantee that Hondurans would be able to work in whatever capacity they wanted without competition from West Indians. Some went so far as to suggest that Honduran workers "were just as, if not more, capable of filling the positions that Spaniards, North Americans, Italians, or Blacks were occupying."[57]

Wrapped in the cloak of patriotism, Honduran officials argued that Hondurans should not imitate North Americans and allow themselves to be subjugated by outside forces. Part of this subjugation came at the hands of companies that substituted foreign labor for local Honduran workers even though Hondurans could fill these positions.[58] This claim about the tendency to substitute local workers with foreign labor bears some merit, considering the fact that the United Fruit Company was reported to have replaced local workers with Jamaicans in La Lima as early as 1932.[59] While the company hired Jamaicans throughout the period, the case in 1932 also emphasized the fact that the company commissaries hurt the local Honduran business economy. From the viewpoint of the local population, not only were Hondurans deprived of a livelihood, but the practice displaced Hondurans from participation in local economic activity.

Considering that the Spanish, North American, and Italian immigrants that Honduran "patriots" frequently criticized came to Honduras as owners of businesses and corporations, the only groups in position to take jobs away from Hondurans were the West Indians. As a result of increased pressure from both intellectuals and the local population of the North Coast, the 1934 immigration law was more thorough in stating which groups were allowed into the country and under what circumstances.

Article 14 of the 1934 immigration law clarifies the status of West Indians by prohibiting the entrance of blacks (along with Chinese, Gypsies, and East Indians) into Honduran territory under any circumstances. These groups were even excluded from receiving three-month tourist visas.[60] Surprisingly, previously excluded Arabic-speaking groups such as the Arabs, Syrians, Palestinians, and Lebanese were allowed entrance into the country. Poles, Czechoslovakians, and Armenians were also given the right to immigrate to Honduras. The only conditions for these groups was that they dedicate themselves exclusively to agriculture or to the introduction and improvement of new industries and that they deposit a sum of 2,000 Honduran *lempiras* (about U.S. $1,000 at the time) upon entrance into the country.

The concessions made to these latter groups of immigrants were reminiscent of those given to North American and European capitalists in previous generations. More important, the 1934 law of immigration sealed the fate of most West Indians in Honduras and facilitated a dramatic decline in the population over the next decade. The political and intellectual discourse that led to the passage of the 1934 law focused almost exclusively on the West Indian community in Honduras. That previously excluded populations were allowed entrance after 1934 demonstrates the preoccupation of Hondurans with the growing West Indian presence on the North Coast. Hondurans generally perceived West Indians, more than any other immigrant population, as the greatest challenge to the economic, political, and cultural autonomy of the nation.

4

WEST INDIAN CULTURAL RETENTION
AND COMMUNITY FORMATION
ON THE NORTH COAST

The social and cultural values that developed among West Indians in Honduras are best examined within the context of the postemancipation experience in the British West Indies. Marked by very blurred perceptions of slavery and freedom, the apprenticeship system that preceded full emancipation did little to improve the situation of blacks in the Caribbean. In many ways an extension of slavery, the system allowed for little upward mobility of the newly freed population. The conditions prevalent in the British Caribbean during the late nineteenth and early twentieth centuries made migration an attractive alternative to conditions of semiservitude in the Caribbean. For instance, in British Honduras, O. Nigel Bolland maintains, the "control of labor and land were two dialectically related aspects of a changing, but persistent structure of colonial domination that continued even after the end of apprenticeship in 1838."[1] The mechanisms that maintained the power differential between whites and blacks during enslavement remained in the postemancipation era. White Belizeans monopolized land ownership, systems of labor, the police force as a means of labor control, and the use of churches, schools, and missionaries as vehicles for instilling within black Belizeans the virtues of subordination and obedience to white authority.[2] In addition to the unequal distribution of power and wealth in the colony, the log wood and mahogany export industries continued to decline between 1885 and 1900, making it harder for a large segment of the population to obtain a livable wage.[3]

By the 1930s, the majority of black Belizeans continued to live in lamentable circumstances. Labor and living conditions were similar to what they had been in the previous century. Most British Hondurans of African descent never owned land and were forced to eke out an existence as subsistence farmers on squatted land or hire out their labor once their crops failed to yield enough produce for sale or consumption.[4] For almost half the population, the colony offered little opportunity for a better life.

Generally, the most destitute of West Indians were more concerned with keeping their families alive and eking out an existence than with risking immigration to unfamiliar countries in Central America. Immigration required savings and marketable skills, two things the average West Indian did not possess. As a result, a disproportionate number of skilled artisans, mechanics, and other members of the middle class were among the first West Indians to seek opportunity abroad.[5] This trend has enormous implications for understanding the history of West Indians in Honduras during the fruit company period, as this skilled group of West Indians disassociated themselves from the black masses in their home countries prior to immigration.

Much like their British Honduran brethren, the Jamaicans who chose to immigrate to Honduras during this period fled the constraints of economic deprivation caused by the decreased importance of the West Indies in the international sugar trade. After emancipation, most freedmen in Jamaica had no access to land and relied solely on agricultural wages for subsistence. Thus the power base in Jamaica was located in the estates and the Jamaican Assembly's policies of creating a landless black peasantry.[6] As Dorsey Walker maintains, the population of Jamaica was not rewarded either politically or economically as a consequence of emancipation.[7] According to Patrick Bryan, as early as 1846 the free trade policy that removed the protection given to British West Indian sugar aided in the declining conditions of the sugar islands.[8] The shortage of vehicles to generate capital and improve production techniques meant that the daily operations of the sugar industry retained the character of pre-emancipation society. Jamaican workers, according to Thomas Holt, "were dispossessed of political defenses and were a heavily exploited group."[9] Add to this the fact that by 1910 the number of sugar estates on the island was reduced to only one-third of what they had been on the eve of emancipation, and the situation for the Jamaican worker proved dismal.[10] Malnutrition and poor housing were the norm and undoubtedly were the causes of the high rate of infant mortality. As a result of the increased economic hardship, many displaced and dispossessed Jamaican workers began to seek opportunities abroad.[11] As evidenced in an article from a New Orleans newspaper reporting on the conditions of the sugar industry in Jamaica, workers were being paid a mere twenty-five cents per day for their labor and were attracted to the higher wages of the canal zone.[12]

While much has been written on the experiences of the Jamaican workers in Panama and in Central American nations such as Costa Rica, the Jamaican demographic of the West Indian community in Honduras has not received significant scholarly consideration, considering that the island was instrumental in the banana trade from its inception. In order to understand the organization of the West Indian community in Honduras, it is essential to understand the role Jamaica played in the trade from its inception.

Introduced to Jamaica from Martinique by the French botanist Jean François Pouyat in 1835, the Gros Michel variety of banana quickly became popular among the peasantry as a highly sustainable crop. With the decline in the sugar industry, banana production soon became the primary agricultural crop in the parishes of St. Mary, Portland, and St. Thomas.[13] Labor on banana plantations was easier than on sugar estates and thus required lower overhead. Local producers actively engaged in the emerging banana industry, forming growing cooperatives to protect their interests.

The banana export trade began in Jamaica in 1866 when George Bosch, an American sea captain, purchased five hundred stems of bananas from Jamaican producers and loaded them into a schooner at Oracabessa, Jamaica, bound for Boston, Massachusetts. Bosch remained in business for a year but suffered significant financial losses during this period because the majority of his banana crop spoiled prior to arrival in Boston.[14] It was not until Lorenzo Dow Baker arrived on the scene in 1870 that the export banana trade between the United States and Jamaica began to flourish. According to Sealy and Hart, Baker created a two-way profit system in which he brought cargo from the United States consisting of flour, pork, salted cod, shoes, and textiles to sell on the Jamaican market, the profits from which he invested in purchasing bananas and selling them in Boston. By 1880 Baker merged his enterprise with the Boston Fruit Company and purchased banana plantations in Jamaica, thus initiating a business practice of vertical integration for which his subsequent conglomerate, the United Fruit Company, which formed in 1899, became famous. However, the United Fruit Company was never able to exert the same political and economic force on Jamaica that it did in Central American nations.

In the early days of the banana export trade, Jamaican producers supplied 80 percent of the bananas shipped to the United States. The Boston Fruit Company acquired upwards of 13,000 acres of land in Jamaica by 1887, but it could not supplant the political power of the Jamaican banana cooperatives organized by locals to protect their interests. The British colonial government in Jamaica recognized the potential of the export banana industry and created mechanisms to promote the trade.[15] An exposition on the agricultural and industrial products of Jamaica during the 1884–1885 New Orleans World's Exposition revealed the magnitude of the increase in production. In a ten-year period between 1875 and 1884, the number of bananas exported from Jamaica to the United States increased from 58,411 to over 1,842,934 bunches.[16] During this increased trade, the Boston Fruit Company shipped goods primarily to Boston, while Jamaican-owned companies produced and shipped goods primarily to Baltimore, Philadelphia, and New York.[17]

Thomas Holt asserts that there were racial overtones to United Fruit Company policies regarding the Jamaican trade. American capitalists would not invest in Jamaica if the black majority was allowed political equality with whites.[18] Therefore, it became necessary for the white minority to maintain a political and economic system in which the black majority remained in a subordinate position. Many landowners refused to sell or rent land to black Jamaicans and the colonial taxation system on material goods and private possessions inevitably meant that black workers had a minimal chance of maintaining their independence.[19] Many blacks gained valuable experience on the banana plantations in Jamaica. In fact, it was this expertise that prompted the North American fruit companies to hire Jamaicans in Central America.

Though Belize and Jamaica supplied the largest number of West Indian workers to Honduras during the major periods of U.S. fruit company expansion into Honduran territory, the West Indian experience in Honduras did not begin with these two groups. The Bay Islands offer some of the earliest known instances of significant Caribbean immigration to Honduras. The Bay Islands, specifically the island of Roatan, are best known as the location where the British deported the Black Carib (Garífuna) population from St. Vincent in the year 1797 in order to rid the

British settlement of the rebellious population that had proven to be an obstacle to British hegemony on the island. However, the first instances of substantial British settlement in the Bay Islands was in the 1830s, when Cayman Islanders began to migrate to the region.

The first Caymanian settler to the Bay Islands was reported to be one Joseph Cooper, a white male who arrived in Utila with no slaves between 1831 and 1836.[20] Cooper was representative of the initial Caymanian settlers to the Bay Islands, in that most were white or near-white. According to Michael Craton, an 1858 census of the islands' population revealed that the majority of settlers in the Bay Islands were from the Cayman Islands or had Caymanian parentage. In fact, of the 1,548 settlers on the three islands, 600 were from the Cayman Islands and 300 were born on the Bay Islands of Caymanian parentage. The remainder of the population consisted of a handful of Garífuna, Spanish-speaking Hondurans, Jamaicans, and people born in other parts of the British West Indies.[21] The majority of the Bay Island inhabitants resided on Roatan, which was the largest island within the archipelago.

Bay Island society, much like other islands in the British Caribbean, was divided according to color and class. White settlers lived overwhelmingly on the islands of Guanaja and Utila while the majority of blacks lived on the island of Roatan. According to Craton, black Bay Islanders preferred the life of subsistence farming and fishing. Whites were more in a position economically to build boats needed for the establishment of successful trade enterprises.[22] In the early years of the history of the Bay Islands, trade relationships were logically established with the Cayman Islands because of the historical and cultural relationship between the two areas. However, it was the establishment of trade relationships between the Bay Islands and the colonial outpost of British Honduras that planted the seeds for what was later to become United States involvement in the banana industry. Belize would also serve as the closest geographical link to the British Empire for West Indians in Honduras throughout the course of this study.

Though the experiences of British West Indians during the late nineteenth and early twentieth centuries varied depending on the territories in which they resided, the common thread that united them was their need to seek opportunity outside the borders of the British Empire. For a people desperate to sustain themselves, the developmental projects of Central America proved tempting. Whether it was the railroad projects in Guatemala, the various canal projects leading up to the Panama Canal, or the fruit plantations of Costa Rica and Honduras, West Indians were willing to go wherever there was opportunity. In the case of Honduras, this opportunity came in the form of specialized positions for the Standard Fruit and Steamship Company and United Fruit Company and its subsidiaries.

The colonial infrastructure of many of the British Caribbean colonies continued to rely on preconceived notions of black inferiority and offered little economic or educational incentive to promote the upward mobility of the formerly enslaved and their descendants. This group relied on their wits and cultural traditions to sustain themselves. Having roots in West African cultural traditions and the Caribbean plantation experience, many in the Caribbean instituted concepts such as food sharing, rotating credit associations, burial groups, class clubs, and friendly societies in order to survive during periods of economic hardships.[23] Many of these traditions survived migration from the Caribbean to Central America.

One aspect of the West Indian colonial experience that emerged in Honduras was the importance placed on religious institutions within the community. For the masses, religious institutions served as vehicles for community organization, the attainment of basic education, and as a voice for their growing social and political concerns. Baptists, Seventh Day Adventists, Jehovah's Witnesses, the Moravians, and various other Protestant sects common in the British Caribbean had sizable followings in Honduras. The two most prominent groups in the region were the Methodist and Anglican (Episcopal) denominations. These two sects had long been established in the English-speaking world and had the broad-based support of a politically and culturally sanctioned church. In addition, these two churches had the financial means to promote missionary activities abroad.

The Methodist Mission in Honduras was the first organized Protestant denomination in the country to establish permanent religious institutions that catered to the spiritual and religious needs of the immigrant West Indian population. An earlier Anglican mission administered to the Caymanian population on the Bay Islands from Belize as early as 1837.[24] However, attempts to establish a permanent church with a resident clergyman never materialized.

Arriving in 1887 from British Honduras, the Methodist Church established the Wesleyan District that included the Bay Islands and the entire North Coast of Honduras. Eventually changing its name to the Zion Methodist Mission, the church set up branches in Puerto Cortés, Tela, Puerto Castilla, La Ceiba, and the Bay Islands, all of which became the primary areas of West Indian settlement in the country at the turn of the twentieth century.[25] For much of its history, the church relied on British-trained pastors from British Honduras to service its congregations until 1959, when the church became a part of the Wesleyan District of Marion, Indiana, and began receiving pastors from the United States. It was not until recently that Hondurans of West Indian descent received leadership from within their community.

The Episcopal Church in Honduras originated under similar conditions as the Methodist Church. The denomination gained permanency in La Ceiba as a missionary outpost of the established church in British Honduras. The Episcopal Church of the Holy Trinity, as the mission became known, was first organized from Belize as a part of the Diocese of British Honduras with Central America at the turn of the twentieth century. Throughout its history, this church catered to the middle economic sector of the West Indian community, which was composed overwhelmingly of skilled, laborers, shopkeepers, and lower-level fruit company management. For much of its history in the Caribbean, the Episcopal Church, according to Patrick Bryan, was the church of the slaveholder with a marked indifference to the spiritual welfare of the enslaved population.[26] The church in many ways continued to reinforce the status quo of owning-class dominance over the masses after emancipation, whereas the more missionary-oriented Protestant denominations in many ways initiated the introduction of the masses into the political system. Moreover, these churches became a socially accepted medium by which to carry out the organized resistance against black oppression that had been prevalent in Caribbean societies since the arrival of the first enslaved Africans to the region.

Despite the varied perceptions of the Episcopal Church and its relationship with the black masses in the greater Caribbean, this congregation in Honduras provides a window into understanding the nature of West Indian society in the country. Since 1915, the church has kept detailed records regarding baptisms, marriages, and internments of its members. The analysis of these records reveals much about the demography of the closely knit West Indian community in the city of La Ceiba and surrounding municipalities.

Between 1915 and 1954, the Episcopal Church of the Holy Trinity

(Iglesia Episcopal de la Sanctísima Trinidad) was a thriving center of black West Indian and Bay Island cultural and religious life. Marriage records from the period indicate that the congregation represented individuals from every economic strata of society. The majority of the 154 congregants married in the church during this period engaged in independent business ventures or highly skilled trades, though many were employed with the Standard Fruit and Steamship Company. West Indian businessmen and shopkeepers catered to the various consumer needs of fruit company workers and management. They profited due to the skills and trades acquired in their home countries, as well as due to the desire of white North American company employees to patronize those businesspeople who spoke English. Unlike the smaller fruit company towns of Tela and Trujillo, the company commissary was not the main supplier of goods and services. There remained a substantial need for small businesses to cater to the growing foreign population. Ultimately, these West Indian businessmen, along with the growing Palestinian Arab merchant class, were able to monopolize a sector of the economy that prior to their arrival was not fully developed.

Women have generally been absent from the available literature on West Indians in Honduras. Part of this omission stems from the overrepresentation of men in the migrant West Indian population along the North Coast of Honduras. This was very similar to the situations in other areas of Central America with large West Indian migrant populations. Though not the majority, women remained a significant presence in West Indian society in Honduras. Laura Putnam, in her assessment of West Indian women in Costa Rica, maintains that some women came with a male partner by their side, while others made the journey on their own.[27] This also holds true for Honduras. Judging from the available records, the propensity for women to settle with their partners was much greater in Honduras than in other areas. The Bay Islands offer part of the explanation for this. John Soluri maintains that "the historical ties between the islands and Jamaicans blurred socio-political boundaries and made efforts to cut off migration between Honduras and Jamaica problematic."[28] Because West Indians and Bay Islanders shared strong cultural and ethnic ties, the propensity for marriage and sexual unions between the two groups was common, forging a bond that often blurred racial and social distinctions. Although West Indian males came to Honduras in larger numbers, there

TABLE 4.1 Occupations of the Congregation of the Church of the Holy Trinity

OCCUPATION	NO. OF PERSONS
Baker	2
Barber	1
Boilermaker	1
Bookkeeper	1
Cabinet Maker	1
Carpenter	13
Clerk	4
Contractor	2
Cook	1
Dispenser	1
Domestic (women)	18
Druggist	1
Electrical Mechanic	1
Engineer	2
Farmer/Agriculture	2
Fireman	1
Fruit Inspector	1
Hotel Keeper	1
Housewife	10
Laborer	4
Machinist	1
Mechanic	3
Merchant	6
Midwife	1
Nurse	3
Painters	5
Sailor/Stevedore	6
Salesman	1
Seamstress/Dressmaker	9
Secretary	1
Shoemaker	2
Shopkeeper	1
Tailor	3
Teacher	2
Train/Railroad Conductor	2
Washing	1
Watchmaker	1
No job (women)	35
No job (men)	1
Illegible Data	2
Total	154

Source: Register of Marriages, 1915–1954. Church of the Holy Trinity. La Ceiba, Honduras.

were potential partners within the Bay Islands population to offset any gender imbalance. It is this factor that separates Honduras from other Central American banana zones during the period.

The records from the congregation of the Holy Trinity offer some of the only primary documentation on the experiences of women during the period. According to the available data, the majority of the women listed their occupations as housewives, domestic workers, or as having no job at all. The fact that the majority of women did not work outside the home was not uncommon. Judging from the accounts of some, gender roles were very traditional, with the male as the provider and the female as the mother and caregiver.[29] More important, as Putnam notes, in Costa Rican operations, the fruit companies and their subsidiaries generally did not employ women as dockworkers or field laborers.[30] Most of the fruit company workers in Honduras, whether West Indian or native Honduran, were in fact male. Even occupations such as cook that were considered the domain of women in other industries were filled by West Indian men in the banana camps. This appears to have been the case only when it concerned West Indians as there are accounts of mestiza and indigenous women migrating to the banana camps to work as labor camp cooks and washerwomen.[31] Such labor designations further created animosity between native Hondurans and West Indians that persisted throughout the duration of major fruit company operations on the coast.

Full-time domestic life for women was only possible for those West Indian households who could afford it. In the event that a husband could not support his family solely on his earnings, as was often the case, women sought employment as domestics in the homes of white American fruit company executives and as vendors at local markets in town. Many of the white American women preferred black West Indian domestic workers in part because they spoke English, as most white Americans on the coast made no effort to learn Spanish. More important, as many of the fruit company executives were from the southern United States, having black "servants" catered to their notions of white superiority.

Regarding traditional gender roles and family life during this period, West Indian and non–West Indian families were much alike. While the propensity for members of the congregation to prefer stable, monogamous relationships is suggested in the baptismal records of the church, there is not enough evidence to indicate that West Indians were more or less traditional in family matters. The records from the Church of the

Holy Trinity do, however, reveal certain patterns that allow for a broader understanding of the West Indian experience.

Of the 574 children baptized between 1915 and 1954, only 52 were born to single mothers. However, in these 52 cases, the father was known and listed within the records. There were no single mothers listed before 1924 or after 1948.[32] This trend coincides with Honduran census data and the increased anti-immigration sentiment in Honduras. While sources in earlier chapters revealed a current of anti-black sentiment prevalent in Honduras from the arrival of West Indians in the late nineteenth and early twentieth centuries, it is not until the 1920s that many intellectuals and politicians began considering a permanent ban on West Indian immigration to the country. By 1924, the West Indian population in Honduras was less transient and made efforts to establish permanent settlement in all of the North Coast cities. Prior to the 1920s, mobility within the population was greater and the West Indian community and its institutions were not fully entrenched. That no single mothers are listed after 1948 denotes that most West Indians had since left Honduras for other viable economic opportunities in the United States, been deported, or were assimilated into the larger society. The immigration of West Indians into Honduras tapered off considerably after the anti-immigrant legislation of 1929 and 1934, thus hindering the growth of the community.

The small number of single mothers within the West Indian population suggests that monogamous unions were the norm within the community. However, the use of the term *single mother* in the documents does not mean that all other baptized children came from legally or religiously sanctioned marriages. Of the 574 couples, 105 were in "common law" unions.[33] In certain cases, there were siblings baptized with age differences ranging from five to ten years who had the same mother, but different fathers. For example, one Beatrice Wade baptized a total of four children between 1928 and 1936. The first three children were born in 1928, 1929, and 1931, and records list no father. However, in 1936, Wade gave birth to a fourth child whose father was listed as one Leroy Johnson.[34] The close proximity in ages of the children, same place of birth, and the fact that the children had multiple godparents and witnesses at their baptisms all suggest that the community in La Ceiba did not stigmatize Wade for having children with different fathers. Moreover, the fact that she had children prior to her relationship with Leroy Johnson indicates that single motherhood was not a barrier to her contracting marriage with a man who was not the father of her older children.

The example of Rachel Waller bears many similarities to that of Beatrice Wade. In June 1936, Waller gave birth to a daughter with one Glenford Lambert of La Ceiba. Eighteen months later in November 1937, the same Rachel Waller gave birth to a son whose father was listed as Charlie Swarton. Three years later, Waller and Swarton had a daughter together, indicating the two were in a stable relationship. Interestingly enough, Charlie Swarton's occupation was listed as blacksmith, a more stable profession, while Lambert, the father of the first child, was listed as a mechanic/laborer, indicating less stability.[35] Life as a laborer often meant constant movement in search of work. Most labor contracts were extended at six-month intervals and were subject to an unstable banana market, particularly in the 1930s when Panama disease damaged large portions of the Honduran banana crops. In addition to demonstrating the tendency within the West Indian community to engage in serial monogamy, the Rachel Waller example indicates that the nuclear family may have been affected as much by the uncertain demands of an unstable labor market as by West Indian traditions.

West Indian relationship patterns in Honduras were in part a continuation of patterns established in the Caribbean. Common law unions were fairly frequent in the Caribbean. Historians continue to debate the reasons for the proclivity of West Indians from the peasant and laboring classes to forego legal or religiously sanctioned marriages. Some have argued that legal marriage was uncommon because of the exorbitant fees and expenses associated with the institution. Others, mostly British researchers and travelers in the Victorian era, maintained racist notions that the cultural and moral void within African peoples contributed to the absence of the institution of marriage in certain classes.[36] More plausible is the reality that British religious and cultural traditions by which the Afro-Caribbean population was judged were not fully entrenched in Jamaica and other areas of the West Indies until after emancipation. Prior to this period, the enslaved African population relied on African traditions and plantation experiences, these being the two heritages that defined Afro–West Indian identity prior to emancipation. Within this context, the traditional nuclear family was the norm. Nuclear families were also central to the West Indian community in Honduras. Marriage, however loosely defined, and the stability associated with it were the normal and preferred familial arrangement.

The examples of Wade and Waller do more than demonstrate the retention of Caribbean cultural traits in Honduras. They, along with countless other women in the documents, were not necessarily relegated to the "traditional" mother/caregiver roles that men within West Indian society espoused. Many women were able to control the nature and duration of their relationships with men while continuing to be fully engaged in the social and religious life of the community. That many of these women were heads of households, primary caregivers to their children, and negotiated the institutions within the community to the benefit of themselves and their children is a testament to the enduring dedication of women of African descent to persist through adversity.

Statistics regarding the number of marriages recorded by the Honduran government are extremely rare. However, judging from the records of the Church of the Holy Trinity and oral accounts, West Indians tended overwhelmingly to choose partners from within their own ethnic and cultural group. This is not to suggest that intimate relations between West Indians and non–West Indians did not occur. The baptismal records reveal that of the 574 children who received the sacrament, 30 were the product of a union between a West Indian and a Honduran with a Spanish first name and surname. Of the 77 marriages performed at the Church of the Holy Trinity, 9 were between a West Indian and a Honduran with a Spanish first name and surname.[37] Whether the Spanish-speaking partners were mestizo(a) or Garífuna remains unclear, as the latter were a large segment of the population in the rural areas along the coast. Many Garífuna also sought employment as seasonal dockworkers for the fruit companies and would have come into close contact with West Indians both at work and within the city. Moreover, because some of the Spanish-speaking individuals listed their home residence as Corrozal and San Juan, some of the unions may have been between West Indians and Garífuna.[38]

In most cases, foreigners were not registering any type of unions with the Honduran authorities. As most retained the citizenship of their countries of origin, foreigners on the North Coast relied on their own diplomatic representation in these matters. As a result, the propensity for the Church of the Holy Trinity to retain the marriage records of its congregation offers insight into the community that would otherwise not have been documented.

Though marriages and common-law unions between Spanish-speaking Hondurans and English-speaking West Indians were rare, West Indians were not hesitant to marry those from other Caribbean islands. It was common for a Jamaican to marry a Barbadian, Trinidadian, or Caymanian. It was also common for any of these groups to marry Bay Islanders of West Indian descent. In fact, there was a proclivity for many Jamaican men to marry Bay Island women. This arrangement benefited Jamaican men in more than just a cultural sense. Bay Islanders were Honduran citizens by birth. Therefore, to a West Indian man seeking to acquire residency in Honduras in order to stave off deportation as a result of increasingly vigilant anti-black immigration laws, it was in his best interest to contract marriage with a Honduran woman. With such a union, the man could legally acquire a visa to remain in the country, while maintaining his West Indian identity and avoiding the need to learn Spanish. Frederick Douglas Opie observes a similar trend in the Guatemalan railroad camps during the same period; West Indian and Afro–North American men courting and marrying nationals had socioeconomic advantages such as acquiring kinship relations and gaining competitive advantage by learning the local laws and customs.[39] To this day, the descendants of these Jamaican men and Bay Island women are referred to as *caracoles,* a term that translates literally into English as conches. The *caracoles* represent a large segment of the population of Roatán and remain a defining symbol of Bay Island identity.[40] These marriage patterns were not limited to Jamaican men, as many West Indian women also married men of Bay Islands origin when given the opportunity.

Unlike the community in Costa Rica, where employers used island rivalries to pit West Indians against each other, the community in Honduras tended to unite based on an Anglo-Caribbean cultural and historical identity rather than become enmeshed in interisland rivalries. What appears to have been more important in choosing a marriage partner or social circle was whether or not the individual was of English-speaking, West Indian heritage. Requests for marriage certificates from Honduran authorities reveal such trends. For instance, in 1925, one Alejandro Steel, a Bay Islands resident, requested a contract to marry one Rosa May Coocke who was listed as a citizen of Jamaica, thus providing evidence that it was not only West Indian men who chose English-speaking Hondurans as marriage partners.[41] Both were listed as residents of the city of Tela. In another request from Tela, one Cyril Augustus Francis requested a contract to marry one Eugenia Sewill, both listed as residents of that city.[42] There were numerous other requests from this period, some undoubtedly submitted by Bay Islanders, further demonstrating the trend of English speakers' preference for marrying other English speakers, presumably of West Indian heritage.

The various Protestant denominations in Honduras were dedicated to nurturing the educational needs of congregants. Throughout much of the postemancipation period in Caribbean history, the Bible was the building block of education. In fact, for the masses of West Indians, the Bible was the only book with which most were acquainted.[43] In many instances, even the rudimentary Bible education with which most West Indians were indoctrinated had largely racist overtones. This is most evident when assessing the advent of secular and religious education in Jamaica at the turn of the twentieth century. Archbishop Enos Nuttall is credited with leading the way in the expansion of both religious and secular education to the masses of Jamaicans. According to Patrick Bryan, his approach was based largely on a derivative of Christian humanism that faced the fact that blacks would not die out as a racial category in Jamaica and therefore must be dealt with. For Nuttall, the outlook of blacks was not shaped by race, but culture. In order to make blacks respectable, and worthy of equal status with whites, Nuttall believed that it was essential to reshape black culture to Anglo-Saxon norms.[44] Education was the means to do this, and the Anglican Church was the vehicle by which this goal was accomplished.

Religious institutions, specifically the Episcopal Church, satisfied the educational needs of many of the children of West Indian immigrants in the banana centers of Honduras. Deeply rooted in the colonial British educational system, schools in Honduras offered an educational paradigm that emphasized memorization and rote learning. This offered little opportunity for critical thought in students and served as a means of British cultural indoctrination. British Honduran and Jamaican teachers taught the children in English. West Indian parents insisted that their children be taught to speak and master the English language, in many instances to the exclusion of other languages, specifically Spanish.[45] By some accounts, Spanish was not even offered as a second language in many of the schools. Most West Indian children who spoke Spanish learned it from their encounters with the local Honduran population.

The children in the English schools learned to pledge at least nominal allegiance to the British crown through the study of British history, the frequent recitation of the British national anthem, and the celebration of British holidays. This type of education was not uncommon in the British West Indies. In his study of the Barbadian educational system, Robert Proctor asserts that the British colonial government emphasized churches and the educational system as primary socializing institutions reinforcing the message that English ways were superior to all others.[46] Proctor adds that these institutions were not designed to meet the needs of the local society, but rather maintained relevance only as part of the British Empire.[47]

West Indians in Honduras often behaved in ways that some perceived as "too British" and indicative of their intentional nonintegration into larger society. Baron Piñeda noted a similar trend on the Nicaraguan Atlantic coast in which communities of West Indian descent (Creoles) were perceived by other Nicaraguans to "believe they were English."[48] Such observations are a recurring theme in the literature related to West Indians in Central America. The social, economic, linguistic, and educational traditions of the community oriented it more to the English-speaking Caribbean than to the larger mestizo culture on the Spanish-dominated mainland.

In another assessment of the British educational system, George Lamming, the well-known Barbadian novelist, asserted that the colonial system taught West Indians to denigrate, if not totally deny, their place of birth. Culture, according to Lamming, was something that came from abroad, specifically from England.[49] In effect, what these institutions accomplished was the transformation of many West Indians, specifically those of the middle classes, into "Black Englishmen." Many of the institutions established by West Indians in Honduras perpetuated colonial notions of British superiority, rather than the newly emerging ideologies espousing black liberation.

Though not a new educational concept in the Caribbean, such notions of maintaining the British colonial status quo were of little use in a Honduran society that was overwhelmingly Spanish-speaking and mestizo in cultural heritage and tradition. Also, because many of the schools and churches of West Indians, especially in Tela, were built by their American employers, there was a tendency for many within the community to ingratiate themselves with Americans by supporting their political and economic interests. The British and American influence on the West Indian community through employment, education, and religious worship placed them at odds with the local population. By teaching their children in English only, and maintaining their strong cultural ties to the Caribbean, many West Indians ensured that their children would be ill-equipped to live in Honduras in the event that the economic situation changed. Most West Indians in Honduras did not plan to remain in Honduras permanently. Most children of West Indians in Honduras sought educations abroad in British Honduras, the United States, and Jamaica following primary school in Honduras. Many also pursued higher education in the numerous universities throughout the Anglophone world. Very few who left ever returned permanently to the North Coast of Honduras, often finding life in the Anglophone world more agreeable to their own cultural sensibilities.

In addition to maintaining their own churches, schools, and businesses, the black West Indian community in Honduras also preserved many social traditions from the Caribbean. These traditions revolved around the numerous Masonic lodges and clubs in the cities along the North Coast and almost all had their origins with Jamaican workers. The lodges served as the focal points for many of the cultural traditions within the community and were vital in acculturating new Caribbean arrivals to life in Honduras. In cities such as La Ceiba, where the Samaritan, Fellow Men, and Scots Mechanic lodges were prominent, it was not only forbidden for non–West Indians to join, but it was also forbidden to speak Spanish.[50] The lodges hosted picnics, dances with Caribbean music, receptions, funerals, and many other social events that brought people together. They also served as mutual aid societies and offered economic assistance to members in need. Since the early Masonic lodges were reserved for men, many women, particularly in La Ceiba, saw the need to form their own organizations. It was out of these circumstances that the prominent female society Household of Ruth emerged.

Though the lodges ceased to exist after the departure of the West Indians from the North Coast, many of their traditions remained. This is most noticeable in the mutual aid societies. For instance, in Tela, the Asociacion de Tercera Edad (Senior Citizen Association) maintains a burial fund; its members pay a small amount of dues per month in exchange for the guarantee that upon their death, they will be buried in a coffin and their families will receive one thousand *lempiras* cash. The president of the association, Rand Garo, is a Honduran of West Indian descent whose family hailed from the British settlement of Bluefields, Nicaragua. At one time he had been a member of the Scots Mechanic lodge. Though the association comprises Hondurans of both mestizo and West Indian descent, Garo revealed that in the beginning, the association was founded by Hondurans only of West Indian descent.[51] To this day, such mutual aid societies do not exist among the Garífuna or larger mestizo community.

Lodges and mutual aid societies were not the only institutions from the Caribbean transplanted to Honduras during the period. In discussions of the numerous dances and social events, many people questioned referred to the prominence of Liberty Halls in facilitating these events. There were in fact Liberty Halls in Coxen Hole on Roatán, El Porvenir, Tela, and La Ceiba. As one individual claimed, many English-speaking blacks would travel from all over the North Coast to attend dances at the Liberty Halls.[52] In addition to serving as the location for dances and social gatherings, Liberty Halls were perhaps better known as meeting halls of the Universal Negro Improvement Association (UNIA), founded by Marcus Garvey.

The Universal Negro Improvement Association or "Garvey Movement" was relatively small in Honduras compared to other regions of Central America along the Caribbean basin with large West Indian settlements such as Costa Rica, Panama, and Nicaragua. Although there is evidence to suggest that there was contact with the various communities in Central America, black nationalism indicative of the Garvey movement was not pervasive in Honduras. However, apart from the few social events at the various Liberty Halls, the movement had no long-lasting cultural imprint on the West Indian community. Part of the reason for this absence of broad-based support for the movement may lie in the fact that most of the West Indians in Honduras were not representative of the poorest classes by either Honduran or West Indian standards. This community maintained a high level of economic stability and made every effort to recreate middle-class Caribbean institutions in Honduras. West Indians in Honduras prided themselves on their British citizenship and made every effort to reap the benefits of that status, whether real or imagined. The UNIA challenged these notions of allegiance to the British crown and its cultural institutions and threatened the stability of the community. More important, the movement threatened to disfavor West Indians in the eyes of their white, North American employers, perhaps the West Indian community's only allies in the country. Most in the community were not willing to take that chance and were opposed to strong UNIA affiliations in the country.

The discussion on the UNIA in Honduras exposes the diverging views on race and identity within the West Indian population. In a letter sent to the *Negro World* from Tela in 1921, Erastus Thorpe, a UNIA representative, was alarmed at the lack of racial solidarity he witnessed among blacks in the vibrant fruit company town. He was commenting on a funeral proceeding of a UNIA member resident in the town and the refusal of the organization to allow its member to be buried by a newly arrived white pastor from England, Reverend Harold C. Dunn. From the account of the funeral procession, the deceased was buried according to UNIA fashion with the coffin draped in the red, black, and green flag that symbolized the movement. Thorpe reported that the procession was "unique and picturesque and garnered the reverence of all who witnessed it."[53]

Along the way, Thorpe conveyed to the president of the UNIA that the Rev. Dunn was awaiting the procession at his mission station in order to carry out the remaining funeral proceedings. UNIA representatives in Tela explained to the reverend that the deceased had been a member of the UNIA and that the movement would be completely responsible for the funeral of their departed brother. The procession simply dismissed the Rev. Dunn's actions as an attempt to deceive the masses and had their own chaplain perform the funeral rites as planned. What followed arrives at the crux of the issue concerning black West Indians in Tela regarding issues of race and class.

Many West Indians in Tela felt that the UNIA dismissal of the Rev. Dunn was in fact a serious insult to the white man who had come all the way from England to administer to the spiritual needs of the people. Many blacks apologized to the reverend for the actions of the UNIA and began to attend religious services at his mission in an effort to make things right and assure him that all blacks did not embrace the UNIA, Garvey, or his ideology. Observers in the UNIA interpreted the increase in black church attendance at the mission as an attempt to appease the white pastor and send a message to the association that Garvey and his ideals were not welcomed in Tela.

The incident in Tela was the only one on record that displayed the extent of the divide among West Indians regarding black identity in the country. For the most part, the UNIA members in Honduras aligned themselves with the overall agenda of the organization aimed at freeing and redeeming Africa and its descendants from the clutches of colonialism and oppression. This was evident in the strong dedication and commitment exhibited in a letter to *The Negro World* from the branch in El Porvenir pledging its continued support for the movement.[54] West Indians in La Ceiba also made clear their commitment to that goal.[55] Erastus Thorpe, the president of the Tela Division, was even compelled to write to *The Negro World* and apologize for the actions of those blacks in Tela regarding the funeral incident and reiterate that there were still blacks in Tela who remained committed to the movement. However, most West Indians continued to see themselves as part of the global British Empire and the Anglo-Saxon values that it symbolized.

Some have cited that, in addition to identifying with British status, many black West Indians did not embrace Marcus Garvey because the community was for the most part middle class. West Indians had their own neighborhoods, shops, businesses, and steady employment with the fruit companies and their various subsidiaries. In fact, many would argue that the conditions in the banana towns were very similar to those in the Jim Crow United States in that blacks were excluded from patronizing white, North American institutions solely because of their race. "Whites Only" and "Colored Only" signs were present in certain areas around Tela just as they were in any city in the southern United States. In every company town, there was a white section, black section, and an area where local Hondurans lived. However, unlike the United States, there was another component of discrimination that went beyond the distinctions between black and white.

The cities of the North Coast were extremely ethnically diverse. In his famous novel *Prisión Verde,* which details the conditions of life in the banana camps of the North Coast, Ramón Amaya Amador describes an environment in which "whites, blacks, Indians, yellows, salt merchants from the Gulf of Fonseca, tobacco merchants from Copán, horsemen from the plains of Olancho, blacks and *zambos* from Colón and La Mosquitia and Bay Islanders from Guanaja and Roatán, in addition to the many people that arrived from the various countries of Central America and Belize all converged on the area."[56] Some possessed skills, education, and titles, while others were illiterate. None proved to be as isolated as the black West Indian. Part of the reason for this came from the special privileges of this group within the banana industry. However, a greater part of this isolation stemmed from the refusal of West Indians to mix with the local population on a grand scale. West Indians lived in mixed neighborhoods in many cities on the North Coast. They interacted with other communities at work, in the marketplace, and at social settings. However, when it came to the issue of marriage, West Indians were as rigidly biased as many of the other immigrant groups in the region.

Just as white North Americans imposed their own notions of racial superiority onto the West Indian and Honduran populations, West Indians imposed their notions of Anglo-Caribbean superiority onto the local Honduran population. Such notions make sense when juxtaposed with the history of identity politics in the broader Caribbean region. Mark Moberg maintains in his study of the banana industry in Belize that the Anglophone Creoles in the country came to regard "British Honduras" as theirs, defining it as black, Protestant, and English speaking. As a result, all other groups in the British colony were on the margins of society.[57] Although the situation in Honduras differed considerably, the attitudes of British Hondurans in Honduras toward the non-English-speaking population made sense as they, along with Jamaicans, represented the two largest groups of West Indians in the country. In addition, many of the cultural and educational institutions of the West Indians in Honduras looked to British Honduras for inspiration, as it was the closest lifeline to the larger British Caribbean world.

Of the various ethnic groups among the Honduran masses, it would at first seem plausible that West Indians would identify with the Garífuna population because of their shared Caribbean and African origins as well as the racial discrimination to which both groups were subjected. However, this was far from the case. For the West Indians, the Garífuna represented the consummate other. In addition to being Spanish-speaking, Catholic, and Honduran, the Garífuna in many ways represented for the West Indian that which was "uncivilized." One descendant of West Indians in Tela recalled that, as a child, she was taught that the Garífuna were "savage and uncultured."[58] Other West Indian descendants simply stated that, while relations between the two groups were relatively peaceful, all agreed that they were never interested in seeking marriage partners from within the Garífuna community, in part due to cultural differences, but more importantly due to the strains that such unions would place on their relationships with family and the larger West Indian community in Honduras. This would explain the low number of marriages between the two groups in the records of the Church of the Holy Trinity.

Most Garífuna did not work in the banana industry alongside West Indians, but rather opted to stick to traditional forms of subsistence agriculture on community-owned lands, selling the produce in local markets. Those who worked in the banana companies did so primarily on the wharfs and docks of cities such as La Ceiba and Tela seasonally loading fruit onto the numerous fruit company ships destined for markets in the United States and Europe. Apart from work on the docks and in the banana fields, every other job in the companies required knowledge of English. This proved to be a deterrent for many Hondurans in general to gaining better jobs. Once a Honduran acquired English, he stood the chance of obtaining a better job, as was the case with the father of two Garífuna men interviewed in Tela.[59] However, this acquisition of English did not entitle the Garífuna to entrance into West Indian society, nor did they necessarily seek it out.

The Garífuna who were able to acquire upwardly mobile jobs with the fruit companies often chose to settle in the burgeoning neighborhoods in Tela, La Ceiba, and Trujillo near their places of employment. This brought them into closer contact with West Indians. Some Garífuna and West Indians lived in the same neighborhoods. One longtime Garífuna resident of Barrio La Brisas in Tela recalled vividly his observations of his family's West Indian neighbors as a young boy. "The *ingleses* were always well dressed in the latest fashions and had all of the latest popular music from the United States."[60] Many residents attested to these claims, specifically citing the recordings of Nat King Cole as some of the more widely circulated records in Tela during the period. The United Fruit Company had a commissary in Tela that sold all of the latest products from the United States. Additionally, shopkeepers and merchants were able to easily import products from New Orleans because it was a major port of call for the banana industry and all of the fruit companies had big operations there.

The dress and cultural tastes of the West Indians seem at first to link them more to North America than the Caribbean. This was a view held by many on the North Coast, that the allegiance of West Indians to the United States made them adversaries in any disputes with the companies. On further analysis, it is true that some West Indians identified with the United States to the exclusion of their own culture and the situation in Honduras evoked certain class differences and attitudes within a small segment of the West Indian population. But the majority of the community remained deeply rooted in their West Indian culture and traditions, in many instances to the exclusion of all other influences.

The relationship between the West Indian and mestizo communities was very similar to the relationship between the West Indian and the Garífuna. However, there was one major detail that made the relationship between West Indians and mestizos much worse. Mestizo animosity toward the West Indian community centered primarily on competition for jobs and the desire on the part of the former for a higher standard of living. This was the mechanism by which race entered into many of the debates on immigration and labor. The West Indians took issue with mestizo culture for many of the same reasons they did with the Garífuna, often choosing to limit their relationships with the community to a professional level.

In their efforts to maintain a distinct cultural identity, members of the West Indian community positioned themselves to remain at odds with the national agenda of the Honduran state. Initially, the Honduran government created the obstacles to West Indian inclusion into Honduran society. However, by the 1930s the West Indian community on the North Coast institutionalized a cultural and social worldview that contributed to its further marginalization from the masses of Hondurans. Rather than simply being denied full entry into Honduran society based on their race and culture, West Indians were reluctant to be included within the ranks of the masses of Hondurans. The community fully embraced its status as the consummate other within North Coast society and made every effort to maintain it. The ramifications of these attitudes of the early West Indian toward others in Honduran society manifested in West Indians' social, political, and cultural fragmentation from others of African descent in the nation.

5

AN IMAGINED CITIZENRY
The Racial Realities of British Identity among
West Indians in Honduras

The authenticity of West Indian claims of British citizenship and their status in Honduras were recurring themes in the antagonistic relationships among West Indians, Hondurans, and the North American fruit companies. West Indians often exerted their "rights" as British subjects when seeking to extricate themselves from the political and social turmoil that affected the daily lives of most Hondurans. West Indians became a target of Honduran labor organizers who saw them as aligning with the fruit companies to further limit the advances of the downtrodden laborers. Honduran governing officials in many municipalities on the North Coast reported that West Indians often refused to participate in relief efforts to assist them in rebuilding the city after storms, fires, and political violence left sections in turmoil. More important, many in Honduras saw the West Indian as an extension of a growing foreign presence in the country that was draining the economic lifeblood of the nation.

Claims of West Indian indignation toward their Spanish-speaking hosts and their insistence on maintaining a separate, "British" identity permeate the literature on West Indian migrant communities throughout Latin America and the Caribbean. Jorge Giovanetti, in his study of West Indian descent communities in Cuba, encountered a Barbados-born woman in her nineties who claimed that she was "still a British subject" despite the fact that she had spent the majority of her life in the Cuban town of Baraguá and Barbados had long since become an independent nation.[1] Trevor O'Reggio and Philippe Bourgois note similar inclinations in the West Indian communities in Panama and Costa Rica, respectively, during the same time period. The former maintains that the

idea of nationality and citizenship among West Indians in Panama remained British colonial through the 1920s.[2] Much of the change after the
1920s stems from the fact that the British government failed to respond to
the demands of their subjects abroad and left them at the mercy of their
U.S. employers for protection, which given the Jim Crow nature of the
Panama Canal Zone, provided little solace to a community that was ex-
periencing negative attention from Panamanian proponents of anti–West
Indian immigration legislation.[3]

Bourgois argues in the case of Costa Rica that West Indians had very
practical reasons for emphasizing their British origins. In many instances,
the British government "was the only external source of support available
to West Indians during times of crisis."[4] Despite the proclivity for West
Indians to identify with Great Britain, the British government expressed
little interest in coming to the aid of its black citizens abroad. The British
documents related to the situation of West Indians in Honduras reveal
a similar trend in that the government failed to protect its citizens. Yet,
despite this, the propensity for West Indians to adhere to their British
identity persisted for as long as they resided in the country.

The extent to which the British government fully extended the rights
of citizenship to its West Indian subjects on the North Coast remained
inconsistent throughout the period in which their presence in the banana
zones was most significant. For the West Indian, failure on the part of the
British government to validate the authenticity of their citizenship claims
left them in a continuous state of diplomatic uncertainty. Formal recognition of British citizenship did not guarantee West Indians the same rights
and privileges as Anglo-Saxon subjects in the United Kingdom and the
larger British Empire. West Indians were at best second-class citizens.
They were never formally denied British citizenship, but they also were
never able to realize the full benefits of being subjects of the most extensive and powerful empire of its era. This chapter deflates the notions of
politicians and labor organizers that West Indians in Honduras benefited
from British nationality by examining Britain's attitudes toward its black
subjects in the West Indies and the emerging West Indian migrant communities throughout Latin America and the Caribbean. West Indian notions of Britishness in Honduras drew on their prior experiences in the
Caribbean and on colonial perceptions of the superiority of British and
Anglo-Caribbean culture and traditions among all others. Their views did
not necessarily equate with the realities of an Anglo-Saxon racial philoso-

phy that situated colonial subjects at the lower rungs of a rigid hierarchy.

After full emancipation from slavery in 1838, many British politicians and intellectuals questioned the extension of full legal rights to blacks within the Caribbean colonies. Catherine Hall argues that Governor Edward John Eyre of Jamaica maintained that representative institutions could not work in the West Indies (sugar colonies) because the general population was unfit to exercise political privileges.[5] Jamaica, according to Eyre, was not Britain and the Jamaican population was not black Anglo-Saxon.[6] In other words, residing within the British Empire alone did not entitle black West Indians to the rights and privileges of their white counterparts. It was the government in London, specifically those within the political and intellectual elite, who determined British identity for blacks within the empire. Eyre further exhibited his attitude toward blacks in measures taken to quell the Morant Bay Rebellion in 1865. He ordered the killing of 439 black protesters and the execution of 354 others despite no resistance on their part to the white militia and government troops sent to suppress the labor rebellion. Eyre's solution to the Morant Bay rebellion was the culmination of an anti-black sentiment acquired through years of experience working in the colonial bureaucracy in the Caribbean. Prior to his appointment as governor of Jamaica, Eyre served as the lieutenant governor of St. Vincent.[7] While in St. Vincent, Eyre reluctantly tolerated the political and economic advancements of the new freedmen. Despite their numerous accomplishments, he repeatedly referred to freedmen as a "wild and savage" mob and therefore, potential enemies of the crown.[8]

Eyre's distrust of the black population in St. Vincent stemmed in large part from the success of the free colored population in petitioning against legal and political restrictions that continued to subordinate them to the white minority population. Through their efforts, free coloreds acquired equal status with whites before the law.[9] Their advancements led many free coloreds to view themselves as British subjects in every way and they fought bitterly to protect their status through the use of legal petitions to the crown. The same dynamic is witnessed in other areas in the British Caribbean. Recognition of British nationality increased the propensity of free coloreds to cling to British culture and identity.

The migration of West Indians to Central America and the development of Britain's Caribbean policies occurred simultaneously. It is no surprise that in Honduras, the West Indian descendants who clung to their

British identity the longest were Bay Islanders descended from near white and free colored settlers from the Cayman Islands who arrived in the archipelago in the 1830s. The Bay Islands provided a consistent refuge for West Indian culture and traditions throughout the period covered in this study.

For most blacks within the Caribbean, it was impossible to erase the "stain" of slavery. The period following the demise of the institution continued to attach to blacks the stigma of servitude and subordination that so many sought to eradicate. As long as elites and policymakers in London defined what constituted a British subject, nonwhite West Indians were never fully recognized. The small wealthy and intellectual classes in England often determined the complexity of racial and ethnic ideologies within the empire. David Cannadine maintains that England was a hierarchical society in which those at the highest level wielded the power. Elites dictated how colonized and conquered societies were administered.[10] In instances where it seemed that the full rights of citizenship would be extended to all within the empire, there was always a structure in place that subordinated nonwhite segments of the population to white society and Anglo-Saxon power. What emerged was an empire in which race and color were superimposed with social status and class in order to preserve the dominance of the Anglo-Saxon minority.

More important to the discussion on the nature of British citizenship is how the British understood this within the context of their colonial possessions. British society proved completely ignorant of the extent and nature of its colonial possessions and territories on almost every level. As early as the 1840s, noted British intellectuals such as Thomas Carlyle viewed black subjects within the empire as culturally backward. He contended that "blacks maintained a dull mental disposition, but possessed a physical strength that would be useful to the Empire and should be coerced into work."[11] Carlyle's views diverge little from the rhetoric used to sanction the enslavement of African peoples in the Americas. This interpretation of race would come to dominate much of the politics within the British Empire because it classified Africans and their descendants according to the Anglo-Saxon paradigm of their racial superiority. This relegated the West Indian to a perpetual state of inequality.

The importance of West Indians to the empire was determined by their British colonizers. When the British praised West Indians for their contributions to the larger society, they were often relegated to the mixed-race or "colored" demographic that created a buffer between the black and white segments of the population. This group espoused European cultural traditions and upheld the colonial status quo. Blackness remained on the periphery within the colonial system and held an inferior position to other racial and ethnic groups. For the majority of West Indians, conceptions of blackness within the British Empire were often linked to a somewhat rigid caste system in which the British, according to Paul Rich, saw their society in rural, pastoral, and peasant terms. In this context the members of the population perceived as black were confined to the lower economic strata and performed menial agricultural jobs and received agricultural-based technical education. While adherence to such race-based hierarchies enhanced the colonial government's political and economic grasp on their West Indian possessions, it did little to promote the sustainable development of the West Indies.

By the late nineteenth and early twentieth centuries, the focus of the British Empire shifted toward the emerging colonial possessions in Africa and the rise of the black working class in Britain. The lack of a British response to racial discrimination within the empire indicates the failure of British nationality alone to guarantee equal and fair treatment for all of its citizens. The government used growing public animosity toward blacks in Britain as a tool in quelling rising labor tensions between the working class and the government. Elites in government used blacks as scapegoats to explain the decreased employment opportunities for the white working class. Many within British labor circles believed the working class in Britain was poor because blacks were taking jobs away from white Anglo-Saxons, not because of a lack of effort on the part of government officials and industrialists to develop programs at home that would create the infrastructure necessary to guarantee worker stability. For almost the entire duration of the British Empire, the interests of these two groups shifted initially from Ireland to the West Indies, Africa, and lastly to India and Asia. At no point was the British working class the beneficiary of government policies to the same extent as its elite countrymen.

By the turn of the twentieth century, the West Indies had ceased to be the focal point of the empire. The region had stopped producing the kind of economic development that would widen the range of job opportunities and allow its economy to absorb the incremental growth of its population.[12] This was due largely to the demise of the price of sugar on the global market, a trend that began in the mid-nineteenth century. As a result, emigration and immigration in search of job opportunities became enduring features of the region's economy.[13] High rates of unemployment combined with good literacy and low infant mortality served to push high levels of Caribbean migration in the late nineteenth and early twentieth centuries. In countries such as Jamaica, the low mortality rate alone contributed to large numbers of displaced, unemployed laborers.[14]

The failure of the West Indies to produce significant revenues for the mother country and the disinterest of the government in addressing the economic and social concerns of the region translated into apathy for those West Indians who sought better economic opportunities abroad. Many within the colonial administrations of the West Indies felt that migrant workers deserved whatever treatment they got by the host governments in Central America because they had voluntarily abandoned their homelands. This colonial neglect, and in some cases resentment, together with the emergence of Pan-Africanism, trade unionism, and other social and political movements, served as the catalyst for the independence movements that emerged following the Second World War. More important, British views with respect to race and empire, and the declining interest in West Indian affairs, carried over into the communities of West Indians living abroad in Central America, particularly Honduras. Despite the propensity for West Indians to claim British citizenship in Honduras, the British Empire did not take the needs of its black citizenry abroad seriously. British protection of West Indians in Honduras depended almost solely on the racial attitudes of individual British officials in Honduras, and not on formal government policy.

The propensity for West Indians in Honduras to define themselves as British subjects introduces the often neglected issues of colonialism and perceptions of race and nation. Benedict Anderson defines the nation as an imagined political community: even the smallest nation will never know most of its members, but in the mind there is the image of communion.[15] This perception of communion is often fostered through the use of unifying language and customs created for the sole purpose of cultivating a sense of nationalism. In the West Indies, the British sought to accomplish this goal first through Christian missionary activity, and second through the institutionalization of a British colonial education system that glorified the empire. Both institutions integrated the West Indian socially and culturally into the Anglo-Saxon ideal. For the most part, success varied from island to island. Barbados prided itself on its Anglo-Saxon values, while outward manifestations of African cultural traditions remained strong in Jamaica. The implications of the varied expressions of Anglo-Saxon influence are not that the British had a limited impact on the psyche of Caribbean citizens of the empire. The Anglo-Saxon ideal in the Caribbean fostered a strong sense of British nationalism among a significant section of West Indian society. Despite the ill treatment of West Indians within the British colonial system and the halfhearted diplomatic response of the British to issues concerning this group in Honduras, many still clung to their identity as subjects of the British Empire and vehemently defended it.

The status of West Indians as British subjects in Honduras and the attitudes of the British government in defending the legal rights of its black subjects were tested frequently in Honduras. An assessment of an earlier and, until relatively recently, obscure event in the history of West Indian workers in Honduras commonly referred to as the La Masica Incident of 1910, in which two West Indian workers were murdered by Honduran soldiers, reaffirms this trend. Moreover, the fallout from the incident set the precedent for how matters pertaining to West Indians in Honduras would be handled by both the British and Honduran authorities until the departure of most of the population by World War II. Echeverri-Gent maintained that the incident served as a warning to the Honduran government of the potential liability large numbers of West Indian workers represented to the nation.[16] However, a further examination of the event suggests that the failure of the British government to fully hold the Honduran government accountable for the murders questions the value the former placed on West Indian life.

The incident was one of numerous examples of brutality directed against West Indians by the Honduran military that ended in controversy. On June 16, 1910, the Vaccaro Brothers Fruit Company celebrated the completion of a railway line from their main headquarters at the port of La Ceiba to the town of La Masica. The celebration included an excursion on the rail line followed by a picnic. Three Jamaican employees of the company, Alexander Thurston, Wilfred Robinson, and Joseph Holland, along with two white American employees listed only as Macnamara and Bacussi, operated the train for the celebration.[17]

Once the train arrived at La Masica, witnesses stated that a drunken Alexander Thurston was involved in an altercation with several people in the vicinity of the train. Witnesses summoned the police, who arrived at the scene within a matter of minutes. Officers maintained that Thurston refused their commands to settle down and dispel the situation. Instead, Thurston and the two other Jamaicans ignored the officers and returned to their duties.[18] The policemen later summoned the military and a squad of Honduran soldiers, and their commander Major Joaquín Medina Planas returned to the train and ordered the two white Vaccaro employees to get down from the train and told the Jamaicans to remain. All men reportedly complied with the commander. Once the white men were out of harm's way, the soldiers opened fire on the Jamaicans, killing Thurston and seriously wounding Robinson. The soldiers later struck Holland to the ground and severely beat him. Afterward, he was taken to the village of La Masica, placed in chains, and sent to La Ceiba with Thurston's body, while Robinson remained under arrest. Initially, the Honduran government charged Robinson with the shooting of Thurston and the wounding of Holland. Holland was not charged with a crime.

During the trial, Robinson, along with Curtis Sinclair, John Stewart, and other West Indian witnesses, declared that Major Medina Planas and two soldiers fired on Thurston and Robinson. The witnesses stated that the major fired a revolver and the soldiers used rifles. The courts ordered the disinterment of Thurston's body and from it investigators extracted a .43 caliber Remington rifle bullet that belonged to one of the soldiers. As a result, the courts exonerated both Robinson and the major of murder charges. However, Holland subsequently suffered internal injuries and died a few months later. Throughout the course of the trial, investigators discovered that Holland was not present at the earlier incident leading up to the confrontation with the police at the rail engine.

At the conclusion of the trials of Medina Planas and Robinson, the Honduran government felt that any claim the British made regarding compensation would be dropped. To the Hondurans, the trial not only exonerated those individuals tried, but also cleared the government of culpability. Though the courts acquitted Major Medina Planas, the British government maintained that the Honduran government was still culpable for the outcome of the incident because the soldiers responsible were in his command. As a result, the British pressed for an indemnity to be paid by the Honduran government as compensation for the death of its citizens.

In August 1911, the British chargé d'affaires in Tegucigalpa reported that the Honduran minister of foreign affairs accepted in principle the British claim concerning the Masica incident. However, the two governments reached no monetary settlement.[19] The British ultimately appealed to the president of Honduras, Manuel Policarpo Bonilla, for a resolution to the Masica claim and for the Honduran government to accept responsibility for the murders.[20] This action never occurred and an arbitration hearing followed, with the king of Spain serving as the principal arbitrator.

The British eventually won the arbitration, but the Honduran government continued to maintain that the soldiers acted as individuals and not as representatives of the government. The British replied that because the soldiers were in official uniform and therefore represented the Honduran army, the Republic of Honduras was still culpable in the case.[21] Eventually the Honduran government paid the indemnity claim to the British but did not formally disclose the terms of the settlement. However, the British claimed that the award was substantially lower than their original request.

British insistence that those responsible for the incident at La Masica be punished and that the Honduran government accept responsibility for the murders through the payment of an indemnity gave the impression that the British government advocated on the behalf of its West Indian citizens in Honduras. However, once the arbitration hearings were completed and the indemnity paid, the British never pressed for the prosecution of the soldiers responsible for the crimes. Moreover, none of the indemnity rendered in favor of the British was distributed to the surviving relatives of the two victims. Though the case began as an attempt to bring justice to the West Indian victims of Honduran police brutality, politics intervened and the relationship between West Indians and Hondurans continued to disintegrate.

Following the La Masica incident, the number of violent encounters between West Indians and Honduran authorities increased. Skirmishes usually resulted in West Indians suffering beatings and incarcerations regardless of guilt. In most instances, the West Indians were innocent and acquitted of charges once cases went to trial. However, the costs of a legal defense and the mental anxiety created by the tensions between the community and the government were constant reminders of the fragile status of West Indians in the region.

Most West Indians in Honduras were hard-working, law-abiding members of the community. However, there were instances in which West Indians, like their Honduran contemporaries, were legitimately convicted of crimes. When guilt was certain, the British sided with local authorities. Sometimes the British government accepted the verdict of the Honduran courts without conducting its own investigation to determine the validity of the court's decision. In one case, Samuel Devine, a British subject, was reportedly forced by local authorities to carry a corpse tied around his neck while his hands were chained after he refused to perform conscripted labor.[22] Evidence submitted at the trial revealed that Devine was known within the community as a "notorious thief" and previously served jail time for robbery.[23] The British government agreed with Honduran authorities that Devine should be castigated for his crime, but that the police should be censured for wounding British subjects.

Why Devine, a foreigner, was singled out to perform conscripted labor was never questioned by the British, nor was it clear that the accused had in fact done anything wrong. Devine had already served his time. It is likely that his criminal past made him an easy target for authorities. The case underscored the failure of the British government to fully investigate the situation. They simply maintained that their subjects were in fact subject to comply with the laws of Honduras. No formal action was ever taken to punish the Honduran authorities for the abuse rendered to Samuel Devine during his initial capture.

In the department of Atlántida where the La Masica incident took place, a British resident at La Ceiba, J. Gallop, reported that there had been ten to twelve cases of ill treatment of British subjects by Honduran authorities since the incident. In addition to the reports of violence, Gallop pressed for government action in the La Masica situation and complained that the British vice consul was not taking their situation in the country seriously and that West Indians were left at the mercy of the anti-black Honduran authorities who abused them. Gallop linked the cases of ill treatment of members of the West Indian community in La Ceiba with the La Masica incident and mobilized protests around this unfortunate event. He also demanded in his formal written protest to the British consul that they address the need for political action and protection.

The West Indian community in Honduras was organized into various social networks and often sought assistance through the proper diplomatic channels. The British Legation in Central America was based in Guatemala City, Guatemala, some three hundred miles across mountainous terrain from the North Coast of Honduras. Satellite offices were situated in La Ceiba and Trujillo depending on the budgetary allocations for a specific year, making representation sporadic for the duration of West Indian immigration to the country. The colonial government in British Honduras received numerous complaints from West Indians in Honduras because many in Honduras originated from the British colony, which was only ninety miles from Tela. The Bay Islands also maintained a relationship with the colony that dated back to the 1830s when West Indians originally settled the area.

Despite distance and inconsistency on the part of the British in maintaining the proper diplomatic channels with communities in Honduras, West Indians continued to have faith in due process and believed that the British government would ultimately come to their aid. The numerous complaints of ill treatment by Honduran authorities submitted by West Indians were viewed as a nuisance by some British officials. The British chargé d'affaires in Tegucigalpa, Jack Armstrong, was fed up with the complaints of West Indian subjects and deemed most of their grievances insignificant and unfounded.[24] Armstrong maintained that the population of "colored" British subjects in La Ceiba was "comprised chiefly of laborers employed in loading and discharging ships and were therefore of a rough type." He felt that the local authorities had been "lenient if only 10–12 cases of ill-treatment were reported in the 2 years since La Masica." Blacks in the area, according to Armstrong, were "drunkards, and because most were Jamaican, their character was turbulent and the local authorities were obliged to maintain a firm hand on that population in order to check disturbances."[25] Armstrong insisted that blacks in La Ceiba were making claims with British authorities because they thought that there would be a cash indemnity in their favor, despite the inexistence of such demands in West Indian petitions to the government. He even made unsubstantiated accusations that the British vice consul in the area encouraged indemnity claims by sending "trivial" cases to Armstrong without discretion.[26]

There was the occasional West Indian claim of mistreatment by Honduran authorities that proved to be frivolous.[27] However, British authorities were obligated by their position to investigate all claims filed by its citizens. Instead, Armstrong dismissed West Indian complaints in La Ceiba on the grounds that there were no reports of similar claims filed by West Indians against the Honduran authorities in San Pedro Sula and Puerto Cortés, two major cities in the region. The implication was that there was a problem with West Indian behavior in the banana enclaves. Armstrong failed to mention in this assessment that the West Indian population in the two cities was almost nonexistent. There were no problems with West Indians in San Pedro Sula and Puerto Cortés because there were no West

Indians there. Instances of abuse would have been more prevalent in La Ceiba, Tela, and Trujillo because these cities were the main centers of operations for the fruit companies and were, therefore, large centers of West Indian settlement and had a stronger diplomatic presence. They were also cities in which anti-black sentiment in the country aimed at the Garífuna had an enduring history, making the probability of attacks against West Indians more likely in this intense racial climate.

The diplomatic fallout after the La Masica incident did not simply expose the nonchalant attitude of the British government in protecting its black subjects, nor did it simply highlight the propensity for violence as the preferred method of interaction between Honduran authorities and West Indians. Both these trends were common in the region. Newly exposed were the inadequacies in British diplomatic representation in Honduras and its inability to exert political force in the region. The British conceded many of their colonial possessions and territories in 1859 when the Mosquito Coast and the Bay Islands were ceded to Honduras at the urging of the United States. By severing political ties with the region, the British had also decreased economic activity along the North Coast of Honduras.

Corruption was widespread among British diplomats in Honduras. Many were more concerned with their own personal economic gain than with the welfare of British subjects working and residing in the country. There was little incentive to help West Indians with political issues when there was more to be gained from siding with the fruit companies and the Honduran government. The case of British Vice Consul Alfred Tayelor is evidence of this. Tayelor's name often surfaced in testimonies associated with corruption. In the aftermath of the La Masica incident, Tayelor attempted to relieve himself of financial burdens brought on by personal mismanagement of funds and bad business investments. Echeverri-Gent asserts that Tayelor's insistence on pursuing the incident caused the fruit companies to exert financial pressure on him because the case would expose their unscrupulous business practices in the country.[28] While the role of the fruit companies in suppressing the details of the case are plausible, Tayelor's financial woes were of his own making.

In June 1912, Tayelor requested a grant of £500 to cover losses he claimed were sustained as a result of his involvement in the Masica claim. Though he could not produce any data to substantiate his contention, Tayelor maintained that he incurred the enmity of the United Fruit Company and the Vaccaro Brothers Company because he was unable to re-pay the advance allotted him to work their farms. According to Tayelor, a storm destroyed most of his banana crop at Masica, which left the vice consul unable to work and therefore obliged to quit his plantation. Despite this presumed setback, Tayelor purchased another plantation but was unable to plant due to a lack of funds.[29] The British chargé d'affaires, Jack Armstrong, stated that Tayelor was very unpopular with local businessmen but felt that this was due to the vice consul's history of debt. At the time of his grant request, he owed £300 locally and had accumulated other debts in excess of £1,500.[30]

Tayelor's attempts to collect funds from the British government did not begin with the British chargé d'affaires. A month earlier, he wrote the Foreign Office in London asserting that because he refused to suppress the truth of the Masica incident as desired by local authorities, hostility developed against him and his commercial interests suffered, due to local merchants desiring to curry favor with the government. In the letter, Tayelor estimated his losses at £2,000 not including the losses due to enmity.[31] By the time he had written Armstrong, the losses Tayelor claimed were considerably lower. Such discrepancies in the amount of debt incurred and the inability to connect his losses to the killings of Thurston and Holland and the beating of Robinson made the vice consul appear to be an opportunist. Most of Tayelor's superiors carried the same sentiment, but given the delicate nature of the Masica situation and the desire for the British to win their indemnity claim, the government conceded to Tayelor and awarded him £500, for fear that the destitution of a British diplomat and the negative attention it would bring to the government would have a damaging effect on the outcome of the case.[32]

There is no record of either the British or Honduran authorities questioning the conflict of interest raised by Tayelor serving as a British vice consul in charge of handling the affairs of British citizens in Honduras, most of whom were workers in the banana industry, and owning and operating banana plantations and making side deals with fruit companies. West Indians apparently respected Tayelor's position because they continued to bring complaints to him throughout his tenure as vice consul, each time expecting appropriate attention to be given to their grievances. Their claims went unnoticed by the British in part because the latter allocated resources to investigate Tayelor's repeated attempts to use his position for profit.

Ultimately, the La Masica incident generated no drastic change in relations between Britain and Honduras. The attacks on West Indians were not enough to warrant a shift in Honduran policy toward West Indians. In fact, they may have initiated the dialogue regarding a reassessment of Honduran immigration law that was unabashedly anti-black. The British never again brought indemnity charges against the Honduran government for the murder of one of their West Indian subjects.[33] The inability of the British government to gain substantially from the indemnity claim in the La Masica incident and its limited influence on the Honduran government sealed the fate of the West Indian population. If they were to advance on the North Coast, it would have to be through alliances with the fruit companies and not with the British government.

The colonial governments on the various Caribbean islands were equally unenthusiastic about involvement in the issues of West Indians abroad. From British Colonial Office correspondence, it is clear that workers in Honduras were part of a massive migration of West Indians working abroad in Latin America. West Indians were employed in such diverse countries as Venezuela, Cuba, Colombia, Peru, Haiti, Ecuador, Bolivia, Mexico, and the Danish West Indies in addition to the more established Panama Canal Zone and Costa Rica. In many of these countries, West Indians suffered from the same anti-immigrant and anti-black sentiments that plagued their countrymen in Honduras. Legislation ordering deportation or violence on the part of native workers forced them to return to their home islands.

Ironically, most colonial governments in the West Indies, though critical of their citizens for seeking work abroad in the first place, were not keen on the idea of workers returning home after deportation. The British government organized a commission in 1931 to enquire into the capacity of its Caribbean colonies to repatriate those West Indians working abroad. Part of the government's concern was the amount of distress and violence these workers faced in their countries of employment and the number of complaints received by the British Foreign Office concerning incidents of violence against British subjects. In most cases, the Caribbean governments were more concerned with the trauma that repatriation would cause on the existing colonial structure and internal affairs of the colonies than with the needs of its citizens.

One report from the Colonial Office described West Indians who emigrated to Central America and Panama as virile young men discontented with the economic conditions in their home colonies. The belief was that these workers would not be content to work as laborers on sugar estates for relatively low wages or as subsistence farmers on small landholdings.[34] The situation in the West Indies had in many ways become worse as the global economic depression had disastrous effects on the Caribbean region. Furthermore, the report suggested that West Indians abroad sent considerable remittances to their families at home and bought houses and clothing for their near relatives when they returned home temporarily.[35] It was in the best interest of colonial governments to have workers abroad to boost the economies of the colonies. In the event that large numbers of West Indians returned from work abroad, the governments feared they would not only lose the much needed remittances, but that these workers would be more apt to rebel and create political tension at home because of disenchantment at the lack of change in the social and economic situation. Many returnees were already politicized due to the fact that conditions in the countries they immigrated to forced them to unionize in order to protect their economic interests.

While rebellion and the loss of remittances were justifiable concerns for the colonial governments in the various Caribbean islands, there was also another reason that repatriation of West Indians was a cause for concern. Governments profited from the recruitment of West Indian workers. For every person under contract to work abroad, the treasuries of the home colonies earned a fee of ten shillings. That number was later reduced to five shillings in 1931 by an amendment to the Emigrants Protection Ordinance.[36] There were some ten thousand West Indians in Honduras at the time, one of the least traveled countries for West Indians. Added to the amount gained by local governments for the entire West Indian population abroad, emigration could be quite lucrative.

Jamaica and British Honduras were more than willing to welcome their citizens home despite the hesitancy of colonial governments to concede to repatriation. The former set up offices to aide displaced and distressed workers in Cuba and other popular destinations for migrant Jamaicans in order to facilitate their return home.[37] British Honduras was less concerned with any ill effects of repatriation because the colony was underpopulated and could easily reabsorb the influx of displaced workers. Most of its citizens had sought employment in neighboring Honduras and Guatemala, logistically making return easier. However, the governor also felt that anti-black and anti-immigrant sentiment in Latin American countries, particularly Honduras, was not permanent. The governor of British Honduras maintained that repatriation was only a temporary situation. The belief was that once the economic depression in those countries with significant West Indian workers subsided and conditions normalized, anti-black sentiment would diminish and workers would be able to return to work.[38] The governor did not understand the gravity of the situation facing West Indians in Honduras. He considered that the displacement and distress encountered by the workers was simply part of the experience of working abroad.

Despite indifference toward repatriation, the governments of Jamaica and British Honduras supported the implementation of the policy in principle. However, problems arose with the execution because the British government, though responsible for introducing repatriation of West Indians abroad as a political agenda, failed to finance the endeavor. Government officials contended that the individual colonies were expected to incur the costs of repatriating citizens. The poor economic state of the region made such a venture highly unlikely.

In an effort to circumvent costs, the West India Commission and the colonial governments of British Honduras, British Guiana, and the Leeward Islands offered to have displaced West Indian migrant workers relocated to their colonies since these territories had an abundance of available land. However, the governments would require investment and the development of agricultural infrastructure. There was the accepted belief that proposals of repatriation would only work if there was an agricultural base within the receiving colonies organized by an agricultural officer under the employ of the government.[39] Settlement of surplus populations of West Indians to the aforementioned territories was the topic of debate for several years prior to the introduction of the repatriation schemes of the 1930s. The colonies always dismissed the possibility, with lack of funding cited as the reason. In order to bypass funding concerns, Governor Robertson of Barbados offered an interesting alternative to resettlement.

The governor maintained that since blacks in the West Indies were descended from West Africans, it was only fitting that the displaced population be returned to their land of origin. Robertson went on to maintain that Africa provided the proper climatic conditions for blacks and that their education, intelligence, and experience would give them the best opportunities of finding prosperity in the British colonies of West Africa.[40] Governor Robertson made no reference in his suggestion for African repatriation to the ill effects British colonialism had on the indigenous African populations. He also did not factor in the expense of such a project. In all likelihood if funding was a concern in repatriating West Indian citizens from Latin America back to their homes in the Caribbean, it would certainly prove more difficult and expensive to transport this population to Africa. The British government subsequently rejected the proposal due to logistical and financial concerns.[41] In addition, most West Indians working abroad did not favor the African proposal. Resettlement in West Africa was deemed a viable option primarily to those West Indians influenced by the Garvey movement.

The repatriation scheme to the West Indies proposed by the British government never fully materialized. The investment required to create the infrastructure to sustain the population influx proved too much of a financial burden for the British. British interest in the West Indies had declined substantially since the emancipation of slavery and the imperial government stood the most to gain from its colonies in Asia. More important, it took more than the desire on the part of the government to relocate the masses of West Indian workers abroad. The workers had to be willing to accept the government's offer to repatriate them. In most instances, the workers refused to return to the West Indies while conditions remained the same as when they left. Specifically in Honduras, the United Fruit Company offered on repeated occasions to provide passage for discharged employees to return to their respective colonies, but most declined the offer. One example from 1936 indicates that only thirty-eight Jamaicans and a similar number of British Hondurans accepted passage to their home colonies.[42] It was more practical for workers to remain in the various Latin American countries and ride out the economic depression than return to the West Indies where opportunities were nonexistent.

Employment was not the only reason West Indians chose to remain in Honduras despite the hostile conditions. By the 1930s, the number of children born to West Indian parents in Honduras was on the rise. Technically, these children would have been Honduran citizens. According to Honduran law, anyone born in Honduras was a Honduran citizen. However, under British law, a Honduran of West Indian parentage could claim the right to British nationality. At most, such an individual could claim dual citizenship. However, dual status had little bearing on the children of West Indian workers in Honduras because the British government offered no legal protection as long as they resided in their country of birth.[43] Apparently prior to the clarification of their status by the British government, British consuls regarded the children of West Indians born in Honduras as British rather than Honduran.[44] As a result, it is likely that many of the claims of British citizenship filed by self-professed West Indians against the Honduran government were in fact claims by Honduran citizens and therefore, limited the power of British consular officials to protect them. The West Indian community in Honduras was thus divided between those born in the British West Indies with the rights of British citizenship, and their offspring who were culturally West Indian but politically Honduran.

The extent to which the issue of nationality created problems within the West Indian community in Honduras remains unclear. The only group that consistently tested the limits of the British government regarding this issue was the Bay Islanders. However, the dilemma of Honduran-born children of West Indians cannot be ignored, as it was through these children that the community in Honduras persisted.

The West Indian community in Honduras gained from its experiences in the country just as much as it was hindered by them. Many were able to establish a semblance of community centered on the cultural traditions and institutions brought from the Caribbean. However, the inability of these people, whether Caribbean or Honduran-born, to envision themselves as part of the broader Honduran nation hindered their acceptance by Honduran society. The local population was sensitive to the status of West Indians within the country and often expressed its animosity for this group through violent protest. The Honduran government saw the group as an obstacle to the nation-building process and in the end enacted legislation to eradicate the group from the country.

The experiences of West Indians in Honduras highlighted the struggles of West Indian migrant workers in the larger Caribbean world, with their status as both British subjects and citizens of colonial governments. The attitudes of the respective governments to the complaints of their citizens abroad, as well as the inability and disinterest of these governments to provide opportunities for citizens at home, demonstrated an occurrence all too common in the study of colonialism. The benefits of British nationality were reserved for only a small segment of the population. In the end, West Indians abroad, just like those at home, had to rely on themselves, and not their governments, to improve their situation.

6

ERADICATING THE BLACK PERIL

The Deportation of West Indian Workers from Tela
and Trujillo, Honduras, 1930–1939

The 1930s proved to be a tumultuous time for West Indians and others of African descent on the North Coast of Honduras. Efforts to halt black immigration to Honduras were officially sanctioned between 1929 and 1934 with the legislation of immigration reform. The reforms initiated a drastic shift in the racial dynamics of the banana industry and demonstrated extreme xenophobia and racism through the establishment of entrance restrictions on certain ethnicities and nationalities into Honduran territory.[1] All of the major West Indian settlements along the North Coast of Honduras felt the impact of the growing anti-immigrant sentiment. However, Tela and Trujillo were most affected by government strategies to eradicate the West Indian presence from the nation.

The history of West Indians in Tela, like other cities on the North Coast of Honduras, is directly tied to the emergence of the banana industry in the early decades of the twentieth century. At the center of this development was the Tela Railroad Company. The Honduran government recognized the Tela Railroad Company and granted concessions to its owners in 1913. From the onset, the company followed the same strategy as earlier fruit companies in Honduras by developing the infrastructure of the town by building ports, railroad lines, housing, and other services geared toward large-scale banana production. Much like the Cuyamel Fruit Company in Puerto Cortés and Standard Fruit Company in La Ceiba, the Tela Railroad Company employed significant numbers of foreign, mostly West Indian laborers in the early years of its development. The Honduran press reported a large influx of West Indians into Tela as early as November 1913. Journalists made the argument that the preferential hiring practices of the fruit company toward West Indians fostered high unemployment rates among the local population.[2] This was a recurring theme throughout the period and resurfaced wherever West Indians settled. As the debate on West Indian labor intensified over the next two decades, the Tela Railroad Company, after merging with the United Fruit Company, was forced to act.

The initial deportation of West Indians from Tela coincided with a less productive banana season in 1930. This led to the curtailment of operations by the Tela Railroad Company and the subsequent layoff of some two thousand workers. Though most of the workers in the district were Honduran and Salvadoran, almost all of the men laid off were Jamaican. Company officials felt it was safer to lay off West Indians and return them to their home islands than to dismiss Hondurans or Salvadorans because they believed the latter would incite riots and restrict company operations. Stereotypes of West Indians by company officials portrayed them as "peaceful and very seldom engaged in riots, murders, outrage, or other disturbances."[3] This was quite different from the Honduran government view, which consistently portrayed West Indians as a criminal element in society.

Race was a determining factor in the laying off and subsequent deportation of West Indians from Tela. West Indians were susceptible to such treatment due in part to their reluctance to organize politically and advocate on their own behalf. Throughout the history of commercial banana cultivation on the North Coast, Salvadoran and Honduran workers organized collectively to demand higher wages, better working conditions, housing, and other necessities for an improved quality of life. West Indians were generally in a better position than local workers and accepted the policies of the fruit companies throughout most of their tenure in the banana zones. Only when the Honduran government presented an obstacle for them did West Indians demonstrate the ability to organize collectively. Even then, it was often at the discretion of their employers.

Company officials feared discharging large numbers of Salvadoran and Honduran workers because of their propensity for inciting large-scale protests and strikes that halted fruit production. Rather than allow such actions to materialize, it was easier for the fruit companies to lay off and deport West Indians. Such actions appeased both local workers and the Honduran government. Local workers viewed the actions as a victory for their cause of creating an entirely "native" work force. The government saw the deportation as a means of ridding the country of an undesirable immigrant population. Ironically, throughout the entire discourse, Salvadorans were never viewed by the local population as foreigners. Their shared mestizo and Central American identity protected them from outward anti-immigrant hostility, even though they represented the majority of the foreign-born labor force.

The deportation of West Indians from Tela went forward without incident. The deportees were all nationals of British West Indian colonies. British Honduras and Jamaica were the most represented. Deportation did not solve the labor problem in Tela. C. Oury-Jackson, the American vice consul in Tela, reported in 1936 that the "continuous discharge of workers from the Tela Railroad Company was increasing the ranks of the unemployed" in the area.[4] Those workers who were not laid off were relegated to part-time positions. By this period, most of these workers were Honduran, indicating that West Indians were not the root cause of depressed economic conditions in the area. Honduran workers succeeded in reducing competition by advocating the deportation of West Indians, but they could not change the effect plant disease and a depressed global economy had on the industry.

Though the estimates vary, many Hondurans of West Indian descent resided in Tela during this period and chose to remain in the country. As late as 1950, May and Plaza in the assessment of United Fruit Company operations in Latin America maintained that Tela remained heavily populated by Hondurans of West Indian descent.[5] The same did not hold true in Trujillo and Puerto Castilla.

The town of Trujillo, situated on the far North Coast of Honduras in the department of Colón, had long been an outpost for the Spanish colonial government in Honduras. Founded in 1525, the port served as the transshipment point for gold from the Honduran interior to Spain. Taylor Mack documents that the trade lasted until the 1550s when most of the easily removed gold had been mined and the indigenous labor supply dwindled due to overwork, malnutrition, disease, and marronage.[6] In the aftermath of the decline in gold mining, the Spanish shifted their focus to the interior by moving operations to Comayagua. The Catholic Church made the move in 1558. Those who remained in Trujillo engaged in the sarsaparilla and cattle hide trade through the 1630s to limited degrees of success.[7]

Throughout much of the period from the 1630s through the turn of the eighteenth century, the city suffered from recurring Dutch and English pirate attacks as the latter sought to disrupt Spanish dominance in the region. By 1683, most of the city had been abandoned and the people of the town moved into the Aguán Valley, a region that would later become a major center of fruit production in the first half of the twentieth century. Many of these settlers engaged in the burgeoning contraband trade in gold, sarsaparilla, silver, indigo, log wood, cattle, balsam, and hides in exchange for British textiles and clothing.[8] Taylor Mack maintains that the contraband network went as far as Comayagua and Tegucigalpa and involved many mulattoes as smugglers. Manuel Rubio Sánchez asserts that as early as the 1630s, mulattoes and mestizos were a large portion of the population living in the haciendas in Trujillo and its vicinity.[9]

The significant presence of blacks and mulattoes in Trujillo as documented by Mack and others was not limited to involvement in the contraband trade. Paul Lokken documents the existence of black and mulatto militiamen in the area as far back as the late sixteenth century. In order to counter the aforementioned pirate attacks on the coast of Central America, the Spanish authorities in Central America authorized the arming of black and mulatto residents in coastal areas to defend against recurring attacks.[10] By the mid-seventeenth century, Central America boasted sixteen black and mulatto units of militiamen with two based on the North Coast of Honduras.[11] The history of Hondurans of African descent involved in the early defense and economic activity of the nation indicates the enduring contribution of this population in shaping the identity of Honduras. While discourses on black identity in Honduras were historically void in other regions of the country, such debates on the North Coast, particularly the Trujillo area, date from the earliest period of the colonial era.

The long-standing history of internationalism and a consistent population of African descent make Trujillo pivotal in understanding the West Indian experience in Honduras during the first half of the twentieth century. Trujillo served as a foundation for several key cultural transitions regarding Honduran identity. The city was the location from which the Garífuna culture spread throughout Central America following the group's settlement of the area after branching out from its original establishments on the island of Roatan. An 1821 census of the city and its surrounding areas reveals that the Garífuna represented some 65 percent of the total population. Whites, primarily Spaniards, only represented some 4 percent of the entire population of the area, with the remainder of the inhabitants comprised overwhelmingly of a diverse group of blacks and mulattoes, some of whose origins were Haitian and British Caribbean.[12] Judging from this data, Trujillo would have fallen outside the scope of a mestizo national identity as defined by Hondurans who viewed their nation as a mixture of Indian and Spanish ancestry. Instead, Trujillo was a city where blackness, or at least individuals claiming some black ancestry, was the norm. The international origins of many within the population made Trujillo much more conducive to later immigration, especially black immigration. Most of the early arrivals to Trujillo from the British Caribbean were more than likely enslaved Africans, and the arrivals from the French Caribbean were most often mulattoes fleeing the Saint Domingue Revolution. The multicultural, multiracial character of the Trujillo population in many ways resembled the broader Caribbean Antilles.

In addition to its colorful history, the city also served as the place where Honduran authorities captured and executed the infamous North American filibuster, William Walker, in his foiled attempt to invade the country in 1860. This event was central in shaping Honduran identity as it represented the efforts of the populace to defend its political integrity from foreign invaders. More important, in recent historical memory, Trujillo and the neighboring city of Puerto Castilla and surrounding areas served as the headquarters of the Trujillo Railroad Company, a subsidiary of the multinational United Fruit Company from 1913 to 1939.

Between 1900 and 1930, the United Fruit Company spread banana production over multiple sites and contracted with local producers in order to avoid risks associated with both agricultural diseases and labor organizing. According to the historian Steve Striffler, a wider area of production also allowed the fruit company to wait out isolated strikes, repress workers, or simply abandon production in particular locales when suitable conditions changed or when more lucrative opportunities became available in newly expanding territories.[13] In addition to the thriving banana industry in Jamaica and other islands in the eastern Caribbean, the agro-industrial production of bananas by the United Fruit Company and its subsidiaries persisted in Central American countries such as Panama, Honduras, Costa Rica, and Guatemala, and later extended to encompass the South American nations of Colombia and Ecuador.

The mass production, mass consumption, low risk strategy of the banana industry during the first half of the twentieth century falls within the paradigm of what many scholars refer to as the Fordist model of agro-export capitalism. More important, the strategies employed by the company regarding plantation management, discipline, and the paternalistic attitude toward company workers proved beneficial in maintaining control of labor forces. Initially, one way to maintain order in the plantations was to hire workers with whom the company had been familiar. In the case of Panama and Costa Rica, this meant hiring workers from the various Caribbean islands. The company relied on the agricultural knowledge and skills these workers had acquired through many years of banana cultivation in their home countries.[14] Many West Indians found themselves in positions as overseers on the plantations because of their expertise on the inner workings of the banana industry. Such perceived favoritism created animosity between these overseers and the local workers and would be the catalyst for much of the anti-immigrant sentiment that spread throughout Central American nations in which the banana industry dominated and the West Indian populations were significant.

With the increased industrialization of the banana industry, the multinational fruit companies were vulnerable to many diseases associated with monocultural agricultural practices, most notably Panama disease. The disease was so named because its first known occurrence surfaced in the Bocas del Toro region of Panama in the 1890s. The disease stunted the growth of the fruit and often killed the banana tree itself. The leaves of the tree, normally a dark green, turned a vivid yellow and then brown, only to fall to the ground when the plant had been totally consumed by the disease.[15] What happened in essence was the rapid death of the banana plant, leading to inedible fruit and an enormous decline in profits for the fruit companies.

Though initially confined to the coastal regions of Panama and Costa Rica, the disease was making inroads in the newer United Fruit company divisions of Honduras and Guatemala by the 1920s. The impact of the disease was so devastating in the Trujillo Railroad Company Division that United Fruit was forced to abandon the division entirely in 1939. In addition to the effects of Panama disease on banana production in the Trujillo Division, the company was also suffering from the cutbacks within the industry as a result of decreased demand for tropical fruits because of the global economic depression of 1929. The estimated value of United Fruit bananas decreased from U.S. $17,306,318 in 1930 to U.S. $9,776,901 by 1934. This paralleled a decline in the number of bananas exported from Honduras during the same period from 28,960,948 stems to 19,462,596 stems.[16]

The effects of Panama disease, the depression of 1929, and the resulting reduction in employment, combined with increased anti-black immigration legislation in the form of the 1929 and 1934 immigration laws, created a volatile environment in the various banana enclaves along the northern coast of Honduras. In the Trujillo–Puerto Castilla region such factors ultimately escalated the deportation of many West Indians from the country. This problem was exacerbated in 1934 when conditions left some six hundred Honduran workers unemployed in the Puerto Castilla region. Because the probability of obtaining employment was low due to the fact that the banana industry was the sole employer in the area and no bananas were being shipped out, the government proposed the idea of sending workers to other locales within the United Fruit Company divisions such as La Lima and Tela in order to find work.[17] However, these areas were engaged in their own labor problems since the cutbacks within the banana industry were nationwide.

Judging from local government correspondence a month later, the situation of the workers did not improve. Unemployed Hondurans and other Latinos from neighboring Central American nations began to equate their own lack of opportunity with the "preferential" hiring practices of the company toward West Indians. To the Honduran, West Indian success in the banana industry, at least in terms of company jobs, came at the expense of local workers. Honduran workers argued that they were starving while West Indians earned good wages. To make matters worse, Honduran workers suggested that West Indians entered the country without passports or other documentation verifying their origins. In many cases these claims were legitimate, but they were exaggerated in order to further the cause of native workers.

Most West Indians who settled in Honduras came to the country independently. Many chose to enter the country through legal means using their British passports. However, illegal immigration was common and relatively easy. Gerald Meade, the British chargé d'affaires in Honduras, maintained that many government officials along the coast supplemented their incomes by allowing the illicit entry of West Indians into the country. Because work was plentiful in the early days of the industry, and the fruit companies were in de facto control of the North Coast, circumventing immigration law was easy.[18] Meade estimated that at any given period, West Indian workers represented no less than 40 percent of all workers for the fruit company. Of these, he maintained that 90 percent lacked the proper documentation to live and work in the country. Meade's assessment of the situation failed to mention that most West Indians initially possessed the proper visas to work in the country. The conflict arose when many chose to remain in the country after their visas had expired and increased anti-black sentiment made it nearly impossible to renew documentation.

The Honduran government issued a mandate after the immigration law of 1934 that required foreigners to register with the government, regardless of race, and they were issued identification cards. This policy proved problematic for many. The Honduran government lacked the infrastructure to administer the registration and identification process efficiently. Many foreigners in Tela and Trujillo were unable to obtain the documentation because the closest offices in San Pedro and Yoro were two days' journey by mule. Workers could not afford to take off the four days necessary to acquire the documentation and there was no guarantee that the process would be successful if they did. Even if they traveled to La Ceiba, the most developed of North Coast cities, immigration officers often requested bribes in exchange for services.[19] Rather than confront these issues, many foreigners chose to remain in Honduras illegally. The population that remained by 1934 was much smaller than in previous decades.

Evidence from company reports prior to 1934 indicates that West Indian employees of the Trujillo Railroad Company did not exceed 10 percent of the workers, including those workers from neighboring British Honduras whose numbers declined in population between 1929 and 1931. In fact, there was a slight decrease in the number of all Trujillo Railroad Company employees, and West Indians in particular.[20] This trend demonstrates the effectiveness of the immigration legislation of 1929 in making it more difficult for West Indians to enter the country both legally and illegally. The downward trend in the number of West Indians within the company continued, and by 1935, the West Indian labor force for the Trujillo Railroad Company had been reduced from 678 in 1929 to 181 by 1935.[21] Regardless of the inaccuracy of the local government official's remarks, his perceptions that West Indians were taking jobs away from local workers permeated the attitudes of Hondurans throughout the country.

The issue regarding the six hundred unemployed Honduran and Central American workers in 1934 was an exceptional situation considering the Trujillo Railroad Company had previously acquiesced to Honduran governmental pressure to replace West Indians with local workers. In fact, the company began a policy of deporting West Indians back to British Honduras and Jamaica as early as January 1934. Initially, the numbers of workers being sent back to their home countries was relatively small. On January 4, 1934, the Trujillo Railroad Company shipped fourteen former employees from Puerto Castilla to ports in British Honduras and Jamaica.[22] A few weeks later on January 26, the company shipped another fourteen workers from Puerto Castilla to Jamaica and five to British Honduras. In both instances, the workers worked for the Trujillo Railroad Company up to a few days prior to being sent home on company vessels.[23] The workers had very little time to settle affairs or make other preparations before their departure to their home countries. They also were not given a choice as to whether they wanted to remain in the country as employees within another capacity of the company.

On March 2, 1934, twenty-seven West Indians had their jobs terminated with the Trujillo Railroad Company and the company immediately deported them from the country. However, in this particular instance, the workers did not go peacefully. Rather than accept their fate as did their brethren in Tela, these individuals, both male and female, refused to board the ships that would take them to Jamaica and British Honduras. Instead, they chose to return to the Trujillo Railroad Company compound and force the company and local authorities to take a position regarding their fate. By returning to the company compound rather than board the ships, the workers were in effect hindering the agenda of the Honduran government and the fruit company to make a smooth transition to an all-Honduran labor force. Unable to deal with the situation, the local authorities appealed to the government in Tegucigalpa for help.[24] A few days later, the workers acquiesced and accepted their deportation to their home countries. The West Indians' compliance with the deportation order was due largely to the lack of legal recourse with which to challenge immigration policy because of their status as foreign contract workers. Once the Trujillo Railroad Company canceled their jobs, their visas were subsequently voided and their status in the country was illegal, facilitating deportation. Also, because the banana industry in the country had been in decline, remaining in the country illegally would not have been a suitable option as there was no other means of immediate employment anywhere along the North Coast.

On the same day these workers were shipped home, the Trujillo Railroad company transported another twenty-two former employees on a vessel destined for Kingston, Jamaica.[25] Such random orders of deportation continued throughout 1934, almost all of which involved West Indians whose jobs had been recently canceled by the Trujillo Railroad Company.

Many government officials felt that the "problem" of West Indian workers in Trujillo would cease to exist if the government and the fruit companies enforced deportation policies. However, these officials did not grasp that West Indian workers were leaving their countries to seek employment in Honduras because there was no opportunity for gainful employment in the various Caribbean islands. The historian Thomas O'Brien articulates this point in his assertion that the collapse of the West Indian sugar industry in the last quarter of the nineteenth century sent wave after wave of black workers into the economies of the Caribbean Basin. He notes that "West Indians labored in the sugar fields of Cuba, the Panama Canal, and the United Fruit company plantations throughout Latin America.[26] For most of the workers, there was simply no reason to return home. In fact, the British chargé d'affaires in Tegucigalpa maintained that it would be easy to arrange for the repatriation of unemployed West Indians to their native countries, but he felt that most would not want to return home because of the fear of being unable to find work.[27] West Indians were also well aware of the difficulties of returning to Honduras once they left, so many decided to risk remaining in the country illegally with the hopes that the banana industry would eventually improve.

The situation of West Indians in Trujillo proved to be heightened compared to other areas along the North Coast. For much of 1933–34, issues arose regarding the return of West Indians who had gone abroad either to Jamaica or to British Honduras for various reasons. In one situation, West Indian athletes listed as British nationals were returning from a sporting event in British Honduras and were scrutinized by immigration officials upon their return to Honduras as to the validity of their Honduran residency status. Several spectators, most likely friends and family of the athletes, accompanied the group and found themselves questioned and sequestered by immigration authorities as well.[28] Eventually the group was allowed to return to Honduras on a technicality because there was a discrepancy as to when the law was effective due to the issuance of a government circular on July 25, 1933, prohibiting the re-entry of blacks to the country but that was not received in Trujillo until August 12, 1933. This was during the period when the group of athletes and spectators were already outside of the country. Therefore, the government interpreted this particular situation as an accidental departure and granted concessions allowing the group's re-entry.

Another incident involved the re-entry of schoolchildren into Honduras after studying abroad in Jamaica, a practice very common among West Indian families on the North Coast and the Bay Islands during this period. In one case, Matilde Reid had to request permission from Honduran authorities for her daughters to return to the country. Reid maintained that her daughters lived in Puerto Castilla for eight years prior to studying abroad.[29] The Reid case was exceptional because most children of West Indians in Honduras who sought education abroad did not return to the country once their education was complete. After secondary education in places like British Honduras, Jamaica, and the United States, many children of West Indians pursued their livelihood in the United States or Britain, finding the cultural life and economic possibilities more agreeable than life in the banana enclaves of Honduras.

Special permission was granted to Matilde Reide for her children to be returned to her. The example in this particular instance had more to do with preserving the structure of the family. While such gestures on the part of the Honduran government at first appear quite noble, there were several occasions in which families remained separated due to officials withholding entry visas into Honduras. In addition to not allowing West Indians to return to Honduras once they left, even after proving that they had taken domicile in the country, the government also did not always extend permanent visas to West Indian wives seeking to join their husbands in the country.

In a conversation with the Honduran minister of foreign affairs, the British chargé d'affaires in Honduras reported that the former maintained that visas for up to six months were not refused to the wives of West Indians, but that in any case, the ultimate goal was for the husbands to return to their wives.[30] In other words, the government was not in the business of promoting the permanent settlement of West Indians in the country. Their eventual return to their native countries was always implied.

The desire for West Indians to remain in the Trujillo area despite the hostile environment is made clear when analyzing the level of return to Honduras among those workers recently deported. As early as January 22, 1934, local authorities complained to officials of the Trujillo Railroad Company that many of the West Indian workers recently deported from the area were returning to the country and resettling specifically in the Trujillo–Puerto Castilla division of the company. From the correspondence, the fruit company appeared to have little control over the camps where the workers lived, which made it possible for people to return and evade detection. Reports of drunkenness and fighting revealed an atmosphere of lawlessness and disorder within the camps that was allowed to persist.[31]

Many in the Honduran press argued that the West Indians returning illegally would be unemployed and therefore would further contribute to the criminal element already out of control in the area. The assumption was that they would become vagrants and engage in illegal activity in order to survive. Neither the Trujillo Railroad Company nor the Honduran government wanted to be held responsible in the event that such predictions came to fruition. There were instances of criminal activity within the banana camps. However, the Honduran press could not substantiate the claims that West Indians were involved in criminal activity to a higher degree than Hondurans and other Central Americans in the camps. Nevertheless, such claims continued to be made in order to facilitate a response from the Honduran government against West Indian immigration.

Deportation for false documentation was enforced almost immediately following the 1929 immigration legislation. However, such policies in the Trujillo–Puerto Castilla area did not commence on a large scale until the Trujillo Railroad Company initiated them. The role of the Trujillo Railroad Company in the deportation of West Indian workers exemplified the fruit company's ability to play both sides in the immigration debate. On the one hand, the company made it clear that it was making a transition from a multicultural labor force that included West Indians and other Central Americans to one that was almost completely Honduran. Such a gesture, along with the actual deportation of West Indians to their home countries on company-owned ships, did much to improve the image of the company locally and appease the growing nationalist sentiment of the Honduran masses. On the other hand, the deportation of the West Indian workers was symbolic of the change in labor demands. Because of the decline in production due to plant disease and the effects of the worldwide depression, the company simply did not need as many employees. The deportation of West Indian workers was as much a business decision as it was a political one.

During the same period that the Honduran government placed restrictions on West Indian immigration and the Trujillo Railroad Company deported its West Indian workers, entry visas for West Indians and their family members continued to be solicited by the United Fruit Company through Honduran consulate offices in New Orleans. In one particular instance, the Honduran government granted Miss Dorothy Davis a two-week visa to visit her father who resided in Puerto Castilla and worked for the Trujillo Railroad Company. In a letter accompanying the visa request, the assistant to the vice president of the United Fruit Company maintained that Miss Davis's father was an old and faithful employee of the company and that she would be traveling exclusively on United Fruit Company steamships from her home in New Orleans to Tela and then on to Puerto Castilla.[32] In addition to demonstrating the power the fruit companies had in bypassing immigration and tourist restrictions placed on West Indians, the case of Dorothy Davis is the first of many examples that show the connection between New Orleans, the Caribbean, and Honduras. Davis was Jamaican born, single, and twenty years of age. She worked as a nurse at Charity Hospital in New Orleans and was also a student.[33] Unlike many West Indian women in Honduras of the previous generation, she was not bound by the gender restrictions that limited her to the status of housewife or domestic worker. Education, and undoubtedly her father's status as a trusted United Fruit Company worker, provided her with the opportunity to improve her status. She was able to do all of this while maintaining a British passport. This was a sore spot in the eyes of Hondurans because they felt that West Indians used their British nationality to circumvent Honduran law. The same situation applied to Davis's two younger brothers, who visited Puerto Castilla the previous June under similar circumstances.

Richard Harvey Davis Jr., sixteen, and David John Davis, fourteen, were both listed as students traveling to see their parents in Puerto Castilla. They made the trip from New Orleans to Tela, and then to Puerto Castilla via United Fruit Company owned and operated steamships. Like their sister, both young men were born in Jamaica and retained their British passports.[34] The case of the Davis family was unique on multiple levels and presents a window into the transnational identities that the banana industry in Honduras created. However, one feature that stands out in their story is that none of them chose to study in Jamaica or British Honduras, as did so many of the other children of West Indians in Honduras. Instead, the family opted to educate their children in New Orleans, perhaps further taking advantage of the relationship between the family and the fruit company, because for much of this period the United Fruit Company maintained an office in the city.

The records of the Honduran Consulate in New Orleans detail additional examples of how West Indians were able to circumvent Honduran laws through their ties to the United Fruit Company. In October 1934, a Jamaican-born employee of the Trujillo Railroad Company, Charles Henry Collingwood Masters, obtained a visa to re-enter Honduras from the consulate in New Orleans after having spent his vacation abroad there. Masters officially resided in Puerto Castilla with his wife, but according to Honduran law he could not re-enter Honduras once he had left due to the fact that he was West Indian, and the 1934 Immigration Law strictly forbade it. Like the others in the examples above, he also maintained his British passport and identity.[35] Through the auspices of the United Fruit Company, he obtained a visa and returned to his family. The Honduran press had long been aware of West Indians and other immigrants deemed undesirable obtaining entry visas through consular agencies abroad similar to the one Charles Masters was issued. Journalists even tried to expose this problem in the hopes that the government would intervene and abate the practice.[36] However, it was often difficult to disseminate information from Tegucigalpa to the various cities on the coast, let alone to Honduran consulate offices overseas. In addition, apart from a few isolated cases of the practice occurring in British Honduras, the problem of falsifying visas did not seem to be as widespread as journalists suggested. Besides, Honduran consulates abroad were known to engage in acts that did not always represent the national interests of the government. The previous scandals regarding the interoceanic railroad and foreign debt involved Honduran consulate officials who had gained personal fortunes by acquiring loans in the name of the people without the consent of the government.[37] In addition, the level of corruption within the Honduran political structure and the overbearing influence of the United Fruit Company in the region made it possible for the company to exert its power whenever and however it chose.

The Honduran government did not encourage the settlement of West Indians in the country and made every effort to make it difficult for spouses to unite with their husbands on the coast. However, in August 1934, during the height of anti–West Indian sentiment in Honduras, Ines May Sharp Foster, a twenty-three-year-old homemaker from Belize, British Honduras, obtained a visa from the Honduran consulate in New

Orleans to travel to Tela in order to be reunited with her husband Franz Foster, an employee of the United Fruit Company. The Honduran consulate issued the visa as a resident permit, with no indication that it was valid only for the six-month period as proscribed by Honduran law.[38]

Honduran animosity toward West Indian workers stemmed from many inconsistencies within the organizational structure of the banana enclaves of the North Coast. The concerns of the local population regarding the competition for jobs with West Indians was just one element. West Indians' privileged status in the banana camps created resentment among Hondurans. The constant reminder that West Indians were British subjects and preferred company employees not subject to the same laws and constraints as Hondurans was most distinguishable in terms of involuntary military and labor conscription.

West Indian workers were subjects in the military conscription debate. Many Honduran military leaders attempted to draft them as soldiers. Following the end of the presidency of Marco Aurelio Soto in 1883, and for much of the early twentieth century, military conspiracies and civil wars associated with elite aspirations for political power, conflicts over disputed elections, and presidential succession plagued Honduras. In order to carry out these wars, it was essential to galvanize armies. The 1930s proved to be a particularly volatile period on the North Coast. Both government and rebel leaders recruited rank-and-file soldiers from the poverty-stricken masses, who promised their services in exchange for a better life if their side was successful. Many were also conscripted. Echeverri-Gent maintains that rebel troops passed through plantation zones on the North Coast and enlisted workers into their ranks on the spot.[39] Honduran government officials at Sonaguera requested assistance from Tegucigalpa regarding whether foreigners, mainly West Indians, could be conscripted into military service during the period immediately prior to the Honduran Civil War of 1932. After an assessment of the laws of Honduras, the government determined that only Honduran citizens could be conscripted into military service and that West Indians, who were British subjects, were exempt from such duties. Honduran citizens of West Indian descent such as Bay Islanders were aware of this and attempted to evade military conscription by claiming British nationality to no avail.[40] Darío Euraque maintains that many Hondurans of West Indian descent sought assistance from within their community, particularly from their pastors, in evading military service on the grounds that they were British subjects. This posed problems with the authorities when the pastor unsuccessfully encouraged the Garífuna to attempt this strategy.[41] While Hondurans were subject to have their lives and stability jeopardized with every political election, West Indians and other foreigners were exempt from such immediate threats.

West Indians presented another dilemma for the Honduran government. Because the government historically made the lives of West Indians difficult on the North Coast, many West Indians did not look with favor on the Honduran political system. There is little evidence to suggest established alliances between West Indians and the rebellions. However, many within the government felt that the large number of West Indians crossing the borders between British Honduras and Honduras posed a threat to the national security of Honduras. Previous examples detail the numerous excursions made by West Indians to compete in athletic events and other social functions in neighboring British Honduras. By the mid-1930s, the Honduran government began to clamp down on such events and prohibited family and spectators from attending. The government rescinded travel permits and visas without explanation. The belief was that many of the spectators at the sporting events were rebel sympathizers and would provide strategic intelligence and resources to those rebels operating out of British Honduras.[42] Such convictions were never substantiated. The incidents demonstrate the fragile existence of West Indians in Honduras in that their loyalties were always suspect. Whether it came from local workers in the fruit companies, the armed services, or the Honduran government, a cloud of suspicion always loomed over West Indians and their descendants in Honduras.

The West Indian situation in Honduras continued to be ambiguous. Though there was no evidence linking the group to rebel movements, and it was clear that the group was not legally required to perform military service, West Indians were not exempt from illegal labor conscription. Labor conscription had been an established practice in Honduras long before the arrival of West Indians and the banana industry. Such mandatory assistance was initiated by local police departments and usually reserved for aiding authorities in times of major catastrophes such as hurricanes, floods, and fires. Because Honduras lacked the resources and infrastructure to handle these situations, everyone in the country, whether foreign or national, was expected to make a contribution. Most did so willingly. However, this was of their own accord as there was no legal precedent mandating free citizens to offer their services in any situation. Instances of compulsory labor were legally relegated "to penal institutions after the conviction of a crime and confirmation of a sentence."[43] Despite the illegality of the practice, local authorities often used this law to harass West Indians and coerce them into performing menial and degrading tasks. West Indians were conscripted to perform tasks such as burying bodies after a yellow fever epidemic, picking up trash and sewage by-products, and moving and hauling illegal contraband for corrupt officials. If they refused, beatings and imprisonment on trumped-up charges were common punishments.

The British vice consul at La Ceiba reported to the British chargé d'affaires in 1935 that the police beat and incarcerated Arnold Bloomfield, a British subject, for refusing to perform labor that he had been ordered to do by local officers. This was five years after the U.S.-backed report on convict and compulsory labor reiterated that such practices did not exist in the country. At first glance, it appeared that Bloomfield simply did not want to help officials in instances of national emergency. However, the local officers had requested Bloomfield and three others to assist with carrying a heavy drum of liquor, as opposed to helping with a situation that was for the common good of the community. Bloomfield maintained that his health did not allow him to perform strenuous tasks and as a result of his refusal to aid the officers, they beat him with the butt ends of their rifles.[44] Immediately upon receipt of the details of the situation, the chargé d'affaires went to the Honduran foreign minister to demand an investigation of the matter. This action immediately led to Mr. Bloomfield's release. However, the Honduran Foreign Ministry attempted to cover up its culpability in the case.

In order to counter the claims of Bloomfield and the British government, the Foreign Ministry produced a medical certificate stating that Bloomfield had not been beaten and presented written accounts of witnesses stating that it was in fact Bloomfield who attacked the officers. The response from the Foreign Ministry displayed some animosity toward Mr. Bloomfield, and West Indians in general; it suggested that they were troublesome and considered themselves above the law because of their nationality. According to the foreign minister, the British government made matters worse because it always came to the aid of its citizens even when they were defiant. The British chargé d'affaires questioned the foreign minister about labor conscription of British subjects. It was at this point that the evidence revealed that Mr. Bloomfield had been asked to move the drum of liquor from the scene of a fire, rather than assist with putting it out. Despite the perceived improprieties on the part of the foreign minister and local authorities, the British chargé d'affaires and Bloomfield decided to let the matter drop, because if the Honduran authorities investigated the matter to its full extent, there was the high probability that they would discover that Bloomfield was in fact residing in the country illegally.

That the chargé d'affaires never took issue with Mr. Bloomfield's status in Honduras and that the former maintained employment in the country is evidence that many of the claims of the foreign minister and anti-black immigration advocates were at least in part true. The chargé d'affaires dropped his inquiry into the case in order to allow Bloomfield to break Honduran law by remaining in the country. The Bloomfield incident exposed many of the problems that plagued West Indian workers on the North Coast. Their race and nationality made them vulnerable to violent attacks from both civilians and government officials. Their status as foreign workers made them beholden to their employers for protection and job security. More important, the ambiguity of their legal status in Honduras gave West Indians little recourse to fight injustices, even if they had representatives of the British Empire behind them. Therefore, when the massive deportations of West Indians took place at Trujillo, most were eventually forced to comply with the orders.

The anti-black sentiment aimed at West Indians that ultimately led to their deportation from Honduras also had a negative impact on the Garífuna population. Many Honduran authorities based black identity solely on phenotype and did not consider the complex historical and cultural realities of class and color in the Caribbean. Therefore, it was inconceivable for some authorities to distinguish the Garífuna from the West Indian, despite the clear ethnic and cultural distinctions between the two groups.

The negative impact of anti-black immigration policy directed at West Indians made the Garífuna targets of border patrols aimed at cracking down on illegal immigration. In September 1934, a group of blacks composed mostly of women and children was captured in the waters near the district of Limón in the Department of Colón. As the identity of these individuals was unclear at the time of the arrest, the police took the group into custody.[45] They eventually deduced that these women and children were in fact residents of the Garífuna settlements of Limón and Cristales and the police subsequently released them. Garífuna settlements historically grew up alongside many of the cities of the North Coast.[46] Therefore, it was not uncommon for the groups to interact in all aspects of life along the coastal cities. Many of the market women in the coastal towns were Garífuna in origin. Also, many Garífuna men engaged in part-time work as stevedores for the fruit companies.[47]

In a similar situation, Honduran authorities captured a boat in an area known as Malaguás near Trujillo. They seized the vessel under suspicion that it was carrying illegal immigrants, but it turned out that a local Honduran operated the boat and the black passengers on board were Garífuna, Honduran, and in fact residents of the municipalities of Limón, Aguán, and Iriona, all within the department of Colón.[48] Authorities did uncover twenty-one sacks of unnamed clandestine merchandise and arrested the crew and passengers. The crew members and passengers were not guilty of being illegal black immigrants, but of smuggling. Interestingly enough, smuggling was a common occurrence along the North Coast, and because the Garífuna worked primarily in the markets and other aspects of the informal economy, in addition to their connections with Garífuna communities in neighboring Guatemala, Belize, and Nicaragua, they were able to gain something of a monopoly in the trade. Accounts of traveling to Belize by canoe during the night in order to acquire goods unavailable in Honduras were very common in the oral history of the Garífuna.[49] Belize offered access to British goods and served as a link between the British Caribbean and Central America.

In addition to affecting the West Indian workers of the Trujillo Railroad Company and the Garífuna, the anti-black immigration legislation in Honduras and the subsequent deportation of West Indians to British Honduras and Jamaica was a cause of concern for the Bay Islander population. It became necessary for these English-speaking Hondurans of West Indian descent to possess proper documentation at all times when they went to the North Coast as workers for the fruit companies. Merrit and Grace Johnson, both of Oakridge, Roatán, were made aware of this when they sought the assistance of the Honduran authorities in Trujillo to have their daughter Eleanor readmitted into the country from Jamaica, where she had been studying. The Johnsons presented birth certificates verifying their Honduran citizenship but could not produce documentation for their daughter. As a result, the authorities in Trujillo were reluctant to get involved in the matter and referred it to authorities in Tegucigalpa.[50] The case was eventually resolved and Eleanor Johnson was allowed to return home to her parents. However, the incident demonstrates the vulnerability of Bay Islanders once they left the islands and settled in the Trujillo area.

The deportation of West Indian workers from Trujillo and Puerto Castilla to their home countries spawned a wide array of issues in the area. The anti-black immigration legislation aimed at West Indians that sparked the initial deportations carried over into the lives of Honduran citizens of all ethnic and racial backgrounds. Deportation of West Indians did little to suppress the massive rates of unemployment in the region due largely to the fact that external forces such as the global depression and the rapidly spreading Panama disease were responsible for the economic decline in the area. However, the masses of Hondurans still equated their suffering with the Trujillo Railroad Company's preference for West Indian labor.

The deportation and its aftermath exposed the social, racial, and economic realities that plagued much of the region. Attacks on West Indians ultimately led to attacks on all people perceived as black or West Indian in Honduras since Bay Islanders, Garífuna, and West Indians were often indistinguishable in the eyes of the Honduran government. Following the events of 1934, the Trujillo Railroad Company continued in a state of decline and by 1939, the United Fruit Company shut down fruit production operations in the area. According to Mark Moberg in his study of the United Fruit Company in Belize, the modus operandi of the multinational organization in closing a production facility due to plant disease was to abandon production in one region or nation for another uninfected and more fertile region. Moberg maintains that during relocation the United Fruit Company systematically destroyed the infrastructure it had constructed in order to prevent local competition from using the resources of the region.[51] Although fruit production ceased in the region, the port remained an important point of shipment for the United Fruit Company in Honduras, but the social and economic issues that arose in the area did not go away. The port alone did not offer many job opportunities to local residents. Instead, the problems among Honduran workers, the fruit companies, and West Indian workers resurfaced in other locales within the vast network of banana enclaves on the North Coast. Eventually, these issues would lead to increased hostilities toward the West Indian population and the subsequent mass exodus of West Indians from the country during the years leading up to the Second World War.

* * *

Although West Indian immigration declined in Honduras after 1934, Honduran political officials and intellectuals persisted in their efforts to unite the nation around a mestizo identity. They proved successful in constructing a national identity that espoused the concepts of *mestizaje* based on Spanish and indigenous ancestry to the exclusion of Hondurans of African descent. It was during the period of intense anti-black sentiment on the North Coast that the image of the indigenous cacique Lempira was promoted as a symbol of Honduran identity. Famous for fighting against Spanish conquerors in the sixteenth century and regarded as the first martyr in the fight for the sovereignty of Honduras, Lempira was elevated to the status of national hero. His image was used as a vehicle to promote the myth of Honduras as a mestizo nation. The image of Lempira was placed side by side with the images of notable Honduran statesmen of Spanish descent such as Francisco Morazán and Marco Aurelio Soto. The fusion of Spanish and indigenous heritage, a result of the biological and cultural miscegenation that took place between the two groups during the Spanish colonial era, was praised.[52] This duality in relegating both the oppressed and the oppressor to equal hero status in Honduran mythology is a testament to the ambiguity of identity politics in the nation. More important, praising the indigenous and Spanish heritages of the nation eliminated those Hondurans of African descent, whether native or foreign born, from the scope of the nation. The deportation of West Indians from the banana enclaves on the North Coast was more than just an effort to eradicate the presence of foreign workers from the nation. This policy was a continuation of a long process aimed at the eradication of blackness from the national character.

EPILOGUE

Emigration is no longer possible, as most countries [in Latin America] have imposed restrictive quotas or barred foreign entry altogether . . . ; thousands of progressive Jamaicans have been hit by the depression abroad and forced to return home."[1] Writing in late 1934, N. A. Rudolf, of Hampstead, Jamaica, thus summarized the end of the West Indian immigrant experience of the late nineteenth and early twentieth centuries. Many West Indians benefited from the economic opportunities provided in the banana enclaves of Honduras and neighboring Central American nations. Representing the first substantial transnational labor force in postemancipation societies, West Indians found themselves at the center of identity politics wherever they settled in Central America. Because of their race, religion, culture, and ties with U.S. interests, their social and political agenda remained outside the scope of the nation-state.

West Indians were ultimately forced out of Honduras in the mid-1930s and found themselves ill-equipped for reintroduction into their own societies. In Jamaica, returning workers from abroad cluttered the restrictive job market, creating competition and labor surplus.[2] West Indian children born abroad experienced difficulties adjusting to Caribbean life. The region was native to them culturally, yet foreign. In Honduras, children of West Indians born in the country acquired citizenship as a birthright. Yet their parents instilled in them the conviction that they were West Indian subjects of the British Empire. Caught between nations and cultures and confronted with a North Coast society in which race and ethnicity continued to stratify not only the Afro-descent population but the nation as a whole, the West Indian community was in constant flux. As a result, the migration process continued for many West Indians, with the United States and Great Britain serving as final destinations.[3] Most West Indians and their descendants who left Honduras never returned. Their experiences in the country remain only as bits and pieces of family history and folklore. Those who remained in the country after the 1930s continued to depend heavily on the fruit companies for their survival and were forced to come to the realization that their status as a preferred labor force had diminished.

The diplomatic pressures to hire Hondurans were successful, and West Indians were phased out of most positions within the companies. In La Ceiba, the English-speaking workers who remained with the fruit companies were Honduran citizens from the Bay Islands employed as sailors for the Standard Fruit and Steamship Company.[4] Bay Islanders continued to represent the most significant English-speaking labor force within the fruit companies. Their presence represented a coming full circle for the West Indians in Honduras. Bay Islanders were some of the first employees of the banana industry and were instrumental in creating the foundation for the West Indian community that emerged on the North Coast during the early twentieth century. After the demise of the West Indian community due to their initial deportation from Honduras and the subsequent emigration of the majority of West Indians to other countries, Bay Islanders continued the rich Caribbean traditions brought initially by their ancestors and later enhanced by their Afro-Caribbean brethren in the banana enclaves.

The West Indian experience in Honduras parallels the modern realities of immigrants around the world. The in-between status afforded most immigrants places them at the center of various debates. "The immigrant," according to Ramon Grosfoguel, "is embedded in social, political, and cultural relations."[5] Grosfoguel's interpretation of the immigrant experience is as valid for the West Indian history in Honduras during the late nineteenth and early twentieth centuries as it is for newly emerging immigrant groups in the twenty-first century. In both cases, whether the host government's policy was one of active support or opposition to the immigrant group, public opinion was reluctant acceptance or discrimination. Issues of political incorporation, assimilation, acculturation, and labor continue to create fervor in societies with large immigrant and migrant populations.

The Honduran government initially turned a blind eye to the affairs on the North Coast and gave economic carte blanche to the banana companies. Politicians viewed the development of the banana industry as beneficial to the overall development of the nation and encouraged it. The various concessions granted to foreigners did not emphasize the source of labor to be used in building the industry, and the growing West Indian presence in the banana industry was met with indifference.

The masses of Hondurans never viewed West Indians with such apathy. Most regarded their presence as a threat to their economic existence. Job availability and security remained a priority. Intellectuals and government officials saw the growing West Indian presence as a threat to mestizo identity and worried that the nation would lose its racial and cultural character. Hondurans also took issue with the British nationality of West Indians. In many ways they regarded the population as agents of the British Empire. The government perceived the British- provided capital and social networks of solidarity to the new arrivals as challenging Honduran sovereignty. These perceptions were never borne out by reality. However, the belief that the British had an imperialistic agenda persisted. The Honduran government hesitated to negotiate with the British regarding the mistreatment of West Indians.

The West Indian community possessed the capital network as employees of the fruit companies and their subsidiaries. They retained the protection of the companies because of the latter's preference for their labor. Socially, the Bay Islands community offered support to the initial wave of West Indian immigrants because they shared a similar historical experience. However, Bay Islanders used the strong West Indian presence and the British diplomatic presence on the North Coast in an attempt to renegotiate their own ambiguous status as Honduran nationals with a British West Indian past.

After 1934, the number of West Indian workers and their descendants decreased significantly on the North Coast. The fruit companies, as a result of plant disease and labor disputes, abandoned Honduras in the years following the Great Depression and sought to expand their economic possibilities in new locales with far less regulation and local opposition through emerging labor unions. The jobs that had long sustained the West Indian population relocated to new territories in Ecuador, Colombia, and other coastal regions of Latin America. However, the experiences of West Indians in Honduras and their ability to establish themselves in the turbulent cultural and political environment of the North Coast are a testament to the determination of this population to both succeed and avoid the possibility of returning to a depressed economy in the Caribbean with few employment options.

Modern immigrant groups, particularly Latino communities in the United States, face similar issues. In the months leading up to major political elections in 2008, immigration surfaced as an important topic of debate. Political and social critics exhibited elements of nativism as they questioned whether Latinos have assimilated American ideals to a level on par with immigrants of generations past. Katz, Stern, and Fader posit that within scholarly communities, many ponder whether Latino immigrants "will retrace the historical route that led Southern and Eastern European immigrants in the early twentieth century to economic parity and success, or will they end up economically marginalized and imperfectly assimilated."[6] Some argue that European immigrants of the early twentieth century embraced the English language and "American values," and fully integrated themselves into American society. Others maintain that the creation of ethnic enclaves, a working-class culture, and American ethnocentrism caused stagnant social and economic mobility within this population. The same holds true for Latino communities in the United States whose status in the country remains in constant flux.

The Latino immigrant experience in the United States and the West Indian experience in Honduras are also similar in that both communities were targeted when issues of job competition arose. Increased job competition in both nations led to a rise in xenophobic and nativist sentiment. Issues of legal status, patriotism, assimilation, and integration emerged within both societies, with each group characterized as an obstacle to homogeneity and a creation of national identity. West Indians were labeled "anti-Honduran" in the same way that the loyalties of many Latinos in the United States were called into question by some.

Throughout this study, I emphasize themes of identity formation within the Afro-descent communities in Honduras. When anti-black sentiment was at its apex, Bay Islanders, West Indians, and Garífuna all found themselves subjected to random acts of violence and racial profiling by Honduran authorities. Though all groups were targeted on the North Coast, there is no evidence of collective organization to combat the situation. The Garvey movement, with its strong Pan-African agenda, failed to gain a following. Ethnicity, culture, language, and economics continued to divide the populations on the North Coast.

Ultimately, ethnocentrism was strongest within the West Indian community. Just as Hondurans were obstacles to the establishment of West Indian communities, chapter 4 reveals, West Indians themselves were equally culpable in many regards. Though stress is placed on the status of West Indians in Honduras and the relationship between the violence committed against them and depressed economic conditions, many of the obstacles to the formation of the West Indian community were instituted by Honduras. By maintaining cultural and social organizations that excluded the local Hispanic population, West Indians aided in the creation of a hostile environment. West Indian parents assured that future generations would be equally at odds with Hondurans as they themselves had been by not integrating their Honduran-born children into the cultural and linguistic fabric of the nation. Perhaps it would have been to the advantage of West Indians to embrace their host country as opposed to denigrating its institutions and its people. However, such rivalries played into the designs of the fruit companies. With no local allegiance or ties to Honduras, the West Indians were often at the mercy of their North American employers, who, as in the case of Trujillo, were not always willing to come to their aid.

West Indians immigrated to Honduras with the intention of eventually returning home as opposed to establishing permanent residence in the country. Stuart Hall suggests that "cultural identity is assumed to be fixed by birth, part of nature, imprinted through kinship and lineage in the genes." For Hall, it is impermeable to something such as temporarily moving one's place of residence.[7] Though conditions in the Caribbean provided the catalyst for immigration, this did not necessarily mean that the immigrants gave up their identity. In the case of Honduras, home was always on the mind of the West Indians, so much so that they actively transmitted their Caribbean culture and the English language to the next generation. The immigrant experience represented one of continuity rather than one of "disruption and uprootedness."[8]

This study centers on the experiences of the West Indian workers in Honduras and the creation of the Afro–West Indian community in the country. However, chapter 5 emphasizes an equally important, but less addressed theme in studies focusing on the migration of Caribbean peoples to Latin America. The West Indian colonies and the British government exhibited indifference in addressing the needs and issues of West Indians working abroad. With the exception of Jamaica and the lesser populated areas of British Honduras, the government took little interest in the repatriation of its citizens. Because the colonial governments in the West Indies were focused on internal problems, there was little concern for matters abroad. In addition, because remittances were vital to West Indian economies, it was in the best interest of colonial governments for the workers to remain abroad, a situation that parallels the experiences of Latino immigrants to the United States and their relationship with their home governments.

British nationality offered no guarantees of support. In fact, the experience of the West Indian subjects in Honduras exposed the inequalities and contradictions within the empire. Race, class, and geographical location had as much to do with levels of citizenship in the British Empire as they did in most societies. This lesson came with a price for West Indians, as property and lives were lost due to the failure of the British government to take the complaints of its subjects seriously.

By midcentury, most workers had long since returned to their home colonies or migrated to other locales. A small minority remained in Honduras and became a part of the nation. Of these, it is impossible to determine the exact numbers. However, judging from discussions with those of West Indian descent in Honduras, choosing to remain in the country called for an inordinate amount of self-examination. Integration and assimilation was a conscious decision. It required learning Spanish, seeking advanced education in Latin American universities for some, and in many cases marrying into Spanish-speaking families. English remains the principal language spoken in the Bay Islands, but the Caribbean culture is slowly eroding due to the aggressive Hispanicization efforts of the Honduran government. In many instances English surnames, religion, music, and cuisine are the only remnants of Honduras's West Indian past on the North Coast. With each generation, the culture inevitably declines.

Many Hondurans of West Indian descent chose to immigrate to the United States. Once settled there, primarily in cities such as New York and Boston, they adopted a broadly defined West Indian identity and assimilated into the larger West Indian immigrant community. While emigration has done much to fracture the West Indian community in Honduras, and despite the efforts of many to assimilate, the experiences of the community remain outside the scope of Honduran history. They are still seen as outsiders by the mestizo majority, and many of the issues that burdened earlier generations are as vital today as they were almost a century ago. The banana enclaves have long since disappeared, but their legacy persists.

This study seeks to broaden the discourse on West Indian immigration to Latin America beyond myopic histories of twentieth-century labor organization in the banana zones. Though the labor needs of the fruit companies were pull factors for West Indian migration to the region, the communities that emerged were not simply accessories to that industry. Their identities were not limited to their occupation. West Indians had to negotiate their existence within the host country, and, equally important, West Indians in Honduras forced the nation to define itself.

In moving away from the numerous Costa Rican and Panamanian examples of West Indian community formation that have dominated the study of West Indians in Latin America, the study of Honduras offers a distinct perspective. Honduras may serve as a jumping-off point for new studies on the West Indian diaspora in other neglected regions in Latin America. Judging from the numerous archival sources surveyed, enormous research possibilities exist for the study of West Indian–descent communities in the Dominican Republic, Cuba, Venezuela, and a host of other countries. These studies are timely given the transnational nature of modern societies. Globalization may be a new concept for North Americans, but in Caribbean societies, from the dawn of colonialism to the present, it has always been the reality. Caribbean peoples, particularly those from the historically British islands, have migrated throughout the region, forcing other nations to redefine themselves, and in the process broadening pre-existing definitions of West Indian identity.

In addition to moving the discussion away from a pure focus on labor, the study of West Indians in Latin America adds a new dimension to definitions of blackness in the region. In Honduras, the presence of a foreign, West Indian "black" community broadened constructions of blackness. As a result, culture and not purely race became the mechanism by which black identity was defined. Black culture and Garífuna culture became synonymous. West Indian culture was often defined by the Garífuna as outside the scope of blackness. This dynamic adds a new dimension to the study of the black diaspora. Too often in black diaspora studies, the research has focused on tracing African tracks and retentions in the Americas in order to demonstrate the interconnectedness of the histories and experiences of Afro-descent peoples.[9] Such goals are important in creating a unifying dialogue among peoples of African descent. However, they do little to highlight the extent to which culture both strengthens and complicates discussions of race and identity within the African diaspora.

The cultural and political fragmentation that exists within the Afro-descent community in Honduras on the surface appears to exist solely among the dominant Garífuna, West Indian, and mestizo populations. However, this conflict exists within the backdrop of larger notions of empire, U.S. expansion, and the early stages of globalization. West Indians in Honduras, like most immigrants, were strangers in a fragile social and political environment, often at the mercy of outside forces for their safety and survival. Despite this, a community did flourish for roughly fifty years, remnants of which are still present on the North Coast. It is hoped that the history of this community in Honduras and its struggles for survival within the nation expand the process by which discussions of race, culture, and migration as they relate to people of African descent can be studied elsewhere in Latin America and beyond.

NOTES

INTRODUCTION

1. Works such as Nancie Gonzalez's *Sojourners of the Caribbean: Ethnogenesis and Ethnohistory of the Garífuna* (Urbana: University of Illinois Press, 1988); Ruy Galvão de Andrade Coelho, *Los Negros caribes de Honduras,* 2d ed. (Tegucigalpa: Editorial Guaymuras, 2002 [1981]); E. Salvador Suazo's *Los deportados de San Vicente* (Tegucigalpa; Editorial Guaymuras, 1997); and numerous other studies in the United States and Honduras have addressed the origins of Garífuna society in Honduras.

2. Kenneth V. Finney, "Rosario and the Election of 1887: The Political Economy of Mining in Honduras," *Hispanic American Historical Review* 59, 1 (February 1979): 81.

3. Mario R. Argueta, *El sector laboral hondureño durante la reforma liberal* (Tegucigalpa: Universitaria Autonoma de Honduras, 1981), 13.

4. Ross Graham, "The Bay Islands English: Stages in the Evolution of a Cultural Identity," in *English-Speaking Communities in Latin America,* ed. Oliver Marshall (New York: St. Martin's Press, 2000), 298.

5. For an analysis of the Anglo-Hispanic conflict in the Bay Islands, see William V. Davidson, *Historical Geography of the Bay Islands, Honduras: Anglo-Hispanic Conflict in the Western Caribbean* (Birmingham, AL: Southern University Press, 1974). In an effort to document the history and culture of the English-speaking peoples of the Bay Islands, Davidson explores the issue of preserving Bay Islands culture in a political and economic climate in which Honduran efforts to Hispanicize the islands, combined with North American tourism, facilitated the demise of the unique culture of the islands.

6. Marvin Barahona, *Evolución histórica de la identidad nacional* (Tegucigalpa: Editorial Guaymuras, 2002), 14–15.

7. See Darío Euraque, *Conversaciones historicas con el mestizaje y su identidad nacional en Honduras* (San Pedro Sula, Honduras: Centro Editorial, 2004). Chapters 5 and 6 are dedicated to issues of blackness in Honduras. In chapter 5 the author focuses on the mulatto communities in the town of Olanchito and chapter 6 is dedicated to the Garífuna experience. Within the context of focusing on the latter, Euraque speaks to relations between the

Garífuna and West Indian communities in Tela and La Ceiba during the height of West Indian settlement in the department of Atlántida during the early twentieth century.

8. Edmund T. Gordon, *Disparate Diasporas: Identity and Politics in an African Nicaraguan Community* (Austin: University of Texas Press, 1998), 30.

9. Euraque, *Conversaciones historicas,* 125.

10. Robinson Herrera notes the variation of slavery in Central America, particularly Guatemala in which Indian labor was exploited in the mines. African labor only became the preferred source of labor once the Spanish officially banned Indian slavery in the sixteenth century. Until then, African slavery was deemed unnecessary except to serve as a status symbol for the elite. See Robinson Herrera, "Porque no sabemos firmar: Black Slaves in Early Guatemala," *The Americas* 57, 2 (October 2000): 247–67. Rafael Leiva Vivas gives a more accurate depiction of the Honduran situation in which the importation of enslaved Africans into Honduras to regions such as Gracias a Dios, Puerto Caballos, Trujillo, San Pedro, Comayagua, and other areas increased in 1542 when the Spanish crown authorized the trade. See Rafael Leiva Vivas, *Tráfico de esclavos negros a Honduras* (Tegucigalpa: Editorial Guaymuras, 1987), 90–94.

11. Linda Newson, *The Cost of Conquest: Indian Decline in Honduras Under Spanish Rule* (Boulder, CO: Westview Press, 1986), 404. Though primarily a study on the indigenous population, Newson devotes attention to the establishment of African Maroon communities on the North Coast and La Mosquitia and the Afro-indigenous culture that emerged there. This culture is not to be confused with the Garífuna or black Carib culture that constitutes a majority in the region.

12. In his assessment of the concept of negritude within the Garífuna community, Euraque highlights the interactions between the Garífuna and West Indians. He maintains that West Indians were rejected not only by nonblack Hondurans, but by Garífuna as well. This was due largely to sociocultural differences and the preferred status of West Indians in the banana industry. See Euraque, *Conversaciones históricas,* 188. Elizet Payne Iglesias argues that the North Coast and the Bay Islands were instrumental in the development of Honduran conceptions of nationhood. She asserts that the obstacle for the North Coast was to create the characteristics of a homogenous identity in line with the rest of the country. This often led to violent encounters between mestizos and blacks as the assimilation of the latter was seen as a major hurdle. See Payne Iglesias, "Identidad y nación: El caso de la Costa Norte e Islas de la Bahía en Honduras, 1876–1930," *Mesoamerica* 42 (December 2001): 75–103.

13. Euraque, *Conversaciones históricas,* 186–90.

14. Aviva Chomsky, "West Indian Workers in Costa Rican Radical and Nationalist Ideology, 1900–1950," *Americas* 51, 1 (July 1994): 12.

15. John Soluri, *Banana Cultures: Agriculture, Consumption and Environmental Change in Honduras and the United States* (Austin: University of Texas Press, 2005), 76.

16. Michael Conniff, *Black Labor on a White Canal: Panama, 1904–1981* (Pittsburgh: University of Pittsburgh Press, 1985), 144. Conniff maintains that West Indians in Panama were not a united group due to the prevalence of interisland rivalries and the strategies of fruit companies to position West Indians against each other to maintain control.

17. Official Honduran census data from 1926, 1930, and 1935 list a foreign West Indian population that averages between 4,000 and 6,000 for these years. Subsequent data from fruit company records, British and U.S. diplomats, unofficial censuses, and works by scholars such as Elisavinda Echeverri-Gent estimate higher numbers. Echeverri-Gent suggests

upwards of 10,000 in her study. See Elisavinda Echeverri-Gent, "Forgotten Workers: British West Indians and the Early Days of the Banana Industry in Costa Rica and Honduras," *Journal of Latin American Studies* 24 (1992): 275–308.

18. See Aviva Chomsky, *West Indian Workers and the United Fruit Company in Costa Rica, 1870–1940* (Baton Rouge: Louisiana State University Press, 1996). Chomsky argues that West Indian artisans and labor unions carried out some of the first strikes in Costa Rica's history. The author emphasizes the predominance of the Jamaican element of the West Indian community within the movement. Philippe Bourgois in *Ethnicity at Work: Divided Labor on a Central American Banana Plantation* (Baltimore, MD: Johns Hopkins University Press, 1989) suggests that the West Indian community was divided, yet labor protest among the various elements of the population was significant.

19. Elisavinda Echeverri-Gent, "Labor, Class, and Political Representation: A Comparative Analysis of Honduras and Costa Rica" (Ph.D. diss., University of Chicago, 1988), 88.

20. Mario Posas, *Breve historia de las organizaciones sindicales de Honduras* (Tegucigalpa: Universidad Pedagógica Nacional Francisco Morazán, 2004), 11–15. Posas employs a Marxist interpretation of labor in which issues of labor and class eschew racial classifications. It is therefore impossible to determine if any of the early mutual aid societies on the North Coast had West Indian members. However, there is a long history of exclusive West Indian lodges and mutual aid societies within North Coast communities that is discussed in chapter 4 of this study.

21. Lester D. Langley and Thomas Schoonover, *The Banana Men: American Mercenaries and Enterpreneurs in Central America, 1880–1930* (Lexington: University Press of Kentucky, 1994), 24.

22. Thomas J. Dodd, *Tiburcio Carías: Portrait of a Honduran Political Leader* (Baton Rouge: Louisiana State University Press, 2005), 139. Tiburcio Carías Andino was the president of Honduras from 1932 to 1948. A controversial figure in Honduras, Carías was viewed by many as an embodiment of the *caudillo* tradition in Latin American politics. To others he was a beloved president. Still others saw him as a cruel, merciless dictator who catered to the interests of the U.S. fruit companies. Mario Argueta depicts Carías as somewhat of an opportunist who used communism and World War II to his benefit in order to garner the support of both the United States government and the UFCO. See Mario Argueta, *La gran huelga bananera: Los 69 días que estremecieron a Honduras* (Tegucigalpa: Editorial Universitaria, 1995), 13, and *Tiburcio Carías: Anatomía de una época, 1923–1948* (Tegucigalpa: Editorial Guaymuras, 1989), 235.

23. Arthur Adair Pollan, *United Fruit Company and Middle America* (New York: New School for Social Research, 1944), 4. The author served as the executive vice president of the United Fruit Company. Much of this work centers on emphasizing the positive benefits of UFCO investment in Central America.

24. Marvin Barahona, *El silencio quedó atrás: Testimonios de la huelga bananera de 1954* (Tegucigalpa: Editorial Guaymuras, 2004), 55.

25. Robert L. Shields, American Vice Consul, Tegucigalpa to Department of State (7/30/1951). Confidential Records Relating to the Internal Affairs of Honduras. U.S. National Archives and Research Administration, College Park, MD.

26. See Rafael Del Cid and Mario Posas, *La construcción del sector publico y del estado nacional en Honduras, 1876–1979* (Ciudad Universitaria Rodrigo Facio, Costa Rica: Editorial Universitaria Centroamericana, 1981), 69–82.

27. Ibid., 71.

28. Francisco Scarano and Lowell Gudmundson, "Conclusion: Imagining the Future of the Subaltern Past—Fragments of Race, Class, and Gender in Central America and the Hispanic Caribbean, 1850–1950," in *Identity and Struggle at the Margins of the Nation State: The Laboring Peoples of Central America and the Hispanic Caribbean*, ed. Aviva Chomsky and Aldo Lauira-Santiago (Chapel Hill, NC: Duke University Press, 1998), 336.

29. See Mark Anderson, "'Existe el racismo en Honduras?': Estereotipas mestizos y discursos Garífunas," *Mesoamérica* 42 (December 2001): 135–63. Anderson agues that racial and cultural blackness are often deployed by mestizos and others in Honduras to marginalize the Garífuna population politically, economically, and socially. Much of this is accomplished by non-Garífuna arguing that notions of mestizaje did away with racism, thereby denying the existence of racism, thus dismissing Garífuna claims of unequal treatment.

30. Michael Conniff, *Black Labor on a White Canal*, 3.

31. Paul Dosal, *Doing Business with the Dictators: A Political History of United Fruit in Guatemala, 1899–1944* (Wilmington, DE: Scholarly Resources, 1993), 121.

32. Stephen Glazer, *Caribbean Ethnicity Revisited* (New York: Gordon and Breach Science Publishers, 1985), 151.

33. H. Hoetnick, *Race and Color in the Caribbean* (Washington, D.C.: Woodrow Wilson International Center for Scholars, 1985), 16.

34. Bonham C. Richardson, *Panama Money in Barbados, 1900–1920* (Knoxville: University of Tennessee Press, 1985), 14.

35. Eve M. Troutt Powell, *A Different Shade of Colonialism: Egypt, Great Britain, and the Mastery of the Sudan* (Berkeley: University of California Press, 2003), 18.

36. Linda Basch et al., *Nations Unbound: Transnational Projects, Postcolonial Predicaments, and Deterritorialized Nation-States* (Amsterdam, The Netherlands: Gordon and Breach Publishers, 1994), 22.

37. Ibid.

1. THE HONDURAN LIBERAL REFORMS AND THE RISE OF WEST INDIAN MIGRATION

1. Darío Euraque, *Reinterpreting the Banana Republic: Region and State in Honduras, 1870–1972* (Chapel Hill: University of North Carolina Press, 1996), 13. In his assessment of why elites abandoned two of the most important coffee-growing regions in Honduras for the North Coast in the late nineteenth century, Euraque maintains that it was due less to impediments to coffee production such as land tenure, but rather to the enormous economic advantages in the burgeoning banana industry.

2. Kenneth V. Finney, "Rosario and the Election of 1887."

3. Marvin Barahona, *La hegemonía de los Estados Unidos en Honduras, 1907–1932* (Tegucigalpa: Centro de Documentación de Honduras, 1989), 41.

4. Darío Euraque, *Estado, poder, nacionalidad y raza en la historia de Honduras: Ensayos* (Obispado de Choluteca, Honduras: Ediciones Subivana, 1996), 12.

5. Darío Euraque maintains that one of the key agendas of the liberal reforms was the regeneration of agriculture, with special attention given from the 1890s onward to the export banana industry to the point that there was almost no opportunity for other agricultural enterprises to flourish. See Euraque, *Reinterpreting the Banana Republic*, 4.

6. Darío Euraque, "La 'reforma' liberal en Honduras y la hipótesis de la oligarquía ausente, 1870–1930," *Revista de historia* 23 (January–June 1991): 39.

7. Euraque, *Reinterpreting the Banana Republic,* 5.

8. Hector Perez Brignoli, "La reforma liberal en Honduras," *Cuadernos de ciencias sociales* 2 (1973): 6.

9. Irma Leticia de Oyuela, *Ramón Rosa: Plenitudes y desengaños* (Tegucigalpa: Editorial Guaymuras, 1994), 33.

10. Ibid.

11. See Brignoli, "La reforma liberal en Honduras," 14, and Euraque, *Reinterpreting the Banana Republic,* 7.

12. Payne Iglesias, "Identidad y nación," 89.

13. Lowell Gudmundson and Héctor Lindo-Fuentes, *Central America, 1821–1871: Liberalism Before Liberal Reform* (Tuscaloosa: University of Alabama Press, 1995), 82.

14. Brignoli, "La reforma liberal," 225.

15. See Taylor E. Mack, "Contraband Trade Through Trujillo, Honduras, 1720s–1782," *Yearbook, Conference of Latin American Geographers* 24 (1998): 50–52. This trade was predicated primarily on British demand for Honduran goods during their colonial exploits in the region. Once the Spanish successfully occupied Trujillo in 1782 and gained possession of Black River from the British in 1786, the contraband trade ceased to produce the enormous profits for smugglers.

16. Gudmundson and Lindo-Fuentes, *Central America,* 224. The Clayton Bulwer Treaty was an agreement between Great Britain and the United States to not seek exclusive control of any canal or territory on either side of such a canal that was to be built in Nicaragua. In addition, the two parties agreed not to fortify any position in the canal area and not to establish colonies in Central America. The treaty was viewed by many in the United States public as a violation of the Monroe Doctrine and many private citizens began private military campaigns (filibusters) to stake claims to the region. The most famous of these filibusters was William Walker.

17. Kenneth Bourne, "The Clayton-Bulwer Treaty and the Decline of British Opposition to the Territorial Expansion of the United States, 1857–1860," *Journal of Modern History* 33, 3 (September 1961): 287.

18. Albert Morlan, *A Hoosier in Honduras* (Indianapolis: El Dorado Publishing Co., 1897), 49. Morlan's account of Honduras, though very general, does make an attempt to discuss at length the role of the development of the banana industry in the country.

19. Frederick Upham Adams, *Conquest of the Tropics: The Story of the Creative Enterprises Conducted by the United Fruit Company* (New York: Arno Press, 1914), 218.

20. Euraque, *Reinterpreting the Banana Republic,* 7.

21. Langley and Schoonover, *The Banana Men,* 10–11.

22. Barahona, *La hegemonía de los Estados Unidos,* 42.

23. Euraque, "La 'reforma' liberal en Honduras," 18.

24. Mario Argueta and Edgardo Quiñones, *Historia de Honduras* (Tegucigalpa: Escuela Superior del Profesorado Francisco Morazan, 1980), 100.

25. James Mahoney, *The Legacies of Liberalism: Path Dependence and Political Regimes in Central America* (Baltimore, MD: Johns Hopkins University Press, 2001), 165.

26. Ibid., 176.

27. Alison Acker, *Honduras: The Making of a Banana Republic* (Boston: South End Press, 1988), 57.

28. Euraque, *Estado, poder, nacionalidad,* 12.

29. Langley and Schoonover, *The Banana Men,* 16.

30. Juan Aranciba C., *Honduras: ¿Un estado nacional?* (Tegucigalpa: Editorial Guaymuras, 2001), 35.

31. For an analysis of the mining industry during this period and the role of the New York and Honduras Rosario Mining Company in Honduras, see Kenneth V. Finney, *In Quest of El Dorado: Precious Metal Mining and the Modernization of Honduras, 1880–1900* (New York: Garland Publishing, Inc., 1987), and "Rosario and the Election of 1887."

32. Aranciba C., *Honduras: ¿Un estado nacional?* 34, 43.

33. Mahoney, *The Legacies of Liberalism,* 175–76.

34. Marco Virgilio Carias V., *La guerra del banano* (Tegucigalpa: Ediciones PAYSA, 1991), 13. Carias maintains that the over 100 Honduran-owned banana companies in operation before the North American domination of the industry were reduced to only 2 after 1910. Also, the author maintains that of all of the capital gained from the banana industry, only 6 percent of the earnings remained in the country in comparison to 50 percent remaining in other countries such as Costa Rica, Guatemala, and El Salvador. Clearly this author sees the Honduran case as unique.

35. Mario Posas, *Luchas del movimiento obrero Hondureño* (Ciudad Universitaria Rodrigo Facio, Costa Rica: Editorial Universitaria Centroamericana, 1981), 26. In addition to Honduran producers on the mainland, Ross Graham documents this trend in the Bay Islands dating back as early as 1850 in which Bay Islanders were producing bananas and selling them to U.S. merchant vessels destined for New Orleans. See Graham, "The Bay Islands English," 294.

36. Emily S. Rosenberg, *Spreading the American Dream: American Economic and Cultural Expansion, 1890–1945* (New York: Hill and Wang, 1982), 12. The author synthesizes her liberal developmentalism theory into five components: (1) Other nations could and should replicate America's own developmental experience. (2) Nations should instill faith in private free-enterprise. (3) There should be government support for free or open access for trade and investment. (4) Nations should promote the free flow of information and culture. (5) Nations should foster a growing acceptance of governmental activity to protect private enterprise, stimulate, and regulate American participation in international economic and cultural exchange. All of these factors come into play in the involvement of the U.S.-owned fruit companies in Honduras.

37. Steve Striffler, *In the Shadows of State and Capital: The United Fruit Company, Popular Struggle, and Agrarian Restructuring in Ecuador, 1900–1995* (Durham, NC: Duke University Press, 2002), 31.

38. Henry R. Blaney, *The Golden Caribbean: A Winter Visit to the Republics of Colombia, Costa Rica, Spanish Honduras, Belize and the Spanish Main via Boston and New Orleans* (Boston: Lee and Shepard Publishers, 1900), 89. Blaney was an independent traveler from New England. His report noted the rise in banana production on the North Coast at the turn of the twentieth century due to increased United States control of the industry. The author's analyses of the local situation are overly general and focus mainly on interpretations of the various republics based on contact with North Americans and Europeans. In

his assessment of Honduras, he fails to account for the presence of English-speaking Bay Islanders, Garífuna, or West Indians on the North Coast.

39. Ramon R. Isaguirre, *Through the Eyes of Diplomats: History of the Bay Islands, 1858–1895, United States Diplomatic Correspondence* (Comayagüela, Honduras: Multigráficos Flores, S. de R. L., 2003), 105.

40. Marcos Carías Zapata, "Honduras: La banana republic," in *Honduras: Del estado-nación a la democracia formal: Lecturas de historia de Honduras del siglo XX*, ed. Rubén Darío Paz (Tegucigalpa: Programa de Formación Continúa, Universidad Pedagogica Nacional Francisco Morazán, 2004), 80.

41. Antonio Canelas Díaz, *El estrangulamiento económica de La Ceiba, 1903–1965* (La Ceiba: Editorial ProCultura, 2001), 188. For more detailed accounts of the development of the Vaccaro Brothers and later Standard Fruit Company in La Ceiba, see Antonio Canelas Díaz, *La Ceiba, sus raices y su historia, 1810–1940* (La Ceiba: Tipografía Ranacimiento, 1999).

42. Mario Argueta, *Bananos y politica: Samuel Zemurray y la Cuyamel Fruit Company en Honduras* (Tegucigalpa: Editorial Universitaria, 1989), 34.

43. "Que se aprueba al traspaso de una concesión," July 1, 1911. Cuyamel Fruit Company Papers, Nettie Lee Benson Collection, University of Texas at Austin.

44. Rubén Bermúdez, "Hay que rehondureñizar Puerto Cortés," in *El drama del Ferrocarril nacional de los Hondureños, recopilación de artículos publicados en El Nacional* (San Pedro Sula, Honduras: Rubén Bermúdez, 1928), 45.

45. Ibid., 46.

46. See Del Cid and Posas, *La construcción*, 71.

47. Adams, *The Conquest of the Tropics*, 279.

48. Ibid., 281.

49. Ethel García Buchard, *Poder político, interés banano e identidad nacional en Centro América, un estudio comparativa: Costa Rica (1884–1938) y Honduras (1902–1958)* (Tegucigalpa: Editorial Universitaria, 1997), 27.

50. Ibid.

51. Antonio Murga Frasinetti, *Enclave y sociedad en Honduras* (Tegucigalpa: Universidad Nacional Autónoma de Honduras, 1978), 15.

52. Carías Zapata, "Honduras: La banana republic," 101.

53. Ibid., 100.

54. Payne Iglesias, "Identidad y nación," 86.

55. Richard Graham, ed., *The Idea of Race in Latin America, 1870–1940* (Austin: University of Texas Press, 1990), 2.

56. Nancy P. Appelbaum et al., *Race and Nation in Modern Latin America* (Chapel Hill: University of North Carolina Press, 2003), 4.

57. Ibid.

58. Ibid., 10.

59. Vincent C. Peloso and Barbara A. Tenenbaum, *Liberals, Politics, and Power: State Formation in Nineteenth-Century Latin America* (Athens: University of Georgia Press, 1996), 4.

60. David Bushnell and Neil Macaulay, *The Emergence of Latin America in the Nineteenth-Century* (New York: Oxford University Press, 1994), 295.

61. For a thorough analysis of the eugenics movement in Latin America, see Nancy Leys Stepan, *The Hour of Eugenics: Race, Gender, and Nation in Latin America* (Ithaca, NY:

Cornell University Press, 1991). Eileen Suárez Findlay's *Imposing Decency: The Politics of Sexuality and Race in Puerto Rico, 1870–1920* (Durham, NC: Duke University Press, 1999), offers a case study of eugenics methods applied in the racially diverse Caribbean island of Puerto Rico.

62. Graham, *The Idea of Race in Latin America*, 4.

63. Ibid.

64. For an analysis of how the racial democracy paradigm played out in Venezuela, see Winthrop R. Wright, *Café con Leche: Race, Class, and National Image in Venezuela* (Austin: University of Texas Press, 1990).

65. Peter Szok, *"La última gaviota:" Liberalism and Nostalgia in Early Twentieth-Century Panamá* (Westport, CT: Greenwood Press, 2001), 15.

66. Gudmundson and Lindo-Fuentes, *Central America, 1821–1871*, 86.

67. Gustavo Zelaya, *El legado de la reforma liberal* (Tegucigalpa: Editorial Guaymuras, 1996), 80.

68. Euraque, *Conversaciones historicas*, 79–80.

69. See George Reid Andrews, *The Afro-Argentines of Buenos Aires, 1800–1900* (Madison: University of Wisconsin Press, 1980). In this work, the author maintains that one of the factors for the decline in the Afro-Argentinian population, in addition to the end of the slave trade and high mortality and low fertility rates, was the very high death rates of black males during wars. This was especially the case with the military campaigns of President Rosas between 1830 and 1870.

70. Jorge Alberto Amaya Banegas, "Reimaginando la nación en Honduras: De la nación homogénea a la nación pluriétnica, los Negros Garífunas de Cristales" (Ph.D. diss., Universidad Complutense de Madrid, 2004), 239.

71. Marvin Barahona, "Del mestizaje a la diversidad etnica y cultural: La contribución del movimiento indígena y negro de Honduras," in *Memorias del mestizaje: Cultura politica en Centroamérica de 1920 al presente*, ed. Dario Euraque, Jeffrey L. Gould, and Charles R. Hale (Antigua, Guatemala: CIRMA, 2004), 249.

72. Ibid., 223–24.

73. See Peter Wade, *Race and Ethnicity in Latin America* (London: Pluto Press, 1997). The bulk of the work is dedicated to analysis of this racial dynamic in Latin American societies.

2. HONDURAN IMMIGRATION LEGISLATION AND THE RISE OF ANTI–WEST INDIAN SENTIMENT

1. George Reid Andrews, *Afro-Latin America, 1800–2000* (New York: Oxford University Press, 2004), 118.

2. Jorge Alberto Amaya Banegas, *Los Árabes y Palestinos en Honduras, 1900–1950* (Tegucigalpa: Editorial Guaymuras, 1997), 57.

3. Mario Argueta, *Los Alemanes en Honduras: Datos para su estudio* (Tegucigalpa: Centro de Documentación de Honduras, 1992), 11.

4. Barahona, *La hegemonía de los Estados Unidos*, 44. The 1866 "Law of Honduras Respecting Immigration" appears in E. G. Squier's *Honduras: Descriptive, Historical, and Statistical* (New York: AMS Press, 1970), 267–68. Squier's account was first published in 1870.

5. República de Honduras, "Constitución de le República de Honduras de 1865," ed.

Jorge A. Coello, *El digesto constitucional de Honduras* (Tegucigalpa: Archivo Nacional de Honduras, 1978), 283.

6. Barahona, *La hegemonía de los Estados Unidos*, 45.

7. Ibid. The exact wording of Rosa according to this source is as follows: "Necesitamos que vengan a nuestro suelo grandes corrientes de inmigración que traigan . . . el espiritú de empresa y el espiritú de libertad que han formado a los Estados Unidos de América."

8. República de Honduras, "Constitución de le República de Honduras de 1873," 312–13.

9. Ibid.

10. Andrews, *Afro-Latin America*, 136.

11. Barahona, *La hegemonía de los Estados Unidos*, 45.

12. Republica de Honduras, "Constitución de le República de Honduras de 1894," 358.

13. Ibid.

14. Barahona, *Evolución histórica*, 261.

15. República de Honduras, *Ley de Inmigración de 1906* (Tegucigalpa: Tipografía Nacional, 1906).

16. "Concesión," *La Gaceta* (Tegucigalpa), 10 December 1906, 553.

17. Ibid., 5.

18. Ibid., 6.

19. República de Honduras, *Ley de Inmigración de 1906*, 3.

20. Ibid.

21. "Ley de Policía," *La Gaceta* (Tegucigalpa), 10 February 1906, 73.

22. Gobernación of Colón to Gobernacion Política in Tegucigalpa, 21 January 1934, Correspondencia telegráfica del Departamento de Colón de Enero a Abril, 1934. Archivo Nacional de Honduras, Tegucigalpa.

23. Rachel McLaren of Puerto Castilla to Gobernacion Política in Tegucigalpa, 28 December 1934. Correspondencia telegráfica del Departamento de Colón de Septiembre a Diciembre, 1934. Archivo Nacional de Honduras, Tegucigalpa.

24. R. Romero, Gobernación de Colón to Gobernación Política in Tegucigalpa, 27–28 June 1934. Correspondencia telegráfica del Departamento de Colón de Mayo a Agosto, 1934. Archivo Nacional de Honduras, Tegucigalpa.

25. Bernardo Reyes, Gobernacion de Atlántida to Gobernación Política in Tegucigalpa, 17 August 1927. Telegramas, Departamento de Atlántida, 1927. Archivo Nacional de Honduras, Tegucigalpa.

26. González, Gobernación de Atlántida to Gobernación Política in Tegucigalpa, 10 August 1928. Telegramas de Departamento de Atlántida de 1928. Archivo Nacional de Honduras, Tegucigalpa. Also see "Informe del Gobernador Político del Departamento de Atlántida. La Ceiba, 28 October 1916," Francisco Mejía, Secretario de Estado. *Memoria de gobernación y justicia 1915–1916* (Tegucigalpa: Tipografia Nacional, 1917), 137.

27. Ibid.

28. Legajo: Gobernación Politica del Republica de Honduras. Departamento de Atlántida, La Ceiba. 2 July 1933. Archivo Nacional de Honduras, Tegucigalpa.

29. "Informe del Gobernador Político del Departamento de las Islas de la Bahía," Francisco Mejía, Secretario de Estado, *Memoria de gobernación y justicia 1915–1916* (Tegucigalpa: Tipografia Nacional, 1917), 153. Of the 213 crimes, 139 were committed on the island of Roatan. On the island of Utila, 27 crimes were committed, with 11 attributed to West Indians.

30. Ibid.

31. Ibid., 154.

32. "Informe del Gobernador Político del Departamento de las Islas de la Bahía," *Memoria de gobernación y justicia 1916–1917* (Tegucigalpa: Tipografía Nacional, 1917), 183.

33. "Ley sobre Misiones Consulares Extranjeras," *La Gaceta* (Tegucigalpa), 27 March 1906, 1.

34. William P. Garrety, American Consul at La Ceiba, Honduras, to the U.S. Secretary of State. Records Relating to the Internal Affairs of Honduras, La Ceiba, 1920. Record Group 59. U.S. National Archives and Records Administration II, College Park, MD.

35. Ramón Rosa Figueroa, Gobernación Política de Atlántida to Ministro de Gobernación in Tegucigalpa recognizing Herbert Adolphus Grant Watson as consul general of England in Honduras, 24 September 1928. Telegramas, Departamento de Atlántida de 1928. Archivo Nacional de Honduras, Tegucigalpa.

36. David J. Hill, Acting Secretary to James G. Bailey, Esquire, Secretary of State, 7/25/1902. Records Relating to Diplomatic Instructions of the Department of State, Central American States, 1801–1906, Record Group 59. U.S. National Archives and Records Administration II, College Park, MD.

37. "Foreigners in Honduras: Trading Under Difficulties," *The London Times,* 11 May 1928, 15.

38. Ibid.

39. U.S Acting Secretary of State to Sir Esme Howard, British Ambassador to the U.S., 26 July 1924, British Public Record Office, FO 115/ 2898, no. 222.

40. Foreign Office to Sir Esme Howard, British Ambassador to the United States, 28 July, 1924, British Public Record Office, FO 115/ 2898, no. 225.

41. Foreign Office to Sir Esme Howard, British Ambassador to the United States, 21 July 1924, British Public Record Office, FO 115/ 2898, no. 220. In this particular telegram, the consul at Trujillo reported that a strike of plantation laborers was taking place with a view of expelling the "colored population," mostly British subjects. The consul maintained that two subjects had already been wounded and four hundred had been displaced. In terms of diplomatic protection, there was none available. The only ordered protection, claimed the consul, was being maintained by armed American civilians.

42. "British Subjects Killed in Honduras: Compensation Claimed," *The London Times,* 3 September 1932, 9.

43. Jorge Alberto Amaya Banegas, *Los Judíos en Honduras* (Tegucigalpa: Editorial Guaymuras, 2000), 37.

44. Republic of Honduras, "Ley de Inmigración de 1934," *Recopilación de leyes migratorias y afines procedimientos prácticos* (Tegucigalpa: Departamento de Inmigración, 1967).

45. "Selected Documents Pertaining to Entrance Visas." Alcaldía Municipal de Olanchito, Departamento de Yoro, 1934–1947. Special thanks to Darío Euraque for allowing me access to his collections.

46. Irma Violeta Suazo Vásquez, "El extranjero ante la legislacion hondureña" (tesis por la licenciada, Universidad Nacional Autónoma de Honduras, 1974), 35–36.

47. Barahona, *El silencio quedó atrás,* 21.

48. Reverend Albert Brooks, pastor of La Iglesia Episcopal del Sanctísima Trinidad in La Ceiba, Honduras, interview by author, La Ceiba, Honduras, 7 October 2004. Rev. Brooks is a descendant of Jamaican and Caymanian immigrants who grew up in Tela.

49. Barahona, *El silencio quedó atrás,* 329.

50. Edwardo Hendricks James, Honduran of West Indian descent, interview by author, Tegucigalpa, Honduras, 28 February, 2005. Mr. Hendricks's father was a Bay Islander of Jamaican parentage who worked as a railroad engineer for the Standard Fruit and Steamship Company in La Ceiba, Honduras.

51. Barahona, *El silencio quedó atrás,* 92.

52. Jesús Aguilar Paz, "Problemas de la cultura Hondureña," *Revista de la universidad nacional autónoma de Honduras* 14, 2 (July–September 1950): 67. The concept of Indo-Spanish heritage most likely refers to those Hondurans of both Indian and Spanish heritage, in other words, the mestizo majority within the country.

53. Mario Posas, "La Huelga de 1954," in *Honduras: Del estado-nación a la democracia formal, lecturas de historia de Honduras del siglo XX,* ed. Rubén Darío Paz (Tegucigalpa: Programa de Formación Continúa UPN, 2004), 281. For a list of all thirty of the demands of the strikers, see "Peticiones de los huelguistas al gerenta general de la United," *El Día* (San Pedro Sula), 16 May 1954, 1–4.

54. Edwardo Hendricks James, Honduran of West Indian descent, interview by author, Tegucigalpa, 28 February 2005.

3. COUNTERING THE "BLACK INVASION"

1. "Alarmamente inmigración," *El Nuevo Tiempo* (Tegucigalpa), 14 November 1913, 3218.

2. "Inmigrantes innecesarios II," *El Nuevo Tiempo* (Tegucigalpa), 15 July 1916, 6490.

3. "Inmigrantes innecesarios III," *El Nuevo Tiempo* (Tegucigalpa), 18 July 1916, 6498.

4. Republic of Honduras, "Informe de gobernador político del Departamento de Cortés, 27 October 1916," in *Memoria de gobernación y justicia, 1915–16* (Tegucigalpa: Tipografía Nacional, 1917), 125.

5. José Antonio Funes, *Froylán Turcios y el modernismo en Honduras* (Tegucigalpa: Banco Central de Honduras, 2006), 98.

6. Republica de Honduras, *Memoria de gobernación y justicia presentada al Congreso Nacional Legislativo* (Tegucigalpa: Tipografía Nacional, 1909), 19.

7. *El Nuevo Tiempo* (Tegucigalpa), 31 October 1913, 3170.

8. Mario Posas, "El problema negro: Racismo y explotación en las bananeras," *Alcaravan* (September 9, 1981): 6.

9. *El Cronista* (Tegucigalpa), 30 September 1914, 3.

10. *El Cronista* (Tegucigalpa), 18 February 1914, 3.

11. "Se introducen 400 operarios de la raza negra cada mes," *La Gaceta* (Tegucigalpa), 8 October 1914, 365.

12. Franklin E. Morales to Assistant Secretary of State (12/11/1922). Records of the Department of State Relating to the Internal Affairs of Honduras, 1910–1929, Record Group 59, U.S. National Archives and Records Administration, College Park, MD.

13. "Conflictos en la Costa Norte," *El Cronista* (Tegucigalpa) (1916), reprinted in *Anales del Archivo Nacional* V (10 May 1971), 62–63.

14. Elisavinda Echeverri-Gent, "Forgotten Workers: British West Indians and the Early Days of the Banana Industry in Costa Rica and Honduras," *Journal of Latin American Studies* 24 (1992): 283.

15. Banegas, *Los Judíos en Honduras*, 39.

16. Alfredo León Gómez, *El escándolo del Ferrocarril: Ensayo histórico* (Tegucigalpa: Imprenta Soto, 1978), 129.

17. Echeverri-Gent, "Forgotten Workers," 279.

18. Barahona, *Evolución histórica*, 263.

19. Banegas, *Los Judíos en Honduras*, 39.

20. William E. Alger, U.S. Consul at Puerto Cortés, Honduras, to David J. Hill, Assistant Secretary of State (7/29/1902). Despatches from U.S. Consuls in Puerto Cortés, 1902–06, Record Group 59. U.S. National Archives and Records Administration II, College Park, MD.

21. Ibid.

22. A. E. Melhado, British Consul at Trujillo to British Consul General Armstrong, 18 October 1911, British Public Record Office, FO 632/ 15, no. 2193.

23. "Informe del gobernador político del departamento de Islas de la Bahía, Roatán, 26 de septiembre de 1917," in *Memoria de gobernación y justicia* (Tegucigalpa: Tipografía Nacional, 1916), 183.

24. Republic of Honduras, *Memoria de la Secretaría de Estado en el despacho de relaciones exteriores presenta al Congreso Nacional , 1920–1921* (Tegucigalpa: Tipografía Nacional, 1922), 20.

25. Ibid.

26. Robert Purdy, American consular agent at Tela, Honduras, to Frederick W. Job of Chicago (10/29/1920). Records of the Department of State Relating to the Internal Affairs of Honduras, 1910–1929, Record Group 59. U.S. National Archives and Records Administration II, College Park, MD.

27. " Proposed Law Restricting Negro Immigration." (1/12/1924). Records of the Department of State Relating to the Internal Affairs of Honduras, 1910–1929, Record Group 59. U.S. National Archives and Records Administration II, College Park, MD.

28. Republic of Honduras, *Memoria de relaciones exteriores presentada al Congreso Nacional 1926–1927* (Tegucigalpa: Tipografía Nacional, 1928), 36–37.

29. Echeverri-Gent, "Forgotten Workers," 283.

30. Dean R. Wood, U.S. Consul to Herbert H. D. Peirce, Assistant Secretary of State. (4/10/1905). Despatches from the U.S. Consuls in La Ceiba, Honduras, 1902–06, Record Group 59. U.S. National Archives and Records Administration II, College Park, MD.

31. Ramón E. Cruz, "La ley de inmigración y el problema de la raza negra en la Costa Norte," *Revista Ariel* (15 October 1926): 700.

32. Carlos González to Ministro de Gobernación Política en Tegucigalpa, 19 December 1928. Telegramas del Departamento de Atlántida de 1928. Archivo Nacional de Honduras, Tegucigalpa.

33. Records of the Department of State Relating to the Internal Affairs of Honduras, 1910–1929, (3/30/1929), Record Group 59. U.S. National Archives and Records Administration II, College Park, MD.

34. Ibid.

35. Republic of Honduras, *Memoria del Secretario de Estado de relaciones exteriores presentado al Congreso Nacional, 1915–1916* (Tegucigalpa: Tipografía Nacional, 1917), 21–22.

36. General Census of the Population of Honduras, 1926. Records of the Department of State Relating to the Internal Affairs of Honduras, 1928, Record Group 59. U.S. National Archives and Records Administration II, College Park, MD.

37. "Buena labor," *Diario del Norte* (San Pedro Sula), 7 September 1927, 1.

38. República de Honduras, *Resumen del censo general de población levantado el 29 de junio de 1930* (Tegucigalpa: Tipografía Nacional, 1932). Census data indicate that 9,964 Central Americans resided in Honduras legally. Of those, 7,692 were Salvadorans.

39. Echeverri-Gent, "Forgotten Workers," 283.

40. "Libro de Extranjeros en el país desde 1898–1926," *La Gaceta* (Tegucigalpa), 7 December 1927, 1.

41. Legajo: Correspondencia recibida de la Gobernación Político del Departamento de Atlántida, January–December 1930. Archivo Nacional de Honduras, Tegucigalpa.

42. "Inmigrantes innecesarios I," *El Nuevo Tiempo* (Tegucigalpa), 7 July 1916, 4514. Turcios maintained that companies did not have to look abroad for a source of labor because there were enough Hondurans to fill these positions. For Turcios, substituting foreign labor for the Honduran worker contributed to impoverishing the masses. This animosity against the foreign worker was only heightened when it was realized that most of the workers imported were blacks from the English-speaking Caribbean.

43. Jose Vasconcelos, "El Capital humano," *El Atlantico* (La Ceiba), 23 December 1926, 5.

44. Bourgois, *Ethnicity at Work*, 51. Though the author focuses on the views expressed by United Fruit Company employees in the Bocas del Toro and Limón provinces of Costa Rica, the hierarchy within the Honduran sections of the company reveals the same propensity to hire West Indians due to their perceived positive "character" traits.

45. Marcus Garvey, "The British West Indies in the Mirror of Civilization, History Making by Colonial Negroes," in *The Birth of Caribbean Civilization: A Century of Ideas about Culture and Identity, Nation and Society* (Kingston, Jamaica: Ian Randle Publishers, 2004), 317.

46. "Individuos escritos en el libro de registro de extranjeros de Atlántida." Legajo: Correspondencia recibida de los Gobernaciones Políticas (Jan.–Dec. 1930). Archivo Nacional de Honduras, Tegucigalpa.

47. Trujillo Railroad Company, "Informe de la Trujillo Railroad Company," in *Memoria de fomento, obras públicas, agricultura y trabajo, 1927–28* (Tegucigalpa: Tipografía Nacional, 1928), 109.

48. Froylán Turcios, "Explicación de nuestra síntesis patriótica," *Revista Ariel* 61, 4 (March 1, 1928): 1151. In this small piece, Turcios described what he viewed as true patriotism. For Turcios, internal conflict was equivalent to slavery because it promoted fratricide and created instability that allowed for foreign incursion into Honduran territory, which would ultimately reduce Honduras to neocolonial status. His efforts were described as an attempt to promote unity within Honduras in particular, and Central America in general, in order to ward off American economic imperialism. However, patriotism quickly turned into racism due to the fact that foreigners, specifically blacks, were viewed as agents of American imperialism.

49. Antonio Zozaya, "Patriotismo y humanismo," *El Cronista* (Tegucigalpa), 31 July 1933, 7.

50. Ibid.

51. "Extiende pasaporte a inmigrantes indeseables un Cónsul Hondureño," *El Pueblo* (Tegucigalpa), 12 March 1932, 5.

52. *El Pueblo* (Tegucigalpa), 12 September 1931, 2.

53. *El Pueblo* (Tegucigalpa), 14 March 1932, 6.

54. Alejandro Martínez, Gobernador de Colón to Ministro de Gobernación Política en Tegucigalpa, 10 August 1933. Correspondencia telegráfica del Departamento de Colón de 1933. Archivo Nacional de Honduras, Tegucigalpa.

55. Alejandro Martínez, Gobernador de Colón to Ministro de Gobernación Política en Tegucigalpa. (08/11/1933). Correspondencia telegráfica del Departamento de Colón de 1933. Archivo Nacional de Honduras, Tegucigalpa.

56. Matilde Reid of Puerto Castilla to Gobernación Politica in Tegucigalpa (08/04/1933). Correspondencia telegráfica del Departamento de Colón de 1933. Archivo Nacional de Honduras, Tegucigalpa.

57. *El Atlántico* (La Ceiba), 25 January 1931, 2.

58. Ibid.

59. "La united sustituye los hondureños con Negros de Jamaica," *El Pueblo* (Tegucigalpa), 12 March 1932, 8.

60. Ibid.

4. WEST INDIAN CULTURAL RETENTION AND COMMUNITY FORMATION ON THE NORTH COAST

1. O. Nigel Bolland, *Colonisation and Resistance in Belize: Essays in Historical Sociology* (Barbados, Jamaica, Trinidad and Tobago: University of the West Indies Press, 2003), 160.

2. Ibid., 163.

3. Wayne M. Clegern, *British Honduras: Colonial Dead End, 1859–1900* (Baton Rouge: Louisiana State University Press, 1967), 92. Clegern discusses the fact that Belize was represented at the New Orleans Expositions of 1885 and 1886 in an attempt to attract increased southern immigration to the colony following the failure of post–Civil War Confederate immigration to regenerate the economy. It was believed by many Belizean officials that sugar planters offered the best possible opportunity to galvanize the economy by introducing large-scale agriculture to the colony. Clegern discerns that nothing materialized out of this strategy.

4. O. Nigel Bolland, *The Formation of a Colonial Society: Belize, from Conquest to Colony* (Baltimore, MD: Johns Hopkins University Press, 1977), 135.

5. Ibid., 102.

6. Philip J. McLewin, *Power and Economic Change: The Response to Emancipation in Jamaica and British Guiana, 1840–1865* (New York: Garland Publishing, 1987), 167.

7. Dorsey E. Walker, "Some Realistic Aspects of the Progress of Jamaica, 1895–1947," *Journal of Negro Education* 20, 2 (Spring 1951): 150.

8. Patrick Bryan, *The Jamaican People, 1880–1902: Race, Class, and Social Control* (Kingston, Jamaica: University of the West Indies Press, 2000), 1.

9. Thomas C. Holt, *The Problem of Freedom: Race, Labor, and Politics in Jamaica and Britain, 1832–1938* (Baltimore, MD: Johns Hopkins University Press, 1992), 317.

10. Winston James, "Becoming the People's Poet: Claude McKay's Jamaican Years, 1889–1912," *Small Axe* 13 (March 2003): 20. The author maintains that there were 670 sugar estates in Jamaica in 1836. However, by 1910 the number of estates numbered a mere 74.

11. Elizabeth McLean Petras, *Jamaican Labor Migration: White Capital and Black Labor, 1850–1930* (Boulder, CO: Westview Press, 1988), 66.

12. "Slavery in Jamaica," *New Orleans Weekly Planner,* 15 January 1887, 4.

13. Theodore Sealy and Herbert Hart, *Jamaica's Banana Industry: A History of the Banana Industry with Particular Reference to the Part Played by the Jamaica Banana Producers Association, Ltd.* (Kingston, Jamaica: The Jamaica Banana Producers Association, 1984), 9.

14. Ibid., 11.

15. Peter Clegg, *The Caribbean Banana Trade: From Colonialism to Globalization* (New York: Palgrave MacMillan, 2002), 24.

16. Colonial Government of Jamaica, *Jamaica at the Worlds' Exposition: An Official Introduction to the Jamaica Court Containing a Short Description of the Island, its Productions, and its Climate* (Kingston, Jamaica: Office of Colonial Standards at Jamaica, 1884), 27.

17. D. Morris, *New Orleans Worlds' Exposition, 1884–1885: Agricultural and Industrial Products of the Island of Jamaica* (Kingston, Jamaica: DeCordova and Company, 1884), 4.

18. Holt, *The Problem of Freedom,* 316.

19. James, "Becoming the People's Poet," 20.

20. Michael Craton, *Founded upon the Seas: A History of the Cayman Islands and Their People* (Kingston, Jamaica: Ian Randle Publishers, 2003), 133.

21. Ibid., 134.

22. Ibid., 135.

23. Bonham C. Richardson, *Panama Money in Barbados, 1900–1920* (Knoxville: University of Tennessee Press, 1985), 88.

24. C. F. Pascoe, *Two Hundred Years of the S.P.G., An Historical Account of the Society for the Propagation of the Gospel in Foreign Parts* (London: Society for the Propagation of the Gospel, 1901), 238–39.

25. Díaz, *La Ceiba, sus raices y su historia,* 72.

26. Patrick Bryan, "Aiding Imperialism: White Baptists in Nineteenth-Century Jamaica," *Small Axe* 14 (May 2003): 138.

27. Laura Putnam, *The Company They Kept: Migrants and the Politics of Gender in Caribbean Costa Rica, 1870–1960* (Chapel Hill: University of North Carolina Press, 2002), 7.

28. John Soluri, "Landscape and Livelihood: An Agro-ecological History of Export Banana Growing in Honduras, 1870–1975" (Ph.D. diss., University of Michigan, 1998), 241.

29. Edwardo Hendricks James, interview by author, 28 February 2005, Tegucigalpa, Honduras. Mr. Hendricks is a Honduran of West Indian descent born and raised in La Ceiba. The city served as headquarters for the Standard Fruit and Steamship companies and reported some of the largest numbers of West Indians in the province of Atlántida, of which it is the capital. His parents hailed from Jamaica and Grand Cayman.

30. Putnam, *The Company They Kept,* 9.

31. Soluri, *Banana Cultures,* 135.

32. Register of Baptisms, 1915–1954, Church of the Holy Trinity, La Ceiba, Honduras.

33. Within the baptismal records, when a married couple was baptizing a child, the mother and the father had the same family surname. When the couple was not married, the mother's maiden name was always given. If the couple became legally married after the child was baptized, corrections were made to the baptismal record by crossing out the mother's maiden name and adding the name of the husband. This is witnessed in the case of Uriah Houghton and Gertrude Thompson, who baptized their son Frank on July 1, 1920, and were later married on August 26 of the same year. This was a rare occurrence, as most couples in this situation remained in common law unions.

34. Register of Baptisms, 1915–1954. Church of the Holy Trinity. La Ceiba, Honduras, 40, 51.
35. Ibid., 52–57.

36. Brian L. Moore and Michele A. Johnson, *Neither Led nor Driven: Contesting British Cultural Imperialism in Jamaica, 1865–1920* (Kingston, Jamaica: University of the West Indies Press, 2004), 100. The authors make reference to broader historiographical issues when focusing on marriage within Jamaican society in the nineteenth century. Most of the explanations given by intellectuals and travelers were couched in the Victorian missionary agenda of the period, in which the British sought to impose Victorian modes of marriage and gender, cultural, and societal organization in the hopes of bringing Jamaica and its predominantly Afro-descent population under the cultural umbrella of Britishness. Also see Catherine Hall, *Civilising Subjects: Metropole and Colony in the English Imagination, 1830–1867* (Chicago: University of Chicago Press, 2002). Patrick Bryan has also done work on this subject in which he relates the lack of marriage among Jamaicans to a resistance on the part of both men and women to Victorian ideals. To remain in unmarried unions allowed both parties to maintain a sense of independence.

37. Register of Marriages, 1915–1954, Church of the Holy Trinity, La Ceiba, Honduras.

38. Corrozal is a historically Garífuna community in close proximity to La Ceiba. San Juan is a community on the outskirts of Tela. Because the Church of the Holy Trinity was one of the more well-established West Indian churches in Honduras, many came from all over the North Coast to have ceremonies such as baptisms and marriages performed.

39. Frederick Douglass Opie, "Adios Jim Crow: Afro-North American Workers and the Guatemalan Railroad Workers League, 1884–1921" (Ph.D. diss., Syracuse University, 1999), 127.

40. Canelas Díaz, *La Ceiba, sus raices y su historia,* 68.

41. Alejandro Steel, "Alejandro Steel to contract marriage to Rosa May Coocke, 23 October 1925." Telegramas del Departamento de Atlántida de 1925. Archivo Nacional de Honduras, Tegucigalpa.

42. Cyril Augustis Francis, "Cyril Augustis Francis to contract marriage to Eugenia Sewill, 9 July 1928." Telegramas del Departamento de Atlántida de 1928. Archivo Nacional de Honduras, Tegucigalpa.

43. Nathaniel Samuell Murrell, "Dangerous Memories, Underdevelopment, and the Bible in the Colonial Caribbean Experience," in *Religion, Culture and Tradition in the Caribbean,* ed. Hemchand Gossai and Nathaniel Samuel Murrell (New York: St. Martin's Press, 2000), 10.

44. Patrick Bryan, "The White Minority in Jamaica at the End of the Nineteenth Century," in *The White Minority in the Caribbean,* ed. Howard Johnson and Karl Watson (Princeton, NJ: Markus Wiener Publishers, 1998), 124.

45. German Chávez, prod., *Negros Creoles de Tela* (Tegucigalpa: Universidad Pedagógica Nacional Francisco Morazán, 2003), video recording.

46. Robert Proctor, "Early Developments in Barbadian Education," *Journal of Negro Education* 49, 2 (Spring 1980): 190.

47. Ibid., 188.

48. Baron L. Piñeda, *Shipwrecked Identities: Navigating Race in Nicaragua's Mosquito Coast* (New Brunswick, NJ: Rutgers University Press, 2006), 3.

49. Nalini Persram, "The Importance of Being Cultural: Nationalist Thought and Jagan's Colonial World," *Small Axe* 15 (March 2004): 90.

50. Canelas Díaz, 69. Canelas maintains that this ban on the Spanish language within lodge functions lasted until 1945. By then, the majority of West Indians had already abandoned the city for the United States, the United Kingdom, and other areas.

51. Rand Garo, interview by author, 13 December 2004, Tela, Honduras.

52. Edwardo Hendricks James, interview by author, 28 February 2005, Tegucigalpa, Honduras.

53. D. Erastus Thorpe, "D. Erastus Thorpe, U.N.I.A. Divisional President and Commisioner, Tela, Spanish Honduras, to the Negro World," *The Negro World*, 4 March 1922.

54. Leonard Ivey, "Leonard Ivey, Secretary of El Porvenir U.N.I.A. Division to Adolphus Green of Monte Cristo," *The Negro World*, 26 November 1921.

55. William Garrety, American Consul at La Ceiba to the U.S. Secretary of State, 28 June 1920. Records Relating to the Internal Affairs of Honduras. Record Group 59. United States National Archives and Records Administration, College Park, MD. Consul Garrety referred to the UNIA in La Ceiba as the "Black Star Line," the name of the shipping company that the UNIA owned. Garrety noted that several meetings had been held in Ceiba in which "violent" speeches had been made against the white population, specifically in the United States. Such attacks on the U.S. would be problematic for West Indians who worked for the fruit companies, as their bosses were almost always white Americans. Garrety blamed the movement for all of the racial tensions in the United States and elsewhere. Negro agitation was cited specifically as the cause of racial tensions in La Ceiba. Although such assertions were far from the truth, Garrety's position was held by many in Honduras, black, white, or otherwise.

56. Ramón Amaya Amador, *Prisión verde* (El Progreso, Honduras: Editorial Ramón Amaya Amador, 2004), 46–47. Spanish: "blancos, indios, mestizos, negros y hasta algunos amarillos; saliteros del Golfo de Fonseca, tabaqueros de Copán, chalanes de los llanos de Olancho, morenos y zambos de Colón y la Mosquitia, isleños de Guanaja o de Roatán; de todos los rumbos del país y no pocos también de los demás de Centro América y Belice y de más allá."

57. Mark Moberg, *Myths of Ethnicity and Nation: Immigration, Work, and Identity in the Belize Banana Industry* (Knoxville: University of Tennessee Press, 1997), 12.

58. German Chávez, *Negros Creoles de Tela*, 2003.

59. Cruz Bermudez, interview by author, 13 December 2004, Tela, Honduras, and Gilberto Bermudez, interview by author, 14 December 2004, Tela, Honduras. The father of these two brothers was a Garífuna who worked as a timekeeper for the Tela Railroad Company. The reason he was able to obtain this job was because he could speak English. Both men maintained that learning English was essential in order to move up within the fruit company ranks. Those Hondurans who spoke English had the better jobs. Others were simply day laborers.

60. Ibid.

5. AN IMAGINED CITIZENRY

1. Jorge L. Giovanetti, "The Elusive Organization of Identity: Race, Religion, and Empire Among Caribbean Migrants in Cuba," *Small Axe* 19 (February 2006): 3. The towns of Baraguá, Banes, Chaparra, Delicias, and Jobabo were large centers of West Indian settlement

during the early decades of the twentieth century. Many of the West Indians, mostly Barbadians, Jamaicans, and Haitians, came to work in the sugar industry that was dominated by North American companies following the Spanish American War.

2. Trevor O'Reggio, *Between Alienation and Citizenship: The Evolution of Black West Indian Society in Panama, 1914–1964* (Lanham, MD: University Press of America, 2006), 81.

3. Olmaro Alfaro, *El peligro antillano en la América Central: La defensa de la raza* (Ciudád de Panamá: Imprenta Nacional, 1924). In this pamphlet, the author portrays West Indians in Panama as a threat to the national sovereignty of the nation and emphasizes blacks and other less desirables as enemies in the common struggle for political, cultural, and economic autonomy.

4. Bourgois, *Ethnicity at Work,* 94.

5. Catherine Hall, *Civilising Subjects: Metropole and Colony in the English Imagination, 1830–1867* (Chicago: University of Chicago Press, 2002), 58.

6. Ibid.

7. Sheena Boa, "'Setting the Law in Defiance': Urban Protests and Lieutenant-Governor Edward John Eyre in Post-Emancipation St. Vincent, 1838–1861," *Caribbean Studies* 30, 2: 130–70.

8. Ibid., 154.

9. Ibid., 141.

10. David Cannadine, *Ornamentalism: How the British Saw Their Empire* (New York: Oxford University Press, 2001), 11.

11. Ibid., 19.

12. Ransford W. Palmer, ed., *In Search of a Better Life: Perspectives on Migration from the Caribbean* (New York: Praeger, 1990), 3.

13. Eric Williams, in his classic assessment of the decline of the West Indies, argued that the economic decline in West Indian sugar profits was central to the British government's decision to abolish the slave trade in 1807. For Williams and his adherents, slavery's faltering profitability, not altruism or humanitarianism, mandated abolition. The demise of the sugar industry, the abolition of the slave trade, and subsequent emancipation in 1834 created a ravaged economy and a surplus of labor that fueled the labor market in the American-controlled agricultural and construction industries throughout the region. See Eric Williams, *Capitalism and Slavery* (Chapel Hill: University of North Carolina Press, 1994).

14. Elizabeth McLeon Petras, *Jamaican Labor Migration: White Capital and Black Labor, 1850–1930* (Boulder, CO: Westview Press, 1988), 66.

15. Benedict Anderson, *Imagined Communities: Reflections on the Origin and Spread of Nationalism* (New York: Verso, 1991), 6.

16. Echeverri-Gent, "Forgotten Workers," 299.

17. One Alexander Thurston is listed in State Department records four years prior to the La Masica incident as claiming U.S. citizenship. Many West Indians made such claims in the absence of British representation in the hopes that the United States government would advocate on their behalf. West Indians often highlighted shared language and the fact that they worked for U.S. companies as justification for protection. Such desires on the part of West Indians never materialized. For a list of those claiming U.S. citizenship in Honduras, see Dean R. Wood, U.S. Consul to Assistant Secretary of State Herbert H. D. Pierce (2/23/1906), Despatches from the U.S. Consuls in Puerto Cortes, 1902–1906, Record Group 59. U.S. National Archives and Records Administration, College Park, MD.

18. Arbitration before His Catholic Majesty the King of Spain—The Masica Incident, 4 April 1914, British Public Record Office, FO 881/ 1049X.

19. British Chargé d'Affaires Armstong, Tegucigalpa, to Foreign Office, 8 August 1911, British Public Record Office, FO 632/ 15, no. 2115.

20. British Chargé d'Affaires Armstong, Tegucigalpa, to General Manuel Bonilla, President of the Republic of Honduras, 6 May 1912, British Public Record Office, FO 632/ 15, no. 2474.

21. Arbitration before His Catholic Majesty the King of Spain—The Masica Incident (British Reply) 1917, British Public Record Office, FO 881/ 10587X.

22. Echeverri-Gent, "Forgotten Workers," 299. The incident is also recounted in numerous British Foreign Office documents. For a detailed account, see "Out Letters to His Majesty's Legation in Guatemala, Consuls and Foreign Office and Honduras Government Departments." British Chargé d'Affaires Jack Armstrong to Minister of Foreign Affairs Mariano Vazquez, 20 May 1912, British Public Record, FO 632/ 20, no. 2500.

23. British Chargé d'Affaires Armstrong to Godfrey Haggard, British Legation in Guatemala, 6 July 1912, British Public Record Office, FO 632/ 21, no. 2523.

24. The British chargé d'affaires in the capital city of Tegucigalpa dealt with broader diplomatic issues between the British and Honduran governments. His duties were very similar to those of an ambassador. He reported directly to the British Legation in Guatemala City, which remained the center of British representation in northern Central America.

25. British Chargé d'Affaires Armstrong to Godfrey Haggard, British Legation in Guatemala, 6 July 1912, British Public Record Office, FO 632/ 21, no. 2523. The reference to the character of Jamaicans in particular reaffirms the notion held by many within the British establishment that West Indians were morally degenerate and inassimilable into Anglo-Saxon notions of civilization.

26. Ibid.

27. Take for instance the claim of Aubry Spencer, a native of Jamaica, in Chiloteca, in which he claims that he was robbed by police of some seven ounces of gold at the time of his arrest. Claims like this were often unsubstantiated because it was always the word of the accused against the authorities. British Chargé d'Affaires Armstrong to Rafael Alvarado, Honduran Minister of Foreign Relations, 8 December 1911, British Public Record Office, FO 632/ 15, no. 2268.

28. Echeverri-Gent, "Forgotten Workers," 299.

29. British Chargé d'Affaires Armstrong to Godfrey Haggard, British Legation, 29 June 1912, British Public Record Office, FO 632/ 21, no. 2520.

30. Ibid.

31. Letter from British Vice Consul Tayelor to British Foreign Office, London, 20 May 1912, British Public Record Office, FO 632/ 21.

32. British Chargé d'Affaires Armstrong to British Legation in Guatemala, 24 June 1912, British Public Record Office, FO 632/ 21, no. 2520 B.

33. In 1924, Winifred Forbes requested that the British government file an indemnity claim against the Honduran government for the murder of her husband, Herbert Leslie Forbes, a native of Jamaica. Forbes's killer was tried and sentenced to ten years in prison, but his effects were never returned. The British government maintained that Winifred Forbes had no claim. See Petition of Winifred Forbes to Governor of Jamaica, 24 August 1924, British Public Record Office, FO 371/ 9523. Further, in 1924 a massive strike materialized in

Trujillo directed against blacks. Six West Indians were killed. The British sought no indemnity in any of the cases. See Foreign Office memorandum, Murder and Wounding of British Subjects in Honduras, 18 May, 1928, British Public Record Office, FO 371/ A 3400/ 3400/ 8.

34. His Majesty's Minister in Panama to the British Foreign Office, 25 October 1931, British Public Record Office, CO 318/ 404/ 13.

35. Ibid.

36. General Correspondence, 17 November 1931, British Public Record Office, CO 318/ 404/ 10.

37. H. Beckett, Colonial Office, to His Majesty's Representative in Havana, Cuba, 9 May 1933, British Public Record Office, CO 318/ 408/ 3.

38. Governor of British Honduras to Colonial Office, 14 April 1932, British Public Record Office, CO 318/ 406/ 1.

39. His Majesty's Minister in Panama to the Foreign Office, 25 November 1931, British Public Record Office, CO 318/ 404/ 13.

40. Governor Robertson, Barbados, to Sir Philip Cunliffe-Lister, 11 May 1932, British Public Record Office, CO 318/ 406/ 2.

41. Ibid.

42. Annual Report of the Central American Republics, 1936, British Public Record Office, FO 371 A 1787/ 1787/ 8.

43. British Chargé d'Affaires Armstrong to British Legation in Guatemala, 27 November 1911, British Public Record Office, FO 632/ 20, no. 2607.

44. British Chargé d'Affaires Armstrong to Mr. Camden, British Legation in Guatemala, 23 November 1911, British Public Record Office, FO 632/ 15 no. 2255.

6. ERADICATING THE BLACK PERIL

1. Banegas, *Los Judíos en Honduras*, 37.

2. Alarmamente Inmigración," *El Nuevo Tiempo* (Tegucigalpa), 14 November 1913, 3218. This article came out seven months after the Tela Railroad Company established operations in Honduras. The company received recognition from the Honduran government on February 20, 1913.

3. U.S. Consul at Tela, Honduras, to U.S. Department of State (11/21/1930), Confidential Records Relating to the Internal Affairs of Honduras. U.S. National Archives and Research Administration, College Park, MD.

4. C. Oury-Jackson, American Vice Consul at Tela, to Leo J. Keena, American Minister at Tegucigalpa (10/23/1936), Confidential Records Relating to the Internal Affairs of Honduras. U.S. National Archives and Research Administration, College Park, MD.

5. Stacy May and Galo Plaza, *The United Fruit Company in Latin America* (Washington, D.C.: National Planning Association, 1958), 225.

6. Taylor Mack, "Contraband Trade Through Trujillo, Honduras, 1720s-1782," *Yearbook, Conference of Latin Americanist Geographers* 24 (1998): 47.

7. Ibid., 48. Mack argues that although large amounts of both goods were shipped out of Trujillo, the trade did very little to restore wealth to the city.

8. Ibid., 50.

9. Manuel Rubio Sánchez, *Historia del puerto de Trujillo* (Tegucigalpa: Banco Central de Honduras, 1975), 173.

10. Paul Lokken, "Useful Enemies: Seventeenth-Century Piracy and the Rise of Pardo Militias in Spanish Central America," *Journal of Colonialism and Colonial History* 5, 2 (2004): 4. Though the Spanish did not officially endorse the idea of arming black and mulatto residents to defend Spanish colonial interests in Central America until 1612, the practice existed unofficially in Honduras from the 1590s. Lokken references the case of fourteen mulattoes and blacks who were compensated financially for their defense of Puerto de Caballos (Puerto Cortés) against French marauders as early as 1595.

11. Ibid., 8.

12. See *Censo de población del padron de Trujillo, 1821,* Archivo del Departamento de Colón. Special thanks to Darío Euraque for allowing me access to this census information that was discovered in the municipal archives of the city of Trujillo, Honduras. This census was taken just three years before the abolition of slavery in Central America in 1824. Of this population, only 39 of the 3,341 inhabitants were listed as enslaved. Of this enslaved population, 34 were listed as simply "moreno," while 2 were listed as originating from the Congo region of Africa, 1 from Guinea, and another listed simply as "negro africano." Only one of the enslaved Africans had an undetermined identity. All of the "moreno" slaves resided in the city of Trujillo, while the African-born slaves lived in the outlying areas of Quebrada Choro-Rio Negro, Caribal Grande, and Sabana de San Pedro.

13. Steve Striffler, "Wedded to Work: Class Struggles and Gendered Identities in the Restructuring of the Ecuadorian Banana Industry," *Identities* 6, 1 (1999): 96.

14. Steve Marquardt, "Green Havoc: Panama Disease, Environmental Change, and Labor Process in the Central American Banana Industry," *American Historical Review* 106, 1 (February 2001): 57.

15. Ibid., 49.

16. Gerald Meade, British Chargé d'Affaires to Tegucigalpa, compiled a report published September 5, 1935, and sent to the British Foreign Office in London that addressed the state of banana production and the conditions of the West Indian subjects of the British Empire in Honduras. See Gerald Meade, British Chargé d'Affaires to Tegucigalpa, to Sir Samuel Hoare, British Foreign Office in London, 5 September 1935, "Statistics Regarding Exports of Bananas During the Last Few Years," 11. Jamaican National Archives, Spanish Town.

17. Honduran officials acted to appease Honduran workers along the northern coast for fear that they would organize into communist-backed unions and incite rebellion in the region. When work was not available in the Trujillo–Puerta Castilla area, the government proposed sending workers to La Lima and Tela. However, the Tela Railroad Company, another United Fruit Company subsidiary, engaged in the same types of employment practices as the Trujillo Railroad Company and employed a substantial amount of West Indians.

18. Gerald Meade, British Chargé d'Affaires to Tegucigalpa, to Sir Samuel Hoare, British Foreign Office in London, 5 September 1935; "Statistics Regarding Exports of Bananas During the Last Few Years," 3; Jamaican National Archives, Spanish Town.

19. C. Oury-Jackson, American Vice Consul at Tela, to Leo J. Keena, American Minister at Tegucigalpa (1/25/1936). Confidential Records Relating to the Internal Affairs of Honduras. U.S. National Archives and Research Administration, College Park, MD.

20. Republic of Honduras, "Informe de Truxillo Railroad Company, Puerto Castilla, 6 de Septiembre de 1930," in *Memoria de fomento, obras públicas, agricultura y trabajo, 1929–1930* (Tegucigalpa: Tipografía Nacional, 1930), 71.

21. Republic of Honduras, "Informe de Truxillo Railroad Company de 1930–1931," in

Memoria de fomento, agricultura y trabajo, 1930–1931 (Tegucigalpa: Tipografía Litografica Nacional, 1931), 273.

22. Alejandro Martínez E., local government official at Puerto Castilla, to Gobernación Política in Tegucigalpa, 5 January, 1934. Correspondencia telegráfica del Departamento de Colón (January–April 1934). Archivo Nacional de Honduras, Tegucigalpa. Alejandro Martínez E. served as the head of the Gobernación Política at Puerto Castilla in the department of Colón, which also included the neighboring city of Trujillo. He was the highest-ranking Honduran government official in the area and frequently reported political concerns and inquiries to the national government at Tegucigalpa. Much of his correspondence was done by telegraph.

23. Alejandro Martínez E., local government official at Puerto Castilla, to Gobernación Política in Tegucigalpa, 26 January, 1934. Correspondencia telegráfica del Departamento de Colón (January–April 1934). Archivo Nacional de Honduras, Tegucigalpa.

24. Alejandro Martínez E., local government official at Puerto Castilla, to Gobernación Política in Tegucigalpa, 2 March 1934. Correspondencia telegráfica del Departamento de Colón (January–April 1934). Archivo Nacional de Honduras, Tegucigalpa.

25. Alejandro Martínez E., local government official at Puerto Castilla, to Gobernación Política in Tegucigalpa, 7 March 1934. Correspondencia telegráfica del Departamento de Colón (January–April 1934). Archivo Nacional de Honduras, Tegucigalpa.

26. Thomas F. O'Brien, *The Revolutionary Mission: American Enterprise in Latin America, 1900–1945* (New York: Cambridge University Press, 1996), 91.

27. Gerald Meade, British Chargé d'Affaires to Tegucigalpa, to Sir Samuel Hoare, British Foreign Office, 5 September 1935, "Report on the Labour Position in Honduras as it Relates to British Subjects," 7. Jamaican National Archives, Spanish Town.

28. Alejandro Martínez E., local government official at Puerto Castilla, to Gobernación Política in Tegucigalpa, 18 August 1933. Correspondencia telegráfica del Departamento de Colón (May–August 1933). Archivo Nacional de Honduras, Tegucigalpa.

29. Matilde Reid of Puerto Castilla to Gobernación Política in Tegucigalpa, 4 August 1933. Correspondencia telegráfica del Departamento de Colón (May–August 1933). Archivo Nacional de Honduras, Tegucigalpa. Matilde Reid was a West Indian woman working in the Trujillo–Puerto Castilla area. Her complaint stands out in that it was one of the few recorded instances in which a West Indian went directly to the Honduran government to request resolution to an immigration issue. Normally, West Indian complaints were handled by British government officials at satellite consular offices in Trujillo and La Ceiba, or through the British Legation at Guatemala City. Many West Indians also filed complaints with the British government at Belize, British Honduras.

30. Gerald Meade, British Chargé d'Affaires to Tegucigalpa, to Sir Samuel Hoare, British Foreign Office, 5 September 1935, "Report on the Labour Position in Honduras as it Relates to British Subjects," 5. Jamaican National Archives, Spanish Town.

31. Alejandro Martinez E., local government official in Puerto Castilla to Gobernación Política in Tegucigalpa, 22 January 1934. Correspondencia telegráfica del Departamento de Colón (January–April 1934). Archivo Nacional de Honduras, Tegucigalpa.

32. P. D. Parks, Assistant Vice-President of the United Fruit Company, to Vicente Williams, Consul General of Honduras, 1 August 1934, Legajo: Consulado General de Honduras en Nueva Orleans (January–December 1934). Archivo Nacional de Honduras, Tegucigalpa.

33. Consulado General de Honduras, Nueva Orleans, Luisiana: Solicitud de Pasaporte, Visa de Pasaporte—Dorothy May Davis, 7 August 1934, *Legajo: Consulado General de Honduras en Nueva Orleans* (January–December 1934). Archivo Nacional de Honduras, Tegucigalpa.

34. Consulado General de Honduras, Nueva Orleans, Luisiana: Solicitud de Pasaporte, Visa de Pasaporte—Richard Harvey Davis, Jr. and David John Davis, 5 June 1934, *Legajo: Consulado General de Honduras en Nueva Orleans* (January–December 1934). Archivo Nacional de Honduras, Tegucigalpa.

35. Consulado General de Honduras, Nueva Orleans, Luisiana: Solicitud de Pasaporte, Visa de Pasaporte—Charles Henry Collingwood Masters, 25 October 1934, *Legajo: Consulado General de Honduras en Nueva Orleans* (January–December 1934). Archivo Nacional de Honduras, Tegucigalpa.

36. "Sigue la Corriente de Inmigrantes Indeseables Entrando al Pais con Pasaporte de Nuestras Cónsules," *El Pueblo* (Tegucigalpa), 14 March 1932, 6.

37. Samuel MacClintock, "Refunding the Foreign Debt of Honduras," *Journal of Political Economy* 19, 3 (March 1911): 222–23.

38. Consulado General de Honduras, Nueva Orleans, Luisiana: Solicitud de Pasaporte, Visa de Pasaporte—Ines May Sharp Foster, 13 August 1934, *Legajo: Consulado General de Honduras en Nueva Orleans* (January–December 1934). Archivo Nacional de Honduras, Tegucigalpa.

39. Echeverri-Gent, "Labor, Class, and Political Representation," 87.

40. Holness C. Powell and sympathizers to British Foreign Office, London, 20 February 1939, British Public Record Office. FO 371/ A 2411/ 2411/ 8. The claim is made by one Holness C. Powell and the Bay Islands residents of Bonacca, Utila, and Roatan that British subjects were being shot for not appearing in military parade. The Honduran government voiced complaints that they were unable to arouse an army in the Bay Islands due to the failure of Bay Islanders to comply with the conscription policy of the government. As in most cases involving the Bay Islanders, it turns out that they were in fact Honduran and therefore, had no recourse with the British government. Bay Islanders had been maintaining the claim that they were British subjects. This was a carryover from the period of 1851–1859 when the islands were a British colony. Since 1859, the islands have been a part of Honduras and its inhabitants Honduran citizens. However, the islands are ethnically, linguistically, and culturally similar to the British Caribbean.

41. Euraque, *Conversaciones históricas,* 187.

42. C. Oury-Jackson, American Vice Consul at Tela, to Leo J. Keena, American Minister at Tegucigalpa (9/11/1936). Confidential Records Relating to the Internal Affairs of Honduras. U.S. National Archives and Research Administration, College Park, MD. In this particular correspondence, the vice consul reports that a baseball and soccer excursion made up of "colored" players and residents of Tela was threatened when the government rescinded travel permits for everyone except the players. The permits were previously granted by the authorities in Tegucigalpa. The vice consul describes a similar situation occurring in Puerto Cortés. The goal was to prevent contact between rebels and their sympathizers.

43. Consul David J. D. Myers, "Report on Convict and Other Compulsory Labor." Confidential Records of the US Department of State, 15 February 1930, 2.

44. Gerald Meade, British Chargé d'Affaires to Tegucigalpa, to Sir Samuel Hoare, British

Foreign Office. "Report on the Labour Position in Honduras as It Relates to British Subjects," 5 September 1935, Jamaican National Archives, Spanish Town, 5–6.

45. R. Romero, local government official in Trujillo, to Gobernación Política in Tegucigalpa, 11 September 1934. Correspondencia telegráfica del Departamento de Colón de Septiembre a Diciembre de 1934. Archivo Nacional de Honduras, Tegucigalpa. R. Romero replaced Alejandro Martínez E. as head of the Gobernación Política for the department of Colón. He was based at Trujillo.

46. Gloria Lara Pinto, *Perfil de los pueblos indígenes y negros de Honduras* (Tegucigalpa: Unidad Regional de Asistencia Técnica, Banco Mundial, 2002), 15.

47. May and Plaza, *The United Fruit Company in Latin America,* 208.

48. J. Manuel Ribaja, local government official in Trujillo, to Gobernación Política in Tegucigalpa, 11 September 1934. Correspondencia telegráfica del Departamento de Colón de Septiembre a Diciembre de 1934. Archivo Nacional de Honduras, Tegucigalpa. J. Manuel Ribaja was head of the Honduran police at Trujillo.

49. German Álvarez, interview by author, village of San Juan, Tela, Honduras, 15 December 2004. Mr. Alvarez grew up in the Garífuna barrio of San Juan on the outskirts of Tela, Honduras. His father made several trips to Belize by canoe in order to acquire goods that his mother sold in the Tela market.

50. Alejandro Martínez, local government official in Trujillo, to Gobernación Política in Tegucigalpa, 7 March 1934. Correspondencia telegráfica del Departamento de Colón de Enero a Abril de 1934. Archivo Nacional de Honduras, Tegucigalpa.

51. Moberg, *Myths of Ethnicity and Nation,* xvii.

52. Banegas, "Reimaginando," 239.

EPILOGUE

1. N. A. Rudolf, "A West Indian Problem," *West Indian Review* 1, 3 (November 1934): 3.

2. Ibid.

3. See Mark Anderson and Sarah England, "Auténtica Cultura africana en Honduras? Los Afrocentroamericanos desafían el mestizaje indohispano en Honduras," in *Memorias del mestizaje: Cultura política en Centroamérica de 1920 al presente,* ed. Dario Euraque, Jeffrey L. Gould, and Charles R. Hale (Ciudad de Guatemala: CIRMA, 2004), 259. The authors maintain that many West Indians immigrated to New York and other U.S. cities based on their connections with the fruit companies.

4. Wimberley DeR. Coarr, American Vice Consul at La Ceiba to Albert H. Cousins, Jr., American Consul at Tegucigalpa (8/25/1941). Confidential Records Relating to the Internal Affairs of Honduras. U.S. National Archives and Research Administration, College Park, MD. Coarr described a situation in which the personnel of the steamship line were multinational and polyglot. Few Hondurans were employed in this aspect of the company. However, those Hondurans employed were Bay Islanders.

5. Ramón Grosfoguel, "Puerto Ricans in the USA: A Comparative Approach," *Journal of Ethnic and Migration Studies* 25, 2 (April 1999): 239.

6. Michael B. Katz, Mark J. Stern, and Jamie J. Fader, "The Mexican Immigration Debate: The View from History," *Social Science History* 31, 2 (Summer 2007): 158.

7. Stuart Hall, "Thinking the Diaspora: Home—Thoughts from Abroad," *Small Axe* 6 (September 1999): 3.

8. Rose-Marie Chierici, "Caribbean Migration in the Age of Globalization: Transnationalism, Race, and Ethnic Identity," *Reviews in Anthropology* 33 (2004): 45. The author expands on this concept of cultural continuity based on the work of Michel Laguerre in his work on Haitian Americans in the United States. See Michel S. Laguerre, *Diasporic Citizen: Haitian Americans in Transnational America* (New York: St. Martin's Press, 1998).

9. Ronald Segal, *The Black Diaspora* (New York: Farrar, Straus and Giroux, 1995), xiii.

BIBLIOGRAPHY

ARCHIVAL SOURCES—UNITED STATES

Hispanic Division, Library of Congress, Washington, D.C.

República de Honduras. *La población de Honduras en 1901*. Tegucigalpa: Tipografia Nacional, 1902.

República de Honduras. *La poblacion de Honduras en 1905*. Tegucigalpa: Tipografia Nacional, 1906.

República de Honduras. *Resumen del censo general de población levantado el 29 de junio de 1930*. Tegucigalpa, Honduras: Tipografia Nacional, 1932.

República de Honduras. *Resumen del censo general de población levantado el 30 de junio de 1935*. Tegucigalpa, Honduras: Tallero Tipograficos Nacionales, 1936.

República de Honduras. *Resumen del censo general de población levantado el 24 de junio de 1945*. Tegucigalpa, Honduras: Talleres Tipograficos Nacionales, 1947.

Manuscript Division, Library of Congress, Washington, D.C.

Papers of Charles Evans Hughes, 1905–1940.

Papers of Paul J. Pelz, investor in the Honduran Aurora Mining Company, 1890–1917.

National Archives and Research Administration II, College Park, Maryland

Confidential Records of the Department of State Relating to the Internal Affairs of Honduras, 1928–1956.

Diplomatic Instructions of Department of State, Central American States, June 1900–August 1906.

General Census of the Population of Honduras, 1926.

Records of the Department of State Relating to the Internal Affairs of Honduras, La Ceiba, 1902–1906.

Records of the Department of State Relating to the Internal Affairs of Honduras, Omoa, Trujillo, and Roatán, 1831–1893.

Records of the Department of State Relating to the Internal Affairs of Honduras, Puerto Cortés, 1902–1906.

Records of the Department of State Relating to the Internal Affairs of Honduras, Tegucigalpa, 1860–1906.

Records of the Department of State Relating to the Internal Affairs of Honduras, Utila, 1903–1906.

Records of the Department of State Relating to the Internal Affairs of Honduras, 1928.

Records of the Department of State Relating to the Internal Affairs of Honduras, 1930–1939.

University of Texas at Austin, Nettie Lee Benson Latin American Collection

Cuyamel Fruit Company Papers.

Tulane University, New Orleans, Louisiana

Standard Fruit and Steamship Company Papers.

ARCHIVAL SOURCES—HONDURAS

Archivo National de Honduras, Tegucigalpa

República de Honduras. "Constitución de le República de Honduras de 1865." Ed. Jorge A. Coello, *El digesto constitucional de Honduras.*

Legajos
Consulado General de Honduras en Nueva Orleans, 1934.

Correspondencia Recibido de la Policía Nacional, 1934.

Cuentas del Cónsul de Honduras en Panamá, por servicio postal en los vapores, 1923–1929.

Gobernacion Política del República, 1933, 1934.

Informe Estadística Nacional, 1933–1943.

La Dirección General de Estadística, 1937–1938.

Libro copiador de varias notas de Ministerio de Gobernación, 1923.

Ministerio de Relaciones Exteriores, Notas Varias, 1913–1918.

Ministerio de Relaciones Exteriores, Varias Notas, 1933.

Memorias and Informes

"Informe del Gobernador Político del Departamento de Atlántida. La Ceiba, 28 October 1916." Francisco Mejía, Secretario de Estado. *Memoria de gobernación y justicia 1915–1916*. Tegucigalpa: Tipografía Nacional, 1917.

Memoria del Secretario de Estado en despacho de relaciones exteriores por Dr. Mariano Vasquez presentado al Congreso Nacional, 1915–16. Tegucigalpa: Tipografía Nacional, 1917.

Memoria de la Secretaría de Estado en el despacho de relaciones exteriores presenta al Congreso Nacional por el Licenciado Don Antonio R. Reina h., Secretario de Estado, por Ministerio de la Ley, 1920–21. Tegucigalpa: Tipografía Nacional, 1922

Memoria de la Secretaría de Estado de relaciones exteriores por Dr. Don Salvador Zelaya presentada al Congreso Nacional, 1930–31. Tegucigalpa: Tipografía Nacional, 1932.

Memoria de la Secretaría de Estado de relaciones exteriores presentada al Congreso Nacional por Dr. Don Antonio Mermudez M., 1933–34. Tegucigalpa: Tipografía Nacional, 1935.

Memoria de la Secretaría de Estado de relaciones exteriores presentada al Congreso Nacional, 1926–27. Secretario de Estado por la Ley Augusto C. Coello. Tegucigalpa: Tipografía Nacional, 1928.

Memoria de la Secretaría de Estado de relaciones exteriores, 1925–26, Secretario de Estado Dr. Fausto Davila, Tegucigalpa: Tipografía Nacional, 1927.

Republica de Honduras. Departamento de Inmigración. *Recopilación de leyes migratorios y afines procedimientos practicos*. Tegucigalpa: Departamento de Inmigración, 1967.

Republica de Honduras. "Informe de Truxillo Railroad Company, Puerto Castilla, 6 de Septiembre de 1930." In *Memoria de fomento, obras públicas, agricultura y trabajo, 1929–1930*. Tegucigalpa: Tipografía Nacional, 1930.

Republica de Honduras. "Informe de Truxillo Railroad Company de 1930–1931." In *Memoria de fomento, agricultura y trabajo, 1930–1931*. Tegucigalpa: Tipografía Litografica Nacional, 1931. Republica de Honduras. *Memoria de gobernación y justicia presentada al Congreso Nacional Legislativo*. Tegucigalpa: Tipografía Nacional, 1909.

Trujillo Railroad Company. "Informe de la Trujillo Railroad Company," in *Memoria de fomento, obras públicas, agricultura y trabajo, 1927–28*. Tegucigalpa: Tipografía Nacional, 1928.

Telegramas

Correspondencia telegráfica, Departamento de Atlántida, 1927–1928.

Correspondencia telegráfica, Departamento de Colón, 1933.

Correspondencia telegráfica, Departamento de Colón, 1934.

Correspondencia telegráfica, Departamento de Cortés, 1927–1928.

Church Records

Register of Marriages, 1915–1954. Church of the Holy Trinity. La Ceiba, Honduras.

Newspapers and Periodicals

Anales del Archivo Nacional
Boletin de la Oficina de Inmigración y Colonización, 1930–1931
Diario del Norte
El Atlantico
El Cronista
El Nuevo Tiempo
El Pueblo
El Sol
La Gaceta
La Tribuna
Reconciliación
Revista Ariel
Revista Imaginación

ARCHIVAL SOURCES—GREAT BRITAIN

British National Archives—Kew, Richmond, Surrey

FO 371/ 81457   Labour organisation and problems in Honduras (1950).
FO 371/ 90769   Labour situation and social and labour legislation in Honduras (1951).
FO 371/ 108984   Plans for evacuation of British subjects from Honduras in event of an emergency (1954).
FO 371/ 108988   Strike by United Fruit Company workers in Honduras (1954).
FO 371/ 22733   Treatment of British subjects in Honduras (1939).
FO 881/ 10491X   Honduras: Arbitration. Masica incident-memorial of H. M. Government reply and award (1914).
FO 881/ 10587X   Honduras. Arbitration. Masica incident, British reply (1914).
FO 369/ 2924   British Honduras labourers, repatriation of (1943).
FO 369/ 4538   Honduras. Arrest and detention of British subjects (1950).
FO 115/ 2898   Honduras-Immigration. Nos. 1–11 (1924).
FO 115/ 3168   Honduras-Immigration. Nos. 1–33 (1927).
FO 632/ 15   Out Letters to H. M. Legation Guatemala, Consuls and Foreign Office and Honduras Government Departments. July–December (1911).

FO 632/ 20   Out Letters to H. M. Legation Guatemala, Consuls and Foreign Office and Honduras Government Departments. January–June (1912).

FO 632/ 21   Out Letters to H. M. Legation Guatemala, Consuls and Foreign Office and Honduras Government Departments. June–December (1912).

INTERVIEWS

Alvarez, German, Garífuna resident of the village of San Juan and alumnus of the English School in Tela. Interview by author, 15 December 2004, San Juan, Tela, Honduras.

Bermúdez, Cruz, Garífuna artist and long-time resident of Tela, Honduras. Interview by author, 13 December 2004, Tela, Honduras.

Bermúdez, Gilberto, Garífuna artist and long-time resident of Tela, Honduras. Interview by author, 14 December 2004, Tela, Honduras.

Brooks, Reverendo E. Albert, a descendant of Jamaican immigrants and pastor of Iglesia Episcopal de Sanctísima Trinidad, La Ceiba. Interview by author, 7 October 2004, La Ceiba, Honduras.

Garo, Rand, a descendant of English-speaking blacks from Bluefields, Nicaragua, and long-time Tela R.R. Company employee. Interview by author, 13 December 2004, Tela, Honduras.

Hendricks, James Edwardo, Honduran of West Indian descent who grew up in La Ceiba. Interview by author, 28 February 2005, Tegucigalpa, Honduras.

SECONDARY SOURCES

BOOKS

Acker, Alison. *Honduras: The Making of a Banana Republic.* Boston: South End Press, 1988.

Adams, Frederick Upham. *Conquest of the Tropics: The Story of the Creative Enterprises Conducted by the United Fruit Company.* New York: Arno Press, 1976 [1914].

Alfaro, Olmedo. *El Peligro Antillano en la América Central: La Defensa de la Raza.* Ciudad de Panamá: Imprenta Nacional, 1924.

Amaya Amador, Ramon. *Prisión verde.* El Progreso, Honduras: Editorial Ramón Amaya Amador, 2004.

Amaya Banegas, Jorge Alberto. *Los Árabes y Palestinos en Honduras, 1900–1950.* Tegucigalpa: Editorial Guaymuras, 1997.

————. *Los Chinos de Ultramar en Honduras.* Tegucigalpa: Editorial Guaymuras, 2002.

————. *Los Judíos en Honduras.* Tegucigalpa: Editorial Guaymuras, 2000.

Anderson, Benedict. *Imagined Communities: Reflections on the Origin and Spread of Nationalism.* New York: Verso, 1991.

Anderson, Mark, and Sarah England. "Auténtica cultura africana en Honduras? Los Afrocentroamericanos desafían el mestizaje indohispano en Honduras." In *Memorias del mestizaje: Cultura política en Centroamérica de 1920 al presente,* ed. Dario Euraque, Jeffrey L. Gould, and Charles R. Hale. Ciudad de Guatemala: CIRMA, 2004.

Andrade Coelho, Ruy Galvão de. *Los negros caribes de Honduras,* 2d ed. Tegucigalpa: Editorial Guaymuras, 2002 [1981].

Andrews, George Reid. The *Afro-Argentines of Buenos Aires, 1800–1900.* Madison: University of Wisconsin Press, 1980.

————. *Afro-Latin America, 1800–2000.* New York: Oxford University Press, 2004.

Appelbaum, Nancy P., et al. *Race and Nation in Modern Latin America.* Chapel Hill: University of North Carolina Press, 2003.

Aranciba C., Juan *Honduras: ¿Un estado nacional?* Tegucigalpa: Editorial Guaymuras, 2001.

Archivo Nacional de Honduras. *Indice de impresos del siglo XIX.* Tegucigalpa: Instituto Hondureño del Libro y el Documento, Archivo Nacional de Honduras, 1995.

Argueta, Mario. *Bananos y politica: Samuel Zemurray y la Cuyamel Fruit Company en Honduras.* Tegucigalpa: Editorial Universitaria, 1989.

————. *Historia de los sin historia, 1900–1948.* Tegucigalpa: Editorial Guaymuras, 1992.

————. *La gran huelga bananera: Los 69 días que estremecieron a Honduras.* Tegucigalpa: Editorial Universitaria, 1995.

————. *Los Alemanes en Honduras: Datos para su estudio.* Tegucigalpa: Centro de Documentación de Honduras, 1992.

————. *El sector laboral hondureño durante la reforma liberal.* Tegucigalpa: Editorial Universitaria, 1981.

————. *Tiburcio Carías: Anatomía de una época, 1923–1948.* Tegucigalpa: Editorial Guaymuras, 1989.

Argueta, Mario, and Edgardo Quiñones. *Historia de Honduras.* Tegucigalpa: Escuela Superior del Profesorado Francisco Morazan, 1979.

Arnesen, Eric. *Black Protest and the Great Migration.* New York: St. Martin's Press, 2003.

————. *Waterfront Workers of New Orleans: Race, Class, and Politics, 1863–1923.* New York: Oxford University Press, 1991.

Azevedo, Mario. *Africana Studies: A Survey of Africa and the African Diaspora,* 3d ed. Durham, NC: Carolina Academic Press, 2005.

Barahona, Marvin. *El Silencio quedó atras: Testimonios de la huelga bananera de 1954*. Tegucigalpa: Editorial Honduras, 2004.

———. *Evolución histórica de la identidad nacional*. Tegucigalpa: Editorial Guaymuras, 1991.

———. *La Hegemonía de los Estados Unidos en Honduras (1907–1932)*. Tegucigalpa: Centro de Documentación de Honduras, 1989.

———. "Del mestizaje a la diversidad etnica y cultural: La contribución del movimiento indígena y negro de Honduras." In *Memorias del mestizaje: Cultura política en Centroamérica de 1920 al presente*, ed. Dario Euraque, Jeffrey L. Gould, and Charles R. Hale. Antigua, Guatemala: CIRMA, 2004.

Basch, Linda, et al. *Nations Unbound: Transnational Projects, Postcolonial Predicaments, and Deterritorialized Nation-States*. Amsterdam, The Netherlands: Gordon and Breach Publishers, 1994.

Bell, Wendell, and Walter E. Freeman, eds. *Ethnicity and Nation-Building: Comparative, International, and Historical Perspectives*. Beverly Hills, CA: Sage Publications, 1974.

Bermúdez, Rubén. "Hay que rehondureñizar Puerto Cortés." In *El drama del Ferrocarril nacional de los Hondureños, recopilación de artículos publicados en El Nacional*. San Pedro Sula, Honduras: Rubén Bermúdez, 1928.

Bisnauth, Dale. *History of Religions in the Caribbean*. Trenton, NJ: Africa World Press, 1996.

Blaney, Henry R. *The Golden Caribbean: A Winter Visit to the Republics of Colombia, Costa Rica, Spanish Honduras, Belize and the Spanish Main via Boston and New Orleans*. Boston: Lee and Shepard Publishers, 1900.

Blassingame, John W. *Black New Orleans*. Chicago, IL: University of Chicago Press, 1973.

Bolland, O. Nigel. *Colonisation and Resistance in Belize: Essays in Historical Sociology*. Barbados, Jamaica, Trinidad and Tobago: University of the West Indies Press, 2003.

———. *The Formation of a Colonial Society: Belize, from Conquest to Colony*. Baltimore, MD: Johns Hopkins University Press, 1977.

———. *On the March: Labour Rebellions in the British Caribbean, 1934–1939*. Kingston, Jamaica: Ian Randle Publishers, 1995.

———. *The Politics of Labour in the British Caribbean*. Princeton, NJ: Markus Wiener Publishers, 2001.

Bourgois, Philippe I. *Ethnicity at Work: Divided Labor on a Central American Banana Plantation*. Baltimore, MD: Johns Hopkins University Press, 1989.

Brasseaux, Carl, et al. *Creoles of Color in the Bayou Country*. Jackson: University of Mississippi Press, 1994.

Brignoli, Hector Pérez. *A Brief History of Central America*. Berkeley: University of California Press, 1989.

Bryan, Patrick. *The Jamaican People, 1880–1902: Race, Class, and Social Control*. Kingston, Jamaica: University of the West Indies Press, 2000.

———. "The White Minority in Jamaica at the End of the Nineteenth Century." In *The White Minority in the Caribbean,* ed. Howard Johnson and Karl Watson. Princeton, NJ: Markus Wiener Publishers, 1998.

Buchard, Ethel García. *Poder político, interés bananero e identidad nacional en Centro América, un estudio comparativo: Costa Rica (1884–1938) y Honduras (1902–1958).* Tegucigalpa: Editorial Universitaria, 1997.

Burns, E. Bradford. *The Poverty of Progress: Latin America in the Nineteenth Century.* Berkeley: University of California Press, 1980.

Bushnell, David, and Neil Macaulay. *The Emergence of Latin America in the Nineteenth-Century.* New York: Oxford University Press, 1994.

Butler, Kim D. *Freedoms Given, Freedoms Won: Afro-Brazilians in Post-Abolition Sao Paulo and Salvador.* New Brunswick, NJ: Rutgers University Press, 2000.

Canelas Díaz, Antonio. *El estrangulamiento económica de La Ceiba, 1903–1965.* La Ceiba, Honduras: Editorial ProCultura, 2001.

———. *La Ceiba, sus raices y su historia, 1810–1940.* La Ceiba, Honduras: Tipografia Renacimiento, 1999.

Cannadine, David. *Ornamentalism: How the British Saw Their Empire.* New York: Oxford University Press, 2001.

Carías, Virgilio, and Victor Meza. *Compañías bananeras en Honduras: Un poco de historia.* Tegucigalpa: Instituto de Investigaciones Económicas y Sociales-UNAH, 1982.

Carías V., Marco Virgilio. *La guerra del banano.* Tegucigalpa: Ediciones PAYSA, 1991.

Carías Zapata, Marcos. "Honduras: La banana republic." In *Honduras: Del estado-nación a la democracia formal: Lecturas de historia de Honduras del siglo XX,* ed. Rubén Darío Paz. Tegucigalpa: Programa de Formación Continúa, Universidad Pedagogica Nacional Francisco Morazán, 2004.

Casanova, Pablo González, and Marcos Roitman Rosenmann, coodinadores. *La democracia en America Latina: Actualidad y perspectivas.* Madrid, España: Editorial Complutense, 1992.

Casey Gaspar, Jeffrey. *Limón, 1880–1940: Un estudio de la industria bananera.* San José: Editorial Costa Rica, 1979.

Cavero, Manuel. *Guaymura: Truxillo, Truxillo.* Trujillo: Sociedad Paulinos, 1976.

Centeno García, Santos. *Historia del movimiento negro hondureño.* Tegucigalpa: Editorial Guaymuras, 1997.

———. *Historia del Pueblo Negro Caribe y su llegada a Hibueras el 12 de abril de 1797.* Tegucigalpa: Editorial Universitaria, 1996.

Chala, Santiago Valencia. *El Negro en Centroamerica.* Quito, Ecuador: Ediciones Abya-Yala, 1986.

Chamberlain, Mary, ed. *Caribbean Migration: Globalised Identities.* London: Routledge, 1998.

Chomsky, Aviva. *West Indian Workers and the United Fruit Company in Costa Rica, 1870–1940.* Baton Rouge: Louisiana State University Press, 1996.

Chomsky, Aviva, and Aldo Lauira-Santiago, eds. *Identity and Struggle at the Margins of the Nation State: The Laboring Peoples of Central America and the Hispanic Caribbean.* Durham, NC: Duke University Press, 1998.

Clegern, Wayne M. *British Honduras: Colonial Dead End, 1859–1900.* Baton Rouge: Louisiana State University Press, 1967.

Clegg, Peter. *The Caribbean Banana Trade: From Colonialism to Globalization.* New York: Palgrave MacMillan, 2002.

Conniff, Michael. *Black Labor on a White Canal: Panama, 1904–1981.* Pittsburgh: University of Pittsburgh Press, 1985.

Cooper, Frederick, et al. *Beyond Slavery: Explorations of Race, Labor, and Citizenship in Post-Emancipation Societies.* Chapel Hill: University of North Carolina Press, 2000.

Craton, Michael. *Founded upon the Seas: A History of the Cayman Islands and Their People.* Kingston, Jamaica: Ian Randle Publishers, 2003.

Davidson, William V. *Historical Geography of the Bay Islands, Honduras: Anglo-Hispanic Conflict in the Western Caribbean.* Birmingham, AL: Southern University Press, 1974.

De la Fuente, Alejandro. *A Nation for All: Race, Inequality, and Politics in Twentieth-Century Cuba.* Chapel Hill: University of North Carolina Press, 2001.

Del Cid, Rafael, and Mario Posas. *La construcción del sector publico y del estado nacional en Honduras, 1876–1979.* Ciudad Universitaria Rodrigo Facio, Costa Rica: Editorial Universitaria Centroamericana, 1981.

Dodd, Thomas J. *Tiburcio Carías: Portrait of a Honduran Political Leader.* Baton Rouge: Louisiana State University Press, 2005.

Dosal, Paul T. *Doing Business with the Dictators: A Political History of United Fruit in Guatemala, 1899–1944.* Wilmington, DE: Scholarly Resources, 1993.

Duron, Romulo E., ed. *Policarpo Bonilla: Colección de escritos.* Tegucigalpa: Tipografía Nacional, 1899.

Elvir, Rafael Angel. *La villa de Triunfo de la Cruz en la historia.* San Pedro Sula, Honduras: Centro Editorial, 2000.

Euraque, Darío. *Conversaciones históricas con el mestizaje y su identidad nacional en Honduras.* San Pedro Sula, Honduras: Centro Editorial, 2004.

———. *Estado, poder, nacionalidad y raza en la historia de Honduras: Ensayos.* Choluteca, Honduras: Ediciones Subirana, 1996.

———. *Reinterpreting the Banana Republic: Region and State in Honduras, 1870–1972.* Chapel Hill: University of North Carolina Press, 1996.

Euraque, Darío, Jeffrey L. Gould, and Charles R. Hale, eds. *Memorias del mestizaje: Cultura política en Centroamérica de 1920 al presente.* Antigua, Guatemala: Centro de Investigaciones Regionales de Mesoamérica, 2004.

Findlay, Eileen Suarez. *Imposing Decency: The Politics of Sexuality and Race in Puerto Rico, 1870–1920.* Durham, NC: Duke University Press, 1999.

Finney, Kenneth V. *In Quest of El Dorado: Precious Metal Mining and the Modernization of Honduras, 1880–1900.* New York: Garland Publishing, 1987.

Flores Valeriana, Enrique. *La explotación bananera en Honduras.* Tegucigalpa: Editorial Universitaria, 1987 [1979].

Fonseca, Rolando Sierra. *Colonia, independencia y reforma: Introducción a la historiografía Hondureña.* Tegucigalpa: Fondo Editorial UPNFM, 2001.

Franco, Jean. *The Modern Culture of Latin America: Society and the Artist.* New York: Frederick A. Praeger, 1967.

Frank, André Gunder. *Latin America: Underdevelopment or Revolution.* New York: Monthly Review Press, 1969.

———. *Lumpenbourgeoisie, Lumpendevelopment: Dependence, Class, and Politics in Latin America.* New York: Monthly Review Press, 1972.

Freire, Paulo. *Pedagogy of the Oppressed.* New York: Continuum, 2000 [1970].

Funes, José Antonio. *Froylán Turcios y el modernismo en Honduras.* Tegucigalpa: Banco Central de Honduras, 2006.

Garvey, Marcus. "The British West Indies in the Mirror of Civilization, History Making by Colonial Negroes." In *The Birth of Caribbean Civilization: A Century of Ideas about Culture and Identity, Nation and Society,* ed. O. Nigel Bolland. Kingston, Jamaica: Ian Randle Publishers, 2004.

Glazer, Stephen. *Caribbean Ethnicity Revisited.* New York: Gordon and Breach Science Publishers, 1985.

Goldin, Liliana, ed. *Identities on the Move: Transnational Processes in North America and the Caribbean Basin.* Austin: University of Texas Press, 1999.

Gómez, Alfredo León. *El escándolo del Ferrocarril: Ensayo histórico.* Tegucigalpa: Imprenta Soto, 1978.

Gomez, Michael A. *Reversing Sail: A History of the African Diaspora.* New York: Cambridge University Press, 2005.

Gonzalez, Nancie L. *Dollar, Dove, and Eagle: One Hundred Years of Palestinian Migration to Honduras.* Ann Arbor: University of Michigan Press, 1992.

———. *Sojourners of the Caribbean: Ethnogenesis and Ethnohistory of the Garífuna.* Urbana: University of Illinois Press, 1988.

González de Oliva, Alexis. *Gobernantes hondureños: Siglos XIX y XX.* Tegucigalpa: Editorial Universitaria, 1996.

Gordon, Edmund T. *Disparate Diasporas: Identity and Politics in an African Nicaraguan Community.* Austin: University of Texas Press, 1998.

Gossai, Hemchand, and Nathaniel Samuel Murrell, eds. *Religion, Culture and Tradition in the Caribbean.* New York: St. Martin's Press, 2000.

Gottlieb, Peter. *Making Their Own Way: Southern Blacks' Migration to Pittsburgh, 1916–1930.* Urbana: University of Illinois Press, 1987.

Graham, Richard, ed. *The Idea of Race in Latin America, 1870–1940.* Austin: University of Texas Press, 1990.

Graham, Ross. "The Bay Islands English: Stages in the Evolution of a Cultural Identity." In *English-Speaking Communities in Latin America*, ed. Oliver Marshall. New York: St. Martin's Press, 2000.

Grossman, James R. *Land of Hope: Chicago, Black Southerners, and the Great Migration*. Chicago: University of Chicago Press, 1989.

Grossman, Lawrence S. *The Political Economy of Bananas: Contract Farming, Peasants, and Agrarian Change in the Eastern Caribbean*. Chapel Hill: University of North Carolina Press, 1998.

Gruzinski, Serge. *The Mestizo Mind: The Intellectual Dynamics of Colonization and Globalization*. New York: Routledge, 2002.

Gudmundson, Lowell, and Héctor Lindo-Fuentes. *Central America, 1821–1871: Liberalism Before Liberal Reform*. Tuscaloosa: University of Alabama Press, 1995.

Guillamin, Colette. *Racism, Sexism, Power and Ideology*. New York: Routledge, 1995.

Hair, William Ivy. *Bourbonism and Agrarian Protest: Louisiana Politics, 1877–1900*. Baton Rouge: Louisiana State University Press, 1969.

Hall, Catherine. *Civilising Subjects: Metropole and Colony in the English Imagination, 1830–1867*. Chicago: University of Chicago Press, 2002.

Halter, Marilyn. *Between Race and Ethnicity: Cape Verdean American Immigrants, 1860–1965*. Urbana: University of Illinois Press, 1993.

Harpelle, Ronald N. *The West Indians of Costa Rica: Race, Class, and the Integration of an Ethnic Minority*. Montreal: McGill-Queen's University Press, 2001.

Harris, Joseph E. *Global Dimensions of the African Diaspora*. Washington, D.C.: Howard University Press, 1993.

Helg, Aline. *Our Rightful Share: The Afro-Cuban Struggle for Equality, 1886–1912*. Chapel Hill: University of North Carolina Press, 1995.

Herranz, Atanasio. *Estado, sociedad y lenguaje: La política lingüística en Honduras*. Tegucigalpa: Editorial Guaymuras, 1996.

Hoetnick, H. *Race and Color in the Caribbean*. Washington, D.C.: The Woodrow Wilson International Center for Scholars, 1985.

Holt, Thomas C. *The Problem of Freedom: Race, Labor, and Politics in Jamaica and Britain, 1832–1938*. Baltimore, MD: Johns Hopkins University Press, 1992.

Irwin, Graham W. *Africans Abroad: A Documentary History of the Black Diaspora in Asia, Latin America, and the Caribbean During the Age of Slavery*. New York: Columbia University Press, 1977.

Isaguirre, Ramón R. *Through the Eyes of Diplomats: History of the Bay Islands, 1858–1895. United States Diplomatic Correspondence*. Comayagüela, Honduras: Multigráficos Flores, S. de R. L., 2003.

Jackson, Joy J. *New Orleans in the Gilded Age: Politics and Urban Progress, 1880–1896*. Baton Rouge: Louisiana State University Press for the Louisiana Historical Association, 1969.

Jamaica, Colonial Government of. *Jamaica at the Worlds' Exposition: An Official Introduction to the Jamaica Court Containing a Short Description of the Island, its Productions, and its Climate.* Kingston, Jamaica: Office of Colonial Standards at Jamaica, 1884.

James, Ariel. *Banes, imperialism y nación en una plantación azucarera.* La Habana: Editorial Ciencias Sociales, 1976.

Johnson, Howard, and Karl Watson, eds. *The White Minority in the Caribbean.* Princeton, NJ: Markus Wiener Publishers, 1998.

Johnson, Paul Christopher. *Diaspora Conversions: Black Carib Religion and the Recovery of Africa.* Berkeley: University of California Press, 2007.

Karnes, Thomas L. *Tropical Enterprise: The Standard Fruit and Steamship Company in Latin America.* Baton Rouge: Louisiana State University Press, 1978.

Kepner, Charles D. *Social Aspects of the Banana Industry.* New York: AMS Press, 1967.

Kepner, Charles David, and Jay Henry Soothill. *The Banana Republic: A Case Study in Economic Imperialism.* New York: Vanguard Press, 1935.

Klich, Ignacio, and Jeffery Lesser, eds. *Arab and Jewish Immigrants in Latin America: Images and Realities.* London: Frank Cass, 1998.

Knight, Franklin W. *The Caribbean: The Genesis of a Fragmented Nationalism.* New York: Oxford University Press, 1990.

Kraay, Hendrik., ed. *Afro-Brazilian Culture and Politics, Bahia 1790s to 1990s.* Armonk, NY: M. E. Sharpe, 1998.

La Feber, Walter. *The New Empire: An Interpretation of American Expansion, 1860–1898.* Ithaca, NY: Cornell University Press, 1998.

———. *Inevitable Revolutions: The United States in Central America.* New York: W. W. Norton, 1983.

Laguerre, Michel S. *Diasporic Citizen: Haitian Americans in Transnational America.* New York: St. Martin's Press, 1998.

Langley, Lester D., and Thomas Schoonover. *The Banana Men: American Mercenaries and Enterpreneurs in Central America, 1880–1930.* Lexington: University Press of Kentucky, 1995.

Lara, Victor Cáceres. *Gobernantes de Honduras en el siglo XX: De Terencio Sierra a Vicente Tosta.* Tegucigalpa: Litografía Lopez, S. de R.L., 1992.

Larson, Brooke. *Trials of Nation Making: Liberalism, Race and Ethnicity in the Andes, 1810–1910.* Cambridge: Cambridge University Press, 2004.

Lawrence, K. O. *A Question of Labour.* New York: St. Martin's Press, 1994.

Leiva Vivas, Rafael. *Tráfico de esclavos Negros a Honduras.* Tegucigalpa: Editorial Guaymuras, 1982.

Leman, Nicholas. *The Promised Land: The Great Migration and How It Changed America.* New York: Vintage Books, 1991.

López García, Victor Virgilio. *La Bahía del Puerto del Sol y la massacre de los Garífunas de San Juan.* Tegucigalpa: Editorial Guaymuras, 1994.

Mahoney, James. *The Legacies of Liberalism: Path Dependence and Political Regimes in Central America*. Baltimore, MD: Johns Hopkins University Press, 2001.

Marshall, Oliver, ed. *English-Speaking Communities in Latin America*. New York: St. Martin's Press, 2000.

Martínez-Vergne, Teresita. *Nation and Citizen in the Dominican Republic, 1880–1916*. Chapel Hill: University of North Carolina Press, 2005.

May, Robert E. *The Southern Dream of a Caribbean Empire, 1854–1861*. Gainesville: University Press of Florida, 2002.

May, Stacy, and Galo Plaza. *The United Fruit Company in Latin America*. Washington, D.C.: National Planning Association, 1958.

McLewin, Philip J. *Power and Economic Change: The Response to Emancipation in Jamaica and British Guiana, 1840–1865*. New York: Garland Publishing, 1987.

Mejía, Medardo. *Historia de Honduras*. Tegucigalpa: Editorial Universitaria, 1983.

Melendez, Carlos, and Quince Duncan. *El Negro en Costa Rica*. San José: Editorial Costa Rica, 1972.

Meza, Victor. *Historia del movimiento obrero hondureño*. Tegucigalpa: Editorial Guaymuras, 1980.

Moberg, Mark. *Myths of Ethnicity and Nation: Immigration, Work, and Identity in the Belize Banana Industry*. Knoxville: University of Tennessee Press, 1997.

Montiel, Luz María Martínez. *Presencia Africana en Centroamérica*. Ciudad de Mexico: Consejo Nacional para la Cultura y Los Artes, 1993.

Moore, Brian L., and Michele A. Johnson. *Neither Led nor Driven: Contesting British Cultural Imperialism in Jamaica, 1865–1920*. Kingston, Jamaica: University of the West Indies Press, 2004.

Mordecai, Martin, and Pamela Mordecai. *Culture and Customs of Jamaica*. Westport, CT: Greenwood Press, 2001.

Morlan, Albert. *A Hoosier in Honduras*. Indianapolis: El Dorado Publishing Co., 1897.

Morris, D. *New Orleans Worlds' Exposition, 1884–1885: Agricultural and Industrial Products of the Island of Jamaica*. Kingston, Jamaica: DeCordova and Company, 1884.

Morris, James A. *Honduran Caudillos and Military Rulers*. Boulder, CO: Westview Press, 1984.

Moya, José C. *Cousins and Strangers: Spanish Immigrants in Buenos Aires, 1850–1930*. Berkeley: University of California Press, 1998.

Murga Frasinetti, Antonio. *Enclave y sociedad en Honduras*. Tegucigalpa: Universidad Nacional Autónoma de Honduras, 1978.

Navas de Miralda, Paca. *Barro*. Tegucigalpa: Editorial Guaymuras, 1992.

Naylor, Robert A. *Penny Ante Imperialism: The Mosquito Shore and the Bay of Honduras, 1600–1914: A Case Study in British Informal Empire*. London: Associated University Presses, 1989.

Newson, Linda. *The Cost of Conquest: Indian Decline in Honduras Under Spanish Rule.* Boulder, CO: Westview Press, 1986.

Newton, Velma. *The Silver Men: West Indian Labour Migration to Panama, 1850–1914.* Kingston, Jamaica: Ian Randle Publishers, 2004.

Nugent, Walter. *Crossings: The Great Transatlantic Migrations, 1870–1914.* Bloomington: Indiana University Press, 1992.

O'Brien, Thomas F. *The Revolutionary Mission: American Enterprise in Latin America, 1900–1945.* New York: Cambridge University Press, 1996.

Okpewho, Idisore, et al. *The African Diaspora: African Origins and New World Identities.* Bloomington: Indiana University Press, 2001.

O'Reggio, Trevor. *Between Alienation and Citizenship: The Evolution of Black West Indian Society in Panama, 1914–1964.* Lanham, MD: University Press of America, 2006.

Oyuela, Irma Leticia de. *Cuatro hacendados del siglo XIX: Selección de cuatro capítulos de la mujer en la hacienda.* Tegucigalpa: Editorial Universitaria, 1989.

———. *Ramón Rosa: Plenitudes y desengaños.* Tegucigalpa: Editorial Guaymuras, 1994.

Palmer, Frederick. *Central America and Its Problems: An Account of a Journey from the Rio Grande to Panama, with Introductions, Chapters on Mexico, and Her Relations to Her Neighbors.* London: T. Werner Laurie, 1916.

Palmer, Ransford W., ed. *In Search of a Better Life: Perspectives on Migration from the Caribbean.* New York: Praeger, 1990.

Pascoe, C. F. *Two Hundred Years of the S.P.G., An Historical Account of the Society for the Propagation of the Gospel in Foreign Parts.* London: Society for the Propagation of the Gospel, 1901.

Pastor Fasquelle, Rodolfo. *Biografía de San Pedro Sula: 1536–1954.* San Pedro Sula, Honduras: Centro Editorial, 1989.

Paz, Rubén Darío, ed. *Honduras: Del estado-nación a la democracia formal, lecturas de historia de Honduras del siglo XX.* Tegucigalpa: Programa de Formación Continúa UPN, 2004.

Peloso, Vincent C., and Barbara A. Tenenbaum, eds. *Liberals, Politics, and Power: State Formation in Nineteenth-Century Latin America.* Athens: University of Georgia Press, 1996.

Petras, Elizabeth McLean. *Jamaican Labor Migration: White Capital and Black Labor, 1850–1930.* Boulder, CO: Westview Press, 1988.

Piñeda, Baron. *Shipwrecked Identities: Navigating Race on Nicaragua's Mosquito Coast.* New Brunswick, NJ: Rutgers University Press, 2006.

Pinto, Gloria Lara. *Perfil de los pueblos Indígenes y Negros de Honduras.* Tegucigalpa: Unidad Regional de Asistencia Técnica, Banco Mundial, 2002.

Pollan, Arthur Adair. *The United Fruit Company and Middle America.* New York: New School for Social Research, 1944.

Posas, Mario. *Luchas del movimiento obrero Hondureño.* Ciudad Universitaria Rodrigo Facio, Costa Rica: Editorial Universitaria Centroamericana, 1981.

——. *Breve historia de las organizaciones sindicales de Honduras.* Tegucigalpa: Universidad Pedagógica Nacional Francisco Morazán, 2004.

——. "La Huelga de 1954." In *Honduras: Del estado-nación a la democracia formal, lecturas de historia de Honduras del siglo XX,* ed. Rubén Darío Paz. Tegucigalpa: Programa de Formación Continúa UPN, 2004.

Purcell, Trevor W. *Banana Fallout: Class, Color, and Culture Among West Indians in Costa Rica.* Los Angeles: Center for Afro-American Studies, University of California, Los Angeles, 1993.

Putnam, Lara. *The Company They Kept: Migrants and the Politics of Gender in Caribbean Costa Rica, 1870–1960.* Chapel Hill: University of North Carolina Press, 2002.

Raphael-Hernandez, Heike, ed. *Blackening Europe: The African American Presence.* New York: Routledge, 2004.

Rich, Paul B. *Race and Empire in British Politics,* 2d ed. Cambridge: Cambridge University Press, 1990.

Richardson, Bonham C. *Panama Money in Barbados, 1900–1920.* Knoxville: University of Tennessee Press, 1985.

Rodriguez, Mario. *A Palmerstonian Diplomat in Central America: Frederick Chatfield, Esq.* Tucson: University of Arizona Press, 1964.

——. *The Cádiz Experiment in Central America, 1808 to 1826.* Berkeley: University of California Press, 1978.

——. *Central America.* Englewood Cliffs, NJ: Prentice-Hall, 1965.

——. *Chatfield: Consul británico en Centroamérica.* Tegucigalpa: Banco Central de Honduras, 1970.

Rosenberg, Emily S. *Spreading the American Dream: American Economic and Cultural Expansion, 1890–1945.* New York: Hill and Wang, 1982.

RosenGarten, Frederic, Jr. *William Walker y el ocaso del filibusterismo.* Tegucigalpa: Editorial Guaymuras, 2002.

Saakana, Amon Saba. *Colonization and the Destruction of the Mind: Psychosocial Issues of Race, Class, Religion and Sexuality in the Novels of Roy Heath.* Lawrenceville, NJ: Red Sea Press, 1996.

Sánchez, Manuel Rubio. *Historia del puerto de Trujillo.* Tegucigalpa: Banco Central de Honduras, 1975.

Satzewich, Vic. *Racism and the Incorporation of Foreign Labour: Farm Labour Migration to Canada since 1945.* London: Routledge, 1991.

Scarano, Francisco, and Lowell Gudmundson. "Conclusion: Imagining the Future of the Subaltern Past—Fragments of Race, Class, and Gender in Central America and the Hispanic Caribbean, 1850–1950." In *Identity and Struggle at the Margins of the Nation State: The Laboring Peoples of Central America and the Hispanic Caribbean,* ed. Aviva Chomsky and Aldo Lauira-Santiago. Chapel Hill, NC: Duke University Press, 1998.

Schelling, Vivian, ed. *Through the Kaleidoscope: The Experience of Modernity in Latin America.* New York: Verso, 2000.

Schlesinger, Stephen, and Stephen Kinzer. *Bitter Fruit: The Untold Story of the American Coup in Guatemala*. Garden City, NY: Doubleday and Company, 1982.

Schoonover, Thomas. *The French in Central America: Culture and Commerce, 1820–1930*. Wilmington, DE: Scholarly Resources, 2000.

Sealy, Theodore, and Herbert Hart. *Jamaica's Banana Industry: A History of the Banana Industry with Particular Reference to the Part Played by the Jamaica Banana Producers Association, Ltd*. Kingston, Jamaica: The Jamaica Banana Producers Association, 1984.

Segal, Ronald. *The Black Diaspora*. New York: Farrar, Straus and Giroux, 1995.

Sernett, Milton C. *Bound for the Promised Land: African-American Religion and the Great Migration*. Durham, NC: Duke University Press, 1997.

Shugg, Roger W. *Origins of Class Struggle in Louisiana: A Social History of White Farmers and Laborers During Slavery and After, 1840–1875*. Baton Rouge: Louisiana State University Press, 1968.

Simmons, Donald C. *Confederate Settlements in British Honduras*. Jefferson, NC: McFarland and Company, 2001.

Sims, Harold. *Adventures and Proletarians: The Story of Migrants in Latin America*. Pittsburgh: University of Pittsburgh Press, 1977.

Singh, Kelvin. *Race and Class Struggles in a Colonial State: Trinidad, 1917–1945*. Mona, Jamaica: University of the West Indies Press, 1994.

Soluri, John. *Banana Cultures: Agriculture, Consumption, and Environmental Change in Honduras and the United States*. Austin: University of Texas Press, 2006.

Spencer, Sarah. *The Politics of Migration: Managing Opportunity, Conflict and Change*. Malden, MA: Blackwell Publishing, 2003.

Squier, E. G. *Honduras: Descriptive, Historical, and Statistical*. New York: AMS Press, 1970 [1870].

Stanley, Diane. *For the Record: The United Fruit Company's Sixty-six Years in Guatemala*. Guatemala City: Editorial Antigua, S.A. 1994.

Stepan, Nancy Leys. *The Hour of Eugenics: Race, Gender and Nation in Latin America*. Ithaca, NY: Cornell University Press, 1991.

Stokes, William. *Honduras: An Area Study in Government*. Madison: University of Wisconsin Press, 1950.

Striffler, Steve. *In the Shadows of State and Capital: The United Fruit Company, Popular Struggle, and Agrarian Restructuring in Ecuador, 1900–1905*. Durham, NC: Duke University Press, 2002.

Suazo, E. Salvador. *Los deportados de San Vicente*. Tegucigalpa: Editorial Guaymuras, 1997.

Szok, Peter. *"La última gaviota:" Liberalism and Nostalgia in Early Twentieth-Century Panamá*. Westport, CT: Greenwood Press, 2001.

Troutt Powell, Eve M. *A Different Shade of Colonialism: Egypt, Great Britain, and the Mastery of the Sudan*. Berkeley: University of California Press, 2003.

Turcios, Froylán, ed. *Boletin de la defensa nacional.* Tegucigalpa: Editorial Guaymuras, 1980.

United Fruit Company: Un caso del dominio imperialista en Cuba. "Nuestra historia" series. La Habana, Cuba: Editorial de Ciencias Sociales, 1976.

Vargas, Germán Romero. *Historia de la Costa Atlántica.* Managua, Nicaragua: CIDCA, 1996.

Wade, Peter. *Race and Ethnicity in Latin America.* London: Pluto Press, 1997.

Walker, Sheila. *African Roots/American Cultures: Africa in the Creation of the Americas.* New York: Rowman & Littlefield, 2001.

Welcome, Clifford N. *Chattah Talk: The First Dictionary to Detail the Language(s) and Speech Patterns of the Black North Coast Hondurian, Bay Islands, and Caribbean People.* Brooklyn, NY: Clifford N. Welcome, 1999.

Whitten, Norman E., and Arlene Torres, eds. *Blackness in Latin America and the Caribbean: Social Dynamics and Cultural Transformations.* Bloomington: Indiana University Press, 1998.

Williams, Eric. *Capitalism and Slavery.* Chapel Hill: University of North Carolina Press, 1994.

Williams, Robert G. *Export Agriculture and the Crisis in Central America.* Chapel Hill: University of North Carolina Press, 1986.

———. *States and Social Evolution: Coffee and the Rise of National Governments in Central America.* Chapel Hill: University of North Carolina Press, 1994.

Wilson, Charles M. *Empire in Green and Gold: The Story of the American Banana Trade.* New York: Greenwood Press, 1968 [1947].

Winslow, Calvin, ed. *Waterfront Workers: New Perspectives on Race and Class.* Chicago: University of Chicago Press, 1998.

Woodward, Ralph Lee. *Central America: A Nation Divided.* New York: Oxford University Press, 1999 [1976].

Wright, Winthrop R. *Café con Leche: Race, Class, and National Image in Venezuela.* Austin: University of Texas Press, 1990.

Yuscarán, Guillermo. *Gringos in Honduras: The Good, the Bad, and the Ugly.* Tegucigalpa: Nuevo Sol Publications, 1995.

Zelaya, Gustavo. *El legado de la reforma liberal,* 2a ed. Tegucigalpa: Editorial Guaymuras, 2001 [1996].

Zelaya Garay, Oscar, compilador. *Lecturas de historia de Honduras, antología.* Tegucigalpa: Universidad Pedagógica Nacional Francisco Morazán, 1998.

Articles and Pamphlets

Aguilar Paz, Jesús. "Problemas de la cultura Hondureña." *Revista de la universidad nacional autónoma de Honduras* 14, 2 (July–September 1950): 64–68.

Altink, Henrice. "An American Race Laboratory: Jamaica, 1865–1945." *Wadabagei: A Journal of the Caribbean and Its Diaspora* 10, 3 (Fall 2007): 53–83.

Anderson, Mark. "'Existe el racismo en Honduras?' Estereotipos mestizos y discursos Garífunas." *Mesoamérica* 42 (December 2001): 135–63.

Andrews, George Reid. "Review Essay: Latin American Workers." *Journal of Social History* 21 (Winter 1987): 311–26.

Argueta, Mario R. "El sector laboral hondureño durante la reforma liberal." Tegucigalpa: Universitaria Autonoma de Honduras, 1981.

Baracco, Luciano. "Race and Revolution in Bluefields: A History of Nicaragua's Black Sandinista Movement." *Wadabagei: A Journal of the Caribbean and Its Diasporas* 10, 1 (Winter 2007): 4–23.

Boa, Sheena. "'Setting the Law in Defiance': Urban Protests and Lieutenant-Governor Edward John Eyre in Post-Emancipation St. Vincent, 1838–1861." *Caribbean Studies* 30, 2 (December 2002): 130–69.

Bolland, O. Nigel. "Systems of Domination after Slavery: The Control of Land and Labour in the British West Indies after 1838." *Comparative Studies in Society and History* 23, 4 (1981): 591–619.

Bourne, Kenneth. "The Clayton-Bulwer Treaty and the Decline of British Opposition to the Territorial Expansion of the United States, 1857–1860." *Journal of Modern History* 33, 3 (September 1961): 287–91.

Brignoli, Héctor Pérez. "La reforma liberal en Honduras." *Cuaderno de ciencias sociales* 2 (1973): 1–19.

Brown, Jonathan C. "Foreign and Native-Born Workers in Porfirian Mexico." *American Historical Review* 98 (June 1993): 786–818.

Bryan, Patrick. "Aiding Imperialism: White Baptists in Nineteenth-Century Jamaica." *Small Axe* 14 (September 2003): 137–49.

Chierici, Rose-Marie. "Caribbean Migrations in the Age of Globalization: Transnationalism, Race, and Ethnic Identity." *Reviews in Anthropology* 33 (2004): 43–59.

Chomsky, Aviva. "Barbados or Canada? Race, Immigration, and Nation in Early Twentieth-Century Cuba." *Hispanic American Historical Review* 80, 3 (February 2000): 415–62.

———. "West Indian Workers in Costa Rica and Nationalist Ideology, 1900–1950." *The Americas* 51, 1 (July 1994): 11–40.

Cruz, Ramón E. "La ley de inmigración y el problema de la raza negra en la Costa Norte." *Revista Ariel* (15 October 1926): 700.

De la Fuente, Alejandro. "Myths of Racial Democracy: Cuba 1900–1912." *Latin American Research Review* 34, 3 (1999): 39–73.

Devés Valdés, Eduardo. "Afroamericanismo e identidad en el pensamiento latinoamericano en Cuba, Haiti y Brasil, 1900–1940." *Canadian Journal of Latin American and Caribbean Studies* 25, 49 (2000): 53–75.

Echeverri-Gent, Elisavinda. "Forgotten Workers: British West Indians and the Early Days of the Banana Industry in Costa Rica and Honduras." *Journal of Latin American Studies* 24 (1992): 275–308.

Euraque, Darío A. "La 'reforma' liberal en Honduras y la hipótesis de la oligarquía ausente, 1870–1930," *Revista de historia (Heredia, Costa Rica)* 23 (January–June 1991): 7–56.

Ferleger, Louis. "The Problem of Labor in the Post-Reconstruction Louisiana Sugar Industry." *Agricultural History* 72, 2 (Spring 1998): 140–58.

Finney, Kenneth V. "Rosario and the Election of 1887: The Political Economy of Mining in Honduras." *Hispanic American Historical Review* 59, 1 (February 1979): 81–107.

Giovanetti, Jorge L. "The Elusive Organization of "Identity": Race, Religion, and Empire Among Caribbean Migrants in Cuba." *Small Axe* 19 (February 2006): 1–27.

Grosfoguel, Ramon. "Puerto Ricans in the USA: A Comparative Approach." *Journal of Ethnic and Migration Studies* 25, 2 (April 1999): 233–49.

Hale, Charles. "Mestizaje, Hybridity and the Cultural Politics of Difference in Post-Revolutionary Central America." *Journal of Latin American Anthropology* 2, 1 (1996): 34–61.

Hall, Stuart. "Thinking the Diaspora: Home—Thoughts from Abroad." *Small Axe* 6 (September 1999): 1–18.

Harpelle, Ronald. "Racism and Nationalism in the Creation of Costa Rica's Pacific Coast Banana Enclave." *The Americas* 56, 3 (January 2000): 29–51.

Herrera, Robinson. "Porque no sabemos firmar: Black Slaves in Early Guatemala." *The Americas* 57, 2 (October 2000): 247–67.

James, Winston. "Becoming the People's Poet: Claude McKay's Jamaican Years, 1889–1912," *Small Axe* 13 (March 2003): 17–45.

Jones, David W., and Carlyle A. Glean. "The English-speaking Communities of Honduras and Nicaragua." *Caribbean Quarterly* 17, 2 (June 1971): 50–61.

Jong, Greta de. "'With the Aid of God and F.S.A': The Louisiana Farmers' Union and the African American Freedom Struggle in the New Deal Era." *Journal of Social History* 34, 1 (2000): 105–39.

Josiah, Barbara. "After Emancipation: Aspects of Village Life in Guyana, 1869–1911." *The Journal of Negro History* 82, 1 (Winter 1997): 105–21.

Katz, Michael B., Mark J. Stern, and Jamie J. Fader. "The Mexican Immigration Debate: The View from History." *Social Science History* 31, 2 (Summer 2007): 158.

Lokken, Paul. "Useful Enemies: Seventeenth-Century Piracy and the Rise of Pardo Militias in Spanish Central America." *Journal of Colonialism and Colonial History* 5, 2 (2004): 1–18.

Mack, Taylor E. "Contraband Trade Through Trujillo, Honduras, 1720s–1782." *Yearbook, Conference of Latin Americanist Geographers* 24 (1998): 45–46.

Mahoney, James. "Radical Reformist and Aborted Liberalism: Origins of National Regimes in Central America." *Journal of Latin American Studies* 33, 2 (May 2001): 321–56.

Marquardt, Steve. "Green Havoc: Panama Disease, Environmental Change, and

Labor Process in the Central American Banana Industry." *American Histori-cal Review* (February 2001): 49–82.

Marshall, Woodville. "'We Be Wise to Many More Tings': Blacks' Hopes and Ex-pectations of Emancipation." *Social and Economic Studies* 17 (1968).

———. "Peasant Development in the West Indies since 1838." *Social and Economic Studies* 17 (1968): 252–63.

Martínez-Echazabal, Alejandro. "Mestizaje and the Discourse of National/Cultural Identity in Latin America, 1845–1959." *Latin American Perspectives* 25, 3 (May 1998): 21–42.

McCreery, David J. "Coffee and Class: The Structure of Development in Lib-eral Guatemala." *Hispanic American Historical Review* 56, 3 (August 1976): 438–60.

McKeown, Adam. "Global Migration, 1846–1940." *Journal of World History* 15, 2 (2004): 155–89.

Newson, Linda. "Diets, Food Supplies and the African Slave Trade in Early Seven-teenth- Century Spanish America." *The Americas* 63, 4 (April 2007): 517–50.

Norwood, Stephen H. "Bogalusa Burning: The War Against Biracial Unionism in the Deep South, 1919." *Journal of Social History* 63, 3 (August 1997): 591–628.

Offen, Karl H. "British Logwood Extraction from the Mosquitia: The Origin of a Myth." *Hispanic American Historical Review* 80, 1 (2000): 113–37.

Payne Iglesias, Elizet. "Identidad y nación: El caso de la Costa Norte e Islas de la Bahía en Honduras, 1876–1930." *Mesoamérica* 42 (December 2001): 75–103.

Persaud, Anil. "The Civility of Things: 'Unnatural Practices' and the Making of Value(s) in the British Sugar Colonies." *Wadabagei: A Journal of the Carib-bean and Its Diaspora* 10, 3 (Fall 2007): 32–52.

Persram, Nalini. "The Importance of Being Cultural: Nationalist Thought and Jagan's Colonial World." *Small Axe* 15 (March 2004): 82–105.

Piñeda, Baron. "The Chinese Coolies of Nicaragua: Identity, Economy, and Rev-olution in a Caribbean Port City." *Journal of Asian-American Studies* 4, 3 (2001): 209–33.

Posas, Mario. "El problema negro: Racismo y explotación en las bananeras." *Al-caravan* (September 9, 1981): 4–5.

Proctor, Robert. "Early Developments in Barbadian Education." *Journal of Negro Education* 49, 2 (Spring 1980): 184–95.

Putnam, Lara Elizabeth. "Sex and Standing in the Streets of Port Limón, Costa Rica, 1890–1935." Prepared for delivery at the 1998 meeting of the Latin American Studies Association, Chicago, Illinois, September 24–26, 1998.

Reidy, Joseph P. "Mules and Machines and Men: Field Labor on Louisiana Sugar Plantations, 1887–1915." *Agricultural History* 72, 2 (Spring 1998): 183–96.

Revels, Craig S. "Concessions, Conflict, and the Rebirth of the Honduran Ma-hogany Trade." *Journal of Latin American Geography* 2 (2003): 1–17.

Rippy, J. Fred. "The British Bondholders and the Roosevelt Corollary of the Mon-roe Doctrine." *Political Science Quarterly* 49, 2 (June 1934): 195–206.

Rodrigue, John C. "The Great Law of Demand and Supply: The Contest over Wages in Louisiana's Sugar Region, 1870–1880." *Agricultural History* 72, 2 (Spring 1998): 159–82.

———. "Labor Militancy and Black Grassroots Political Mobilization in the Louisiana Sugar Region, 1865–1868." *Journal of Southern History* 67, 1 (February 2001): 115–42.

Rogers, Nicholas. "Caribbean Borderland: Empire Ethnicity, and the Exotic on the Mosquito Coast." *Eighteenth-Century Life* 26, 3 (Fall 2002): 117–39.

Ross, Michael A. "Justice Miller's Reconstruction: The Slaughter-House Cases, Health Codes, and Civil Rights in New Orleans, 1861–1873." *Journal of Social History* 64, 4 (November 1998): 649–76.

Rudolf, N. A. "A West Indian Problem." *West Indian Review* 1, 3 (November 1934): 3–4.

Scott, Rebecca J. "Defining the Boundaries of Freedom in the World of Cane: Cuba, Brazil, and Louisiana after Emancipation." *American Historical Review* 99, 1 (February 1994): 70–102.

Sharman, Russell Leigh. "The Caribbean *Carretera*: Race, Space and Social Liminality in Costa Rica." *Bulletin of Latin American Research* 20, 1 (2001): 46–62.

Soluri, John. "People, Plants, and Pathogens: The Eco-social Dynamics of Export Banana Production in Honduras, 1875–1950." Hispanic American Historical Review 80, 3 (August 2000): 463–501.

Striffler, Steve. "Wedded to Work: Class Struggles and Gendered Identities in the Restructuring of the Ecuadorian Banana Industry." *Identities* 6, 1 (1999): 91–120.

Szok, Peter. "La patria es el recuerdo": Hispanophile Nationalism in Early-Twentieth-Century Panama, 1903–1941." *Journal of Caribbean History* 31 (1997): 149–84.

Turcios, Froylán. "Explicación de nuestra síntesis patriótica." *Revista Ariel* 61, 4 (March 1, 1928): 1151.

Walker, Dorsey E. "Some Realistic Aspects of the Progress of Jamaica, 1895–1947." *Journal of Negro Education* 20, 2 (Spring 1951):148–59.

Woodward, Ralph Lee, Jr. "The Historiography of Modern Central America Since 1960." *Hispanic American Historical Review* 67, 3 (August 1987): 461–96.

———. "The Rise and Decline of Liberalism in Central America: Historical Perspectives on Current Crisis." *Journal of Interamerican Studies and World Affairs* 26, 3 (1984): 291–312.

Louisiana Periodicals

L'Abeille de la Nouvelle-Orléans, 1870–1923
The Crusader, 1890
Daily Picayune, 1900–1914

Louisiana Planter (Alexandria), 1900–1930
New Orleans Times, 1876–81
Southern Republican, 1899–1900
Sugar Planter's Journal (New Orleans), 1900–1930
Weekly Pelican (New Orleans), 1886–1889

Barbados Periodicals

Barbados Agricultural Reporter, 1911–1922
Barbados Globe and Colonial Advocate, 1911–1926
Barbados Standard, 1911–1921
Barbados Times, 1920–1921

Jamaica Periodicals

Daily Gleaner, 1911–1929
Daily Chronicle, 1914–1917
Daily Telegraph and Jamaican Guardian, 1910–1911
Jamaican Times, 1911–1922
The Negro World
West Indian Review, 1930–1940

Dissertations and Theses

Amaya Banegas, Jorge Alberto. "Reimaginando la nación en Honduras: De la nación homogénea a la nación pluriétnica, los Negros Garífunas de Cristales." Ph.D. diss., Universidad Complutense de Madrid, 2004.

Bonner, Donna Maria. "Garífuna Town/Caribbean Nation/Latin American State: Identity and Prejudice in Belize." Ph.D. diss., State University of New York at Buffalo, 1999.

Chen, Wilson Chih-Jong. "Entanglements of U.S. Empire: Race, Nation, and the Problem of Imperialism in the Writings of Carlos Buloson, James Weldon Johnson, and C. L. R. James." Ph.D. diss., University of California-Irvine, 2003.

Echeverri-Gent, Elisavinda. "Labor, Class, and Political Representation: A Comparative Analysis of Honduras and Costa Rica." Ph.D. diss., University of Chicago, 1988.

Euraque, Darío Aquiles. "Merchants and Industrialists in Northern Honduras: The Making of a National Bourgeoisie in Peripheral Capitalism, 1870–1972." Ph.D. diss., University of Wisconsin-Madison, 1990.

Manuel-Scott, Wendi. "Soldiers of the Field: Jamaican Farm Workers in the United States During World War II." Ph.D. diss., Howard University, 2003.

Opie, Frederick Douglass. "Adios Jim Crow: Afro-North American Workers and the Guatemalan Railroad Workers League, 1884–1921." Ph.D. diss., Syracuse University, 1999.

O'Reggio, Trevor. "Between Alienation and Citizenship: The Evolution of Black West Indian Society in Panama, 1914–1964." Ph.D. diss., University of Chicago, 1997.

Soluri, John. "Landscape and Livelihood: An Agro-ecological History of Export Banana Growing in Honduras, 1870–1975." Ph.D. diss., University of Michigan, 1998.

Suazo Vasquez, Irma Violeta. "El extranjero ante la legislación hondureña." Tesis leida por la Licenciada, Universidad Nacional Autónoma de Honduras, 1974.

INDEX

African diaspora: influence in Latin America, 1; West Indians in Central America, 9; identity formation within, 12–13; discourse on migration within, 14; and cultural fragmentation, 142–43

Amaya Amador, Ramón. *See* North Coast

Anderson, Andrés, 45

Anderson, Carlos, 43–44

Anglican Church: early missions to Honduras, 79; and West Indian education, 88

Anglo-Saxon culture: and black labor from colonies, 54; impact on West Indian cultural norms, 93, 98; racial ideology of, 99–103

Anti-black sentiment: directed at West Indians, 5, 20, 49; impact on Garífuna, 9, 108, 132; effect on immigration policy, 84; in West Indian history, 98–99; throughout Latin America, 110; during economic depression, 112; and attitudes toward illegal immigration, 122, 128

Arabs: as immigrants to Honduras, 38–39, 63, 73

Armstrong, Jack, 107, 109

Atlántida, Honduras (department): population of West Indians in, 45, 59–60, 64–65, 67; establishment of British consulate in, 48; fruit industry operations in, 58; site of La Masica incident, 106. *See also* La Ceiba, Honduras

Baker, Lorenzo Dow: business in Jamaica, 76. *See also* Boston Fruit Company

Banana industry: development in Honduras, 26–28, 41, 119–20; origins in Caribbean, 76–77; in British Honduras, 94; in the Bay Islands, 137; political and economic support for, in Honduras, 138

Banco Atlántida, 31. *See also* Standard Fruit and Steamship Company

Baptists, 79

Barbados: class structure of, 13; British identity of, 97; resettlement from Latin America to, 112

Barrio Las Brisas (Tela), 95

Bay Islands: origins of inhabitants, 3; West Indian identity in, 10–11; and criminal activity, 46; citizenship, 58–59, 138; immigration of West Indians to, 77–80; assimilation of West Indian workers, 81–83, 87, 100

Belize. *See* British Honduras

Black Carib. *See* Garífuna

Blackness: Honduran definitions of, 1; Caribbean conceptions of, 9; in the British Empire, 101–2; Honduran challenges to, 142

Bloomfield, Arnold, 131–32

Bocas del Toro (Panama). *See* Panama: agro-industrial production in

Bosch, George, 76